Home is Where We Are

Home is Where We Are

Wang Gungwu
with
Margaret Wang

RIDGE BOOKS
SINGAPORE

Published under the Ridge Books imprint by:

NUS Press
National University of Singapore
AS3-01-02
3 Arts Link
Singapore 117569

Fax: (65) 6774-0652
E-mail: nusbooks@nus.edu.sg
Website: http://nuspress.nus.edu.sg

ISBN 978-981-325-132-8 (casebound)

National Library Board, Singapore Cataloguing in Publication Data

Names: Wang, Gungwu. | Wang, Margaret, author.
Title: Home is where we are / Wang Gungwu with Margaret Wang.
Description: Singapore : Ridge Books, [2021] | Includes index.
Identifiers: OCN 1157277958 | ISBN 978-981-325-132-8 (casebound)
Subjects: LCSH: Wang, Gungwu. | Wang, Margaret. | Historians--Biography. |
        Malaya--History--20th century.
Classification: DDC 950.049510092--dc23

Image 1 is reproduced courtesy of Singapore Press Holdings Limited.
All other images are the author's personal collections.

Typeset by: Ogma Solutions Pvt. Ltd.
Printed by: Markono Print Media Pte Ltd

In Memory of Margaret departed 7 August 2020

Remembering our twenty years
at the University of Malaya in Singapore and Kuala Lumpur
and all our friends and colleagues
who helped us find home

Contents

Before Home

WHEN I WAS growing up, home meant China, the country my parents came from and to which we would one day return. We finally did when I was 16 years old. My parents, however, did not stay and left me to study at the national university in Nanjing. A year later, they asked me to rejoin them in Malaya when the People's Liberation Army was ready to attack Nanjing, the national capital. My book, *Home is not Here* (2018), ends when I was back where I started. My parents' dream to return to the country they loved had ended. Their China was about to be revolutionized in ways they could not comprehend; they no longer talked about going home.

The British-initiated Malayan Union had become a protectorate of Malay States called the Federation of Malaya; the Emergency had been declared against the Malayan National Liberation Army organized by the Malayan Communist Party to liberate the country from British rule. My father saw his work as improving the quality of Chinese education and believed that the local Chinese community should stay out of China's politics. It seemed that he had decided to stay in Malaya and wanted me to have a new start.

I spent most of 1949 preparing to do that. It was a lonely time. My childhood friends had moved to Kuala Lumpur (KL) and my closest school friends were studying in Singapore, at the Raffles College and the King Edward VII College of Medicine. My hope was to continue my university studies. When it was announced that the new University of Malaya (MU) would bring the two colleges together, my father thought I could gain admission because of my Cambridge School Leaving Certificate. However, he was concerned that I might not succeed because I was Chinese and not local-born and, realizing that I could qualify, arranged for me to obtain local citizenship as a naturalized Malayan. Neither of us was conscious of this at the time but, by so doing, I continued to believe that home was tied to a country, in this case one that was yet to be born.

When I continued my story, I recalled that some time ago Margaret had written her story for our children. I asked her if I could weave parts of that into mine to augment and give colour to what I remember of our lives together. I am thankful that she readily agreed.

PART ONE

Fitting In

Soft Landing

ON THE EVE of my 19th birthday, I acquired two new identities. I was a post-colonial undergraduate and a citizen of the Federation of Malaya. I was no longer a foreign Chinese in the eyes of the government and now had the opportunity to go on to learn in a university. In both identities, Malaya loomed large. And I spent the next twenty years of my life wondering how I could make Malaya my country.

I was lucky to have such a soft landing. My father made that possible because he was determined that his only child would not miss out on higher education simply because he had called me back from Nanjing. He could not afford to send me overseas again. When he learnt that MU was being planned, he saw that getting me admitted was the only way I could continue my studies. Fortunately, something he did in the years 1945–47 made that possible. This was when he postponed the family's return to China after the war ended so that I could finish my secondary education. That way, I would not have to start afresh in a high school in China to qualify to sit for a university entrance examination. He had therefore waited until my Cambridge School Certificate results were announced before we left Malaya.

Little did he know what a good decision that was. When we unexpectedly came back, the delay till the middle of 1947 to go to China helped me in two ways. The certificate I had received made me eligible to apply for admission to the new university in Singapore, and the extra two years staying on in Malaya also qualified me to seek Federal citizenship under the new constitution. Given that the anti-British war known as the "Emergency" was underway, my status as a Chinese national who was not local born, someone stateless, could have jeopardized my chances of being admitted. By that time, my father had become open to the idea that Malaya was where we could settle down. My parents never admitted it but I believe they anticipated the political fallout among local Chinese who supported the Republic of China (ROC in Taiwan) against those excited by the New China in Beijing and did not want me to be drawn to one side or the other. I also began to sense that they now thought that living in Malaya was better than anywhere else in the region.

The University of Malaya's primary mission was to train locals to assist British officials in the work of administering their colonies and protectorates. This British-type university set out to transmit ideas and institutions that could help develop the future nation, ideally one that would have goodwill towards British interests. Young Malayans would be selected to take over when the colonial officers eventually left. This was an imperial cause that planned ahead for the end of Empire and its replacement by a new Commonwealth. To accomplish this task, graduates of Britain's best universities were encouraged to go forth to teach in Malaya. It was understood that everything would be done to make MU's degrees recognized and its graduates useful.

⸻◈⸻

The University was formally inaugurated on 8 October 1949. Malcolm MacDonald, the Commissioner General for Southeast Asia, conducted the opening ceremony. Present were Malay monarchs or their representatives as well as political leaders from all parts of the Federation of Malaya and the Colony of Singapore. That campus was renamed University of Singapore in 1962 and then National University of Singapore in 1980. In 1999, when it celebrated the 50th anniversary of its foundation, I described the university as having had a head start preparing for a post-colonial world. At the time, events in Malaya were pointing to some testing years ahead. We were alerted to ready ourselves for major transformations in the region. I suggested that, at the Foundation Ceremony, there was already an air of expectation that this was an institution that would play an important role in the building of a new nation.

The students were new to the idea that Southeast Asia was a region. They were the products of colonial education. The textbooks we used were more or less the same across all the schools in the British Empire and Commonwealth. All students matriculated with certificates provided by the Cambridge Examination Board. As preparation for a future Commonwealth centred in London, the system was skillfully designed, and did the job well. But, as a result of that standardization, most of us arrived at the new university knowing little about Malaya and the countries in the neighbourhood. I was even worse off than most because only half of my education was at a school that looked to England, with the other half being done at a home that focused on the ideal world of ancient China. In addition, my school education was truncated by the Japanese occupation.

Our British teachers hardly knew any more about Malaya. There were a few exceptions among those who had taught in Raffles College before the war and survived three and a half years in Japanese prisons. Not surprisingly, geographers like E.H.G. Dobby led the way. He produced the first geography textbook on the region, which highlighted the strategic importance of Southeast Asia to Britain. Also, there were some in the Economics Department who concentrated on aspects of the Malayan economy, seen as vital to Britain's post-war recovery. T.H. Silcock, in particular, took us through the most recent studies concerning Malaya's tin and rubber industry. In the field of history, Brian Harrison produced the first book on the history of Southeast Asia although it was quickly supplanted by a more comprehensive work by D.G.E. Hall, the former professor of history at Rangoon University.

Most staff and students admitted that they were not sure how the Malayan nation would develop. The idea of "nation" in the West was normally based on the idea of a people having the same language and religion and sharing the same history for a long while. This clearly did not describe the several varieties of polities that were federated in 1948. When I met my new friends coming from all parts of the country, I soon realized that I was one of the least equipped to be Malayan. I knew the parts of Perak I had gone to with my father when he visited in his capacity as inspector of Chinese schools. Some of my school friends had told me about Penang and Kuala Lumpur. More recently, I had read news of the Emergency in parts of the peninsula, the conflict between British troops and the Malayan National Liberation Army led by the Malayan Communist Party (MCP). About Singapore, I knew even less. I had passed through the port on the two trips I made to China but could only remember its railway station.

I was not alone in not knowing enough, but few realized that I had to start almost from scratch to find out what the new country was to be about. In comparison, the local-born from long-settled families were much better informed. Many had visited relatives in different parts of the country or had fathers in business or in government service who had transferred from place to place in their careers. There were also those whose families were forced to move around to escape Japanese mistreatment during the war as well. I also found out that, among the older students, a few had been abroad during the war and observed Malaya from outside. It was fascinating to hear a couple of Malay students tell us about how the Japanese had sent them to Japan for training, and also to meet others from "British India" who had sided with the Indian National Army and seen action in Burma.

My fellow students were a mixed bunch who had very different views of what a future Malaya would be like. I had paid little attention when I lived in Ipoh to local political developments because I was always getting ready to leave for China. Now that I was seeking to be part of a new country, I was keen to find out how I might belong here. I listened to those who described our situation as being part of a larger anti-imperialist movement seeking to transform our world into one of independent nation states. In order to gain a place in that world, we had to prepare for the day when the British withdrew totally. The Emergency was being fought largely in the jungles on the peninsula and was targeted at defeating, not communists (for hardly anyone knew what that really meant), and certainly not nationalists fighting only to free Malaya, but armed men who were called "terrorists" and "bandits". My friends were broadly divided between those who were afraid that the British did not want to leave and would try to stay as long as they could, and those who were fearful of what would happen if the British were to leave without defeating the MCP.

I was conscious that something called decolonization was taking place elsewhere. Burma and Ceylon, like India, had achieved independence. The Philippines had been given theirs. A new people called Indonesians—whose armies like those of the Burmese had been trained by the Japanese—were winning the war to throw out the Dutch. As for the Vietnamese, their cruel fate was to be caught in the larger conflict between Soviet (and Chinese) communism and American capitalism. Located on the frontier between ideologies, theirs was no longer a legitimate war to gain their country's freedom. Instead, it was becoming something much bigger between superpowers, ultimately leading to the hottest war in Asia since 1945.

What then about Malaya? Were the MCP forces really the nationalists who wanted independence for Malaya that they claimed to be? If so, was it necessary to use violent means to achieve that goal if there were non-violent paths towards a peaceful transfer of power? Were the British troops coming in to fight the Emergency or to delay giving the country independence as long as possible? Asking these questions was interesting even though many believed that as long as the MCP was around it would be a mistake to hurry the British along.

I was ignorant about the wide range of interests that were involved in the ongoing struggle. Before I left for China in 1947, I had noted the labour unrest in Ipoh when the British returned after the war. There had been street demonstrations and many arrests. I was curious but decided all that had nothing to do with me because I was going somewhere else. I recalled how the Malayan Union was received with outright opposition among the Malays and considerable scepticism among others who were suspicious of British motives. But as I was waiting to leave for Nanjing, I had not followed what was happening. Now that I was a citizen of the Federation, with the Emergency in full force and strict controls on what we could say and who we associated with, it was time to get my bearings right.

A Mixed Start

I ARRIVED AT the University of Malaya one day before my 19th birthday. Some of my school classmates at the time I left for China had been admitted to the two colleges that had now been merged to become the university. Thus, when I arrived in Singapore, they were my seniors. I was joining schoolmates of a later cohort and meeting other new friends. It seemed strange to have the university for Malaya established in the British colony of Singapore. I was assured that there were at least two good reasons for that: turning the established colleges into the university saved time and money; and in any case, everyone expected Singapore to become a constituent state of the Federation before too long.

The university was very small. The liberal arts faculties admitted 100 students that year, 40 for science (because of the limited laboratory space) and 60 for arts. It could be called a university because it had a medical school. Of the 60 freshmen in arts, I recall that over 40 came from the states of Malaya while the rest were from Singapore (out of a population, including Singapore, of six million). Those of us from the Federation stayed on campus or nearby, with the men in several dormitories and the women stayed in a hostel at Mount Rosie. Only a few Singapore scholarship holders were resident. As a result, the "hostelites" did not really know most of the Singapore students.

I was happy to learn that my fellow students came from different parts of the new country. Learning about where they came from was delightfully instructive. Outside the classroom, in the hostels and sports fields, at our society meetings, over meals and late-night sessions, I asked everyone where they came from. I had never been anywhere apart from a few towns in Perak. The considerable variations described to me were surprising and gave me different perspectives of what a future Malaya might look like. We were not convinced that independent Malaya would be anything like what the British had in mind. We already saw, however vaguely, that the future country was a question mark whose answer depended on those who actively worked to shape it. But when I first arrived on campus, all I wanted was a chance to learn whatever I could.

My hostel mates told me about their hometowns and states, often with intimate details that were more enlightening than what was found in textbooks. Among my seniors on campus, Beda Lim told me about the old families of Penang, and Jack da Silva and Yeo Beng Poh explained why Kuala Lumpur, the new nation's capital, was the place to be. George and James Puthucheary underlined the importance of the state of Johor for both Singapore and the future Malaya. And I recall how Dollah Majid regretted the way everyone ignored his state of Pahang. He told me what his Mandailing ancestors from Sumatra had to do to open up the state. And there was Syed Mahadzar from the small state of Perlis, a state often unnoticed, describing how, together with its larger neighbour Kedah, it had plotted successfully to avoid conflict with the King of Siam.

Among my fellow freshmen, those of us who shared the dormitories got to know one another very well. My closest friend, Thiagarajan, was particularly interesting. His Chinese parents had given him away to their Chettiar friends in Kedah and he grew up as a Tamil. He attracted the whole class's attention when he stood up when his name was called. The lecturer asked him not to be funny and he cheerfully explained that Thiagarajan was indeed his real name. Others who became good friends were Zakaria Haji Ali and Masood Ali, who readily described their kampong lives in the state of Johor. And then there was Hamzah Sendut, who was particularly proud of the exceptional matriarchal nature of his state of Negri Sembilan. He wanted me to understand that its Minangkabau traditions had shaped the Council of Rulers of the new federation. And most fascinating of all was a fun-loving Chinese whose name I have forgotten: he came from Kelantan and told jokes in his local Malay dialect that even his Malay friends could not understand. He would then proudly translate his jokes into English.

—◆◆◆—

There was no talk of politics in any of our courses and no question of trusting our British teachers to talk about our future. It was enough that they did their formal teaching and left us to discuss politics among ourselves. It was just as well that I was not interested in anything overtly political. I was warned that some of my active friends had attracted the attention of the colonial police's Special Branch. But I saw nothing wrong with what they were discussing and often expressed my agreement with what they thought about the British colonial record. It was a measure of my innocence that I was totally surprised when several of the most vocal among my friends were detained the year after I joined their debates.

In particular, I was shocked that Ong Cheng Hui, an Anderson School classmate and a dear friend now in the third year of his medical studies, was one of them. He was the top student in our class of 1946 and had never shown any interest in politics. The Japanese had killed his father during the occupation and I did remember how he had spoken bitterly about Japan's imperial ambitions. The police detained him and his brother for a month and I was sure that their detention was undeserved. If anything, that made him more hostile towards British Malaya. I believe that the experience led him to choose not to serve as a doctor in Malaya but to go to China soon after graduation. Cheng Hui's detention reminded us how fearful the colonial government was of any sign of dissent. Of those arrested, the authorities did not hesitate to banish anyone who was not born in Malaya, whether to Indonesia, China or India. That made those like me who were not born in Malaya all the more cautious about taking part in political activities and expressing anti-imperialist opinions.

Among those arrested with Cheng Hui were new friends I had met on campus, notably James Puthucheary and Dollah Majid who were detained for a year and a half. They were accused of having been members of the Anti-British League (ABL), an underground organization sympathetic to the MCP. We heard that when their rooms were raided, lists of likely recruits were found that included the names of several other students at the university. Stories spread around the campus that my name had been found in some of the ABL documents as a possible future recruit. It was certainly well known that I was James' and Dollah's friend, but I was never able to ascertain if the rumour was true. For myself, while I knew they were both outspokenly anti-colonial, I was not convinced that either of them were communists. When they returned to their studies in 1952, James and I shared a room in the Dunearn Road Hostels and we continued to campaign together for the right to discuss political affairs on campus. We urged the university to allow student political societies, as was common in British campuses, so that students could better understand the democratic process and prepare to play their part in the Malayan nation. Eventually, in 1953, the university agreed and we founded the University Socialist Club.

I am running ahead of my story here but that event was connected with the fact that I was no stranger to the limits on political freedom on university campuses. The year and a half at my first university in Nanjing had taught me that governments could be very suspicious of student activists. Dozens of student leaders from the major universities in and around the capital had been arrested and were still in jail when I arrived in Nanjing in June 1947. My fellow students there had been made to feel that no opposition to the regime of any kind would be tolerated. As a result, the campuses were relatively quiet because no one was sure anymore whom to trust.

In Singapore, English-educated students might have thought that the colonial state respected British liberal traditions and would show them some favour. But in the context of a rebellion that was giving the government its most dangerous moments, to believe that open anti-imperialist sentiments would be tolerated was clearly naïve. I had been sensitized not to take anything for granted from my experience in China where I had learnt to keep my political views to myself. I listened to the anti-colonial arguments and joined some of the discussions but made it clear that my main interest was literary and that I was not inclined to activism. I do not know how much it helped that I was known on campus to have poetic pretensions. If there were suspicions about my politics, they did not seem to have grown and had clearly subsided by 1953 when I was appointed a tutor in history and began to study for my master's degree.

In short, I survived my early years as the foreign-born student who had studied in what had become communist China. I did not think of it at the time but, because I had not been brought up in a family of *colonial* subjects, I had participated in anti-colonial discussions on campus without thinking there was a colonial heritage that I needed to reject. Anti-imperialism was more of an abstract expression to support the idea of national independence. It was not until years later when it became fashionable to display the turning away from the colonial past by talking about being *post-colonial*, that I wondered why I did not share in that many-faceted movement. I then realized that I never felt post-colonial because I had never been a colonial; I was also not attracted to communism whether the scientific or the utopian variety because I had been brought up as a *post-dynastic* Chinese suspended between the modern and the traditional. Perhaps the security authorities knew me better than I did when they left me alone.

Whose Literature?

WHEN I LEFT Ipoh for MU, I did not know I was leaving the town for good. All I wanted was to get back to studying again. After returning from Nanjing, I only thought of Ipoh as a stopover while I waited. It was where my parents lived and it was my town as long as they lived there. After my father was promoted to be Federal Inspector of Chinese Schools and moved to Kuala Lumpur, I had few reasons to visit Ipoh again. It was not until much later that I realized how fond I was of the Kinta valley and that Ipoh was the source of any Malayan consciousness I had to begin with, including what appeared in my early poems. I then knew that it was the only place I could call my hometown.

But at the time, I was excited simply to be studying again. My first thought was to continue with what I thought I knew something about, the English literature that had been my major in Nanjing. But when I arrived on campus, I met friends who thought that Malaya should have its own literature, written in a common language. Some of our British teachers also encouraged us to believe that our plural society, with peoples of largely Malay, Chinese or Indian descent, might have to play down our ancestral languages in favour of the language we were educated in. This underlined the fact that there were few Malay students among us and even fewer were interested in any kind of "Malayanized" English or "Engmalchin" as some had come to call it. My first friend on campus Beda Lim was one of the seniors who was curious about what such a literature might look like. When he found that I was interested in literature, he encouraged me to write poetry and be active in the Raffles Society that he and his classmates had founded. Without being conscious of it at the time, this was to become my entry into a possible Malayan identity.

It all began in the most mundane fashion. Most of us from the northern states took the night train, so that we could arrive in Singapore first thing in the morning, in time for our first day of registration. It was on that night train that the freshmen met our seniors. One of the first I met was Beda. He introduced himself as coming from Penang and asked me what I knew about English poetry. I had been introduced to T.S. Eliot and W.H. Auden by my friend Zhu Yan 祝彦 in Nanjing who was a remarkably well-read student totally immersed in the writings of the literary greats of Europe. He had been keen to educate me in contemporary English literature by poets like Eliot and Auden. Despite my education in English in Ipoh at Anderson School, I had never heard of these authors and Zhu was delighted in telling me about their latest writings, including Auden's anti-war poems and Eliot's Four Quartets. Both their names being still fresh in my mind, I blurted out my admiration for them. Beda was taken aback by my answer and, I think, decided on the spot to adopt me as his freshman. When the train stopped at Kuala Lumpur and other seniors got on board, Beda began to introduce me to his friends as someone who read poetry. Two of them also treated me as special, someone not to be "ragged" with the rest. Jack da Silva and Yeo Beng Poh agreed that if Beda thought I was different they would respect his judgment, and all of us remained good friends thereafter.

It astonished me how my interest in literature began to open doors for me. Unlike the university in Nanjing, however, you could not simply choose to do a degree in literature. Following the Scottish system, we had to select two other subjects for our first three years and graduate with a General degree. Only after that could we specialize in one field. I was disappointed to find that the choices were limited; only three other subjects were available: history, economics and geography. I wanted to do something useful, so I thought I ought to study economics. Between the other two, history was more about people and closer to literature, so I chose that over geography.

Most of our teachers were Europeans. In the three subjects I chose, only two teachers in economics were not from Europe. One was Lim Tay Boh who taught money and finance; he became professor of economics, and later, the vice-chancellor of the university. The other was You Poh Seng who became professor of statistics and helped to found the Singapore

Institute of Management. Having previously attended a university where all our regular teachers, including in English literature, were Chinese (only my German teacher was not), I had to get used to having almost every course taught by Europeans. Economics was totally new to me. History was nearly as alien because the courses were largely about European expansions into Asia, and not about either Chinese or British Empire history. In that way, the only subject I had known something about before coming to this campus was actually English literature.

―◁◇◁▷◇▷―

I had been introduced to some English classics when I was with the Foreign Languages Department in Nanjing, so I thought that I should have little difficulty keeping up. As it turned out, much of what I had to read in Singapore was new. I discovered that there was a great deal more that I knew little about. Nevertheless, English literature was still my priority. I felt I had a good introduction to its history when in Nanjing, and my fellow students there had also taught me something about European literature through works translated into Chinese. I also thought I was well-prepared because my father had an English literature background and had subscribed to English weeklies that he had encouraged me to read. I soon found out how inadequate that was.

Meeting Beda Lim on my way to university provided a big boost to my confidence. He brought me to listen to fellow students of the Raffles Society and I was curious to learn about their idea of a *Malayan* literature. I had never heard of that and they explained that this had to come if the country was to be independent when the British finally left. There I met people for whom the idea that Singapore and Malaya would come together to build a new nation was real. The question for them was, what kind of literature would it have?

I was curious about the new developments occurring almost everywhere I looked but was also aware that I had to be careful of what I said and did. As someone who had come back from a country that was identified as a communist state only a week before our university opened its doors, I had attracted some attention from friends and teachers. While some assumed I must be anti-communist to have left China, others wondered if the sympathy I showed for the anti-colonial cause was inspired by the anti-imperialist rhetoric that the People's Republic openly propagated. I also realized that some of my seniors who led the debate about Malayan literature were considered leftwing radicals, notably the group identified with the *Malayan Orchid* magazine.

Malaya was not England and the politically minded rejected the idea that, even while we wrote in the English language, what we wrote should be a kind of imitation English literature. I found that rejection intriguing. I had never thought that way before. With my background in classical Chinese literature, from the *Book of Poetry* to Tang-Song prose and poetry, and popular novels like *Romance of the Three Kingdoms*, *Journey to the West*, and *The Water Margin*, it had never occurred to me that anyone could write new Chinese literature that did not draw upon that rich legacy. I had read some poetry by Guo Moruo 郭沫若 and Xu Zhimo 徐志摩, some of the short stories by Lu Xun 鲁迅, Mao Dun 矛盾 and Lao She 老舍 and the most popular of Ba Jin's 巴金 novels, his three-volume set of *Family, Spring and Autumn*. I heard my friends discuss the plays by Cao Yu 曹禺 but never had the chance to see them performed. The European inspiration in all of their writings was clear but the responses were always expressed through the Chinese language.

So how could the literature in English language that we wrote not be built on the deep heritage of its literature? I found myself in the curious position of studying English literature in order *not* to write anything that closely followed its traditions. I was not at all sure that could be done but joined my friends to see what could be done, if only in verse.

Verse Making

I NEVER KNEW whether Beda Lim's efforts to make me a budding poet with no head for politics had protected me from closer police scrutiny. He had decided that I was worth befriending as someone who had studied in China and also knew something about English and European literature. My having read Eliot and Auden, whose poetry was not taught in our courses, made me someone with whom he had something to share. In class, we focused on the literary greats from Chaucer and Shakespeare down to 19th-century novels. Anything after that we were encouraged to read for ourselves. I noted that several of our lecturers had a deep interest in the moderns, Thomas Hardy, Joseph Conrad and D.H. Lawrence. One of my teachers in Nanjing had translated some of Hardy's novels and I had greatly enjoyed reading *Tess of the D'Urbervilles*, *The Mayor of Casterbridge* and *Jude the Obscure*. Also, I had been fascinated by Conrad's *The Nigger of the Narcissus* in school and had read his *Lord Jim* and *Heart of Darkness*. As for Lawrence, my father had introduced me to his *Sons and Lovers*. I was, like my classmates, curious about his *Lady Chatterley's Lover*, but we were not able to get a copy to read.

At the same time, I was learning a great deal about Beda. He was someone very different from anyone I had ever known. His father was of Hainanese origin, while his mother was Hakka but grew up *peranakan* and wrote letters to him in Baba Malay. Beda knew no Chinese but spoke excellent English and could communicate in Malay in speech and writing. He had been educated with a deep understanding of literature in English. His father was a professional violinist who played with a travelling band; he told me that British travellers in Rangoon had recorded their appreciation of the band's playing. He himself had an excellent grounding in classical Western music, especially that of the 19th and 20th centuries. What was truly extraordinary was his photographic memory.

Beda encouraged me to talk about poetry. Several fellow students had been publishing poetry in magazines like *The Malayan Orchid* and *The Cauldron* (later *The New Cauldron*). They ranged from rhymed sonnets to various experiments in free verse; the one Beda thought most promising was Richard Ong's "Rhumba". I am not sure how many of these writers thought they might become poets. My friend James Puthucheary, I was sure, saw poetry only as another medium for him to express his anti-imperialist sentiments. His brother George might have been more interested in literary skills. Other seniors who had been publishing in the magazines were also keenly interested in poetry and several continued to write after graduation, notably the Aroozoo sisters, Marie (Bong) and Hedwig (Anuar). Others like Lim Thean Soo and Augustine Goh Sin Tub continued to publish, but the latter two became better known for their novels and short stories.

I asked Beda why he did not write. He admitted to me that every time he wrote, with his remarkable memory, lines he remembered would come to the surface and he could not shake them off. He noted that my memory was merely ordinary so he encouraged me to write. My first poem was done one night when I could not sleep. Sitting on the staircase outside my dormitory, I wrote "Moon Thoughts" and showed it to him. Beda encouraged me to write more. Then he typed 12 of them to make a little booklet that he entitled *Pulse* (the title of one of the poems in the collection) which he then printed and distributed as its publisher in April 1950. We were surprised that it was reported in the local press and was subsequently noted as the first book of poetry published in Singapore.

I was influenced by the free verse popularized by modern English poets to try to capture some of the images of the mixed communities of Chinese, Malays, Indians and Eurasians that characterized Malayan society. We were unclear what language we should be using, so I used Malay and Chinese words in basically English sentence structures. We also thought we should not only use English speech patterns but also seek to capture a local voice or accent. That was how Beda made me a poet in the eyes of some of my teachers as well as a few of my fellow students.

A book of poems comes from a Malayan's pen

TAN TOCK SAIK MEETS VARSITY STUDENT WANG GUNG WU WHO FINDS INSPIRATION AT MIDNIGHT.

THE most surprising thing about Wang Gung Wu, whose poems have just been published in Singapore, in a little book called "Pulse", in his age. This student of Intermediate Arts in the University of Malaya is only 19.

In our University today, where under-graduate verse flourishes as it has never flourished before, the poetry of this teenager stands high above the rest in reflection and poetic expression.

Tall and fair, with handsome delicate features, Gung Wu looks very much like the sensitive poet.

Born in Java, Gung Wu came to Malaya when he was very young. For many years he lived in Ipoh where his father served in the Municipality. He studied in the Anderson School where he was a very good scholar.

☆

IN 1947, the boy was sent to China to read Arts in the National Central University, Nanking. War broke up his studies and he returned to Malaya to join the University here as a private student.

Shyly, Gung Wu told me that he first wrote poetry when he recorded his impressions of China in Chinese. His father, a Chinese scholar, had inculcated a love of Chinese poetry in him.

His first attempts at English poetry were in the University of Malaya. Encouraged by a second-year student Beda Lim, he wrote his first poem "Moon Thoughts" one mid-night.

Even today, he invokes the Muse only at mid-night—when his fellow students have retired and "all is still."

When I voiced my surprise at his youth, he said, "It is not age that matters in writing poetry. It is the changes which take place in a poet's life and it is during this process that he translates his experiences into poetry.

☆

"IT is the ugliness and beauty that he sees that affects him. As for me, the changes have been sudden and frequent. From the sheltered existence of an only child in pre-war Ipoh to the insecure, frenzied life under the Japanese. From post-war Malaya to the poverty and intrigue of China. These experiences, however shocking, have benefitted me in writing poetry."

Gung Wu said that form should come after matter in poetry. "If you have good matter, the form will naturally follow. There should be no restrictions in form. In a variety of metres, more rhythm is found."

He added that he would use any word, no matter how odd, if it expressed his meaning. He uses such words as "marketivity," "factored," "hucksters" and "blachan" in his poems.

☆

IT WAS a most pleasant afternoon I spent that day talking with Gung Wu and listening to Beda Lim reading aloud from a copy of the "Pulse" in the college dining-room.

It was an experience I will not soon forget—Beda reading the opening lines of one of Gung Wu's best poems "Investment":

She was born of a stolen
*   night,*
Of a transient breathless-
*   ness.*

and then these lines from "Three Faces of the Night":

We are the audience
Of the three camps!
We are the campsters, too.
We rush round
To see the others,
But the mirror is a prism
blue.

Wang Gung Wu at work in the room of his friend and encourager, Beda Lim (right), in the University of Malaya hostel.

Gungwu with Beda Lim, on page 3 of the *Singapore Free Press*, 13 May 1951. Photo courtesy of Singapore Press Holdings Limited.

As a first-year student of English literature, I had no thought of being a poet. I simply had too much to learn. We had two tracks in our courses, one tracing the language to its roots, using Otto Jespersen's *Growth and Structure of the English Language*. The other drew on *A History of English Literature* by Emile Legouis and Louis Cazamian. I was fascinated by how Ellis Evans took us through Jespersen's work. He was less interested in the language structure than in its evolution as a means of conveying ideas and thought processes. He was a dedicated teacher very interested in his students and keen to introduce us to some of Wittgenstein's ideas in which he was immersed. I tried to follow him as best I could and discovered two things about myself: one, that I was not inclined to think in the abstract and two, grammar, syntax and phonetics had little appeal. What interested me was how languages change over time and how they influence one another. It was language users and how they cope with languages other than their own that intrigued me most.

As for the history of English literature, it was exhilarating to trace the Anglo-Saxon and Nordic background to Norman writings and how Geoffrey Chaucer's *The Canterbury Tales* came out of that. I found it absorbing to understand how that led to the new poetry of Edmund Spenser and ultimately to William Shakespeare. The two who took us through that class were Roy Morrell and Mary Barker. They stuck closely to the Legouis-Cazamian history and we could follow the long story as it unfolded. But before we reached the Romantics of the 19th century, I for once was drawn to the influence of Renaissance Europe and taken back to Dante, Petrarch and Boccaccio. I was stopped in my tracks here by the realization of how distant I was from the roots of the literature that I admired. For one thing, I had neither Greek nor Latin; only basic French plus the little German that I had begun to learn in Nanjing.

All this reminded me how superficially I understood Eliot's allusions to the classical literature of Europe when I had been reading his works in Nanjing. Even when I looked them up to seek explanations, most of the nuances in his poetry were lost. I could have gone and read the classics in translation, of course, but I found the list long and forbidding. In this university, with its English lecturers well equipped to help, I had hoped to do better. As it turned out, the more I read, the more I knew how far and how much further I would have to go as an apprentice. It was not impossible. If I dedicated the rest of my life to the pursuit of key parts of European civilization, I believed that I could do it. At least that was what I thought. Two years later, I concluded that, even if I could, why would I do that in the midst of all the excitement around me of nation-building and history-making?

By the end of my first year, I already knew that I had a great deal to catch up where English literature was concerned. There were so many gaps in my knowledge, so many writers that I had heard of but not read, and so many volumes of fiction, poetry and plays that I did not know. Without realizing it at the time, my experiments with the poems in *Pulse* had alienated me from the classics of English literature. I had unwittingly subverted my literary education by using the modern writings of Eliot and Auden and later Dylan Thomas as takeoff points for "Malayan" possibilities. I admired these modern authors but they did me no favours; instead, they encouraged me to experiment with styles and images that were no less alien to most of us. As for what I wrote, neither English nor Malayan, what could those poems say? Who would be the audience for something that had no roots in anything meaningful to our soil?

I was no rebel and was ready to learn from my teachers. I read literary criticisms of some of the great works by Shakespeare and the Romantics. I found the scholarship impressive but began to wonder whether that was any use to me as a poet or as a lover of poetry. I was tempted to reject the notes and explications and accept the New Criticism approach which, as I understood it at the time, meant reading each poem for itself and not going too far with the historical and critical baggage. As I recall, the more we were told to read the analyses and admire the scholarship, the less pleasure I found in the poems themselves.

When I heard from Beda Lim that the head of department, Professor Graham Hough, gave more enlightening lectures to his class of second-year students, I followed Beda to attend the lectures whenever I could. Indeed, Hough turned out to be very stimulating. Particularly memorable was his treatment of F.R. Leavis' *New Bearings in English Poetry*. I was not greatly interested in re-reading T.S. Eliot with close attention to the classical allusions, but when Hough introduced us to the metaphysical poets as examples of the kind of writing that preceded Eliot, I was all attention. It opened my eyes to a strain of poetry I had not been aware of. I became an admirer of John Donne and set out to read all the poems that Herbert Grierson had selected in *Metaphysical Lyrics & Poems of the Seventeenth Century*. What I did not immediately see was that my understanding was superficial because I did not share the belief-system that those poets were questioning or celebrating.

What appealed to me was the huge difference between Donne and his contemporaries and the poetry of the Romantics that I had read so much of, notably the works of Wordsworth, Keats and Coleridge. The literature classes I now attended combined those three with Chaucer's *Canterbury Tales* and Shakespeare's *Sonnets* and I found that refreshing. When Hough took us further and compared them to the metaphysical poets, to the heavy religious and philosophical background linked with meditations about man's nature and his relations with God, I found it demanding in a totally new way. It led me to realize that this was taking me deeper into European culture than I was prepared to go. The poetry was beautiful but the underlying assumptions aroused in me a resistance that I did not fully understand.

Nevertheless, I persevered and turned to some of the Greek classics, notably Homer and the Theban plays of Sophocles. I read them in translation and found the experience rather like learning to read classical Chinese while rendering them in the vernacular. The mental exercise was familiar. I enjoyed that and also discovered that knowing them added new dimensions to my understanding of later writings in English, not unlike appreciating Tang and Song poetry better when I recalled allusions to *The Book of Poetry*, the *yuefu* 乐府 lyrics and the *Nineteen Old Poems* 古诗十九首.

I took away another bonus from Hough's lectures. He introduced us to many kinds of satirical writings from the Greek comedies to Jonathan Swift. I was reading George Orwell's *Animal Farm* at the time, and this gave the genre an ancient genealogy that added depth to Orwell's animal story. In particular, taking us back to *Gulliver's Travels* led me to re-read Daniel Defoe's *Robinson Crusoe*, and to re-imagine the time when the world was opening up and Europeans proclaimed how they had "discovered" their new world. This was during the third term of my first year and the history course given by Brian Harrison had just got to the point when Prince Henry the Navigator was helping Portugal to reach south along the West African coast and Columbus and his cohort were preparing to set sail for China and India across the Atlantic.

I had a taste of this story in my Empire and Commonwealth history at school where it all began with the English exploits of Francis Drake and Walter Raleigh. The highlight was Drake's circumnavigation of the world after fighting the Spanish and landing in California. Now we were reading *The Tempest* and *Robinson Crusoe* as literature, and I found Shakespeare's and Defoe's imagined islands much more interesting. It mattered little whether the "natives" were Red Indians or Negro slaves, the evocative words they uttered were memorable. The Western mind's eye looking at the world had augmented the metaphysical transition and saw the world as God's gift, one that imagined a universal mankind that evolved to respond to nature in different ways. From that angle, one could go back to re-visit the Greek and Roman classical traditions or look forward to the Romantic response to the new freedoms that the Europeans now enjoyed. I too found myself in a new world, one that was captured in the layers of modern poetry that I thought I could use to take me out of the English language edifice.

Free to Enjoy

PROFESSOR HOUGH WENT further to broaden my mind in two separate directions. He introduced me to Gerard Manley Hopkins and also encouraged me to take D.H. Lawrence seriously. I was attracted by the way Hopkins played with words and images and tried to read "The Wreck of the Deutschland". But, as I struggled with the poem and its inbuilt religiosity, I was reminded of my many efforts to approach religious faith, without success. I found that I had become stubbornly irreligious. I remembered the times when I visited churches, temples and mosques and came away unbelieving. It confirmed for me that language was pliable but the institutions behind beliefs were more like traps. In contrast, Lawrence represented for me a larger share of freedom and I could understand why my father saw him as quintessentially modern.

When the year ended, I was sorry to hear that Graham Hough was leaving to return to Cambridge and I would not have him as my teacher in my second year. His eventual successor, Roy Morrell, was a caring teacher but more pedestrian in his literary interests. After my second year, when it was time to choose which subject to do my honours degree in, I gave Hough's departure as one of the reasons why I did not continue in English literature. But that was not really fair to the department. Our teachers gave us what they would have given to students in Britain, nothing in their eyes but the best. They also tried to show us how much literature could also be fun. They encouraged us to produce our own literary magazine, *The New Cauldron*. When I became editor of the Students' Union newspaper, *The Malayan Undergrad*, I included a literary section that pushed at the edges of the publishable.

We had our world of earnest effort that might have appeared to others to be no more than make-believe. We wrote about what the future Malayan literature could be like and imagined the role it could play in educating future generations. Some had envisaged the possibility of Chinese, Malays and Indians communicating with one another in an evolving common language. We all knew that the nature of the country was still unclear. But the idea that we could contribute towards defining it by our efforts to promote its literary identity was tantalizing. It led some of us to pay more attention to the political realities of the day, but I shall deal with that in a later chapter.

I had not given up on literature but increasingly felt the limits of being taught the best of *English* literature. Looking back, there was too much missing in our education. Most of us knew little of the classics of Mediterranean Europe so there was no depth in our understanding of later writings. Nor did we know the English language as well as the students from the best English schools, so we were unable to savour the finer points of poetry. Perhaps we could have gained from having something akin to comparative literature, even if confined to other writings in modern Europe. Today, we would also have full access to fine writing in English from America and the Commonwealth. My year in Nanjing in the Foreign Languages Department meant that the English specialists shared classes with students studying French, German and Russian and I could see some of what they were reading. And my friends studying modern Chinese literature were surprisingly well read in the European classics available in translation. I had sensed how that wider access fed their imagination and enriched their insights into their own literary heritage.

Of course, my own schooling or lack of it in Ipoh was partly to blame for my frustrations. I recall how my friend Beda taught me Western symphonic music, introducing me to instrument by instrument as each came on, and how one passage led to the next. He then took me through the elementary stages of development from Vivaldi to Sibelius. I saw why this would have to be replicated to dispel my ignorance of European literature. I would also need to be opened up to the key works of Dante and Cervantes, Moliere and Voltaire, Goethe, Chekov and Tolstoy. The gaps in my knowledge were abysmal. Of course, I could now begin in earnest; our library was good enough and our teachers were willing to help.

But my excitement when joining my English-educated friends and hearing them talk about a future Malayan literature led me to step into the deep end of that pool without learning how to swim. Beda's enthusiasm in publishing the few poems I had written led me further in. Then, out of the blue, I received an invitation to a writers' workshop in Manila where I met real writers from the Philippines and Indonesia. This was to make me realize that the deep end was deeper than I thought. I returned from Manila somewhat chastened, but still willing to pursue Western literature further and also reach out to the literature of my Malay and Indian friends. The visit also spurred me to find out more about local writings in Chinese. I shall write more about the trip in my next chapter.

Literature was not my only activity. I was attending classes in economics and history at the same time. But I remained interested and, in my second year, that was given a boost when a new lecturer arrived. Patrick Anderson had an unusual background. He was a practitioner, not an imperial educator. He had been president of the Oxford Union, a poet who founded *Preview*, a literary magazine in Canada, and also had a left-wing socialist background. Most of all, he was interesting to talk to as someone of the generation of Auden and Spender. He later recounted his two years in Singapore in his book *Snake Wine* and I was surprised to learn how much he had captured of our innocence. For myself, I remember him most for expanding my literary domain through the French writers he admired, notably Albert Camus. I had been reading Marcel Proust but did not take to his volumes of refined writing.

Anderson introduced me to the poetry of Guillaume Apollinaire who was far more interesting and reading him led me to read Charles Baudelaire, Paul Valéry and Arthur Rimbaud. Theirs was an amazing world of artists, musicians and poets and I was transfixed by everything associated with Paris. I had known about Henry James and Ernest Hemingway being inspired by that city. Our lecturers had told us about James Joyce writing about Dublin and finishing his *Ulysses* there, but it was Anderson's insistence that I read *A Portrait of the Artist as a Young Man* that left an indelible mark. When I first came across the phrase "I will not serve", I thought little of it. A few years later, I realized how much the phrase had haunted me and may have turned me away from any career in public service. It was my first retreat, mainly unconscious, from the values that my father and our literati ancestors had left in me. Deep down, the phrase had led me to look for a greater share of freedom, away from the political realm.

Anderson also showed us how literature was fun. As a film-lover, I was always interested in the theatre. But drama in class was remote and largely about words in books, unlike the Chinese opera and Malay *bangsawan* performances we got to see. One of the expatriate wives gathered some of us on campus to produce Merton Hodge's *The Wind and the Rain*, but I found the play quite forgettable and don't think anyone learnt much from acting in it. With Anderson, however, it was different. Dorothy Morrell, wife of our head of department, found him amenable to doing a serious play with the students. This was Sophocles' *Antigone*. Dorothy played Antigone while Anderson played her uncle King Creon. Several of my friends were in the chorus, led by Beda Lim and Jack da Silva. I played the part of Haemon, the man Antigone was supposed to marry. It was a feeble part with no memorable lines, but we had a most enjoyable time and, from then on, I never lost my interest in the theatre.

We read Oscar Wilde and George Bernard Shaw but never saw any of their plays performed. The nearest I got to connecting with some of their writings was when I did readings in my summer job with Radio Malaya in 1950 and took part in a few radio plays. However, the part that really stuck in my mind was when I was the voice of Boxer in the radio version of George Orwell's *Animal Farm*. Orwell had just died and several of us had begun to think of him as a great writer. I had enjoyed his *Burmese Days* and was learning about his involvement in the Spanish Civil War at the time through his *Homage to Catalonia*.

Thus, another aspect of English literature was admitted as a part of my adjustment to political changes. I had become active in the student union and was increasingly drawn into matters with anti-colonial overtones, some of which we equated with resistance against capitalism. In my case, I was leaning towards the British Labour Party variety of socialism. Underlying that was a rejection of violence and a preference for measures that promoted freedom. Like "I will not serve", it was a way of thinking that seemed to be rooted in the literature that the enlightened West stood for.

After the departure of Patrick Anderson, we found a lively replacement in Eric Mottram. Anderson had given us insights into North American writings, but it was Eric who was determined to make American literature essential to our understanding of modern literature in English. With Eric we moved beyond T.S. Eliot to a wider group that ranged from the highly-disciplined Wallace Stevens to Allen Ginsberg and the Beat Generation. In particular, Eric taught me to admire the work of Lionel Trilling, especially *The Liberal Imagination*, and made me aware how much I had become sympathetic towards that worldview.

By the end of my second year, I decided that, although I still loved literature and continued to write a few poems, I did not want to be a literary scholar. Apart from not being keen to do research on the works of poets, novelists and playwrights, I was not interested in literary theory and also could not see myself writing literary criticism as a profession. Once I was clear about that, I had to consider which of the other two subjects I should continue to study for my honours degree. I had by that time spent too much time in student union affairs. I shall write later about what I thought about the Malaya I looked forward to belonging to.

Manila Alert

I WAS AWARE when Beda Lim published my poems that most of my fellow students did not take what I wrote seriously; some openly told me I was wasting my time. It surprised me, however, when some of my British teachers thought it their duty to encourage me to keep going with my experiments in verse. Even more surprising was when, a few months after *Pulse* was published in 1950, I received an invitation to attend a Manila symposium for young writers. I never knew how I came to be invited. I assumed that the organizers had learnt from the newspapers about my book of verse and thought I would benefit from the experience. My friends suggested that one of our teachers might have given my name to the organizers and I recall thinking it might have been Ellis Evans who had shown particular interest in what I was doing with the English language.

The invitation came from the Rockefeller Foundation. It had launched a programme for young writers of Southeast Asia and had asked Wallace Stegner, a novelist of the American West, to teach "writers in the Far East". They sent him to the University of the Philippines (UP) where a well-known Filipino short-story writer and professor of English literature, N.V.M. Gonzalez, had started a UP Writers' Workshop for students and other young writers. The two were asked to organize a symposium that included other writers from the region. I was keen to learn from practitioners even though the symposium was focused on fiction rather than poetry. I include an account here not only because it was my first chance to learn about another Southeast Asian country but also because it taught me what national literature might mean.

I knew little about the Philippines and could only recall some American war films about the Japanese driving General MacArthur out in 1942 and his having said "I shall return", and about how he finally did so. I also remember listening to American and British news broadcasts during the last months of the Pacific War in 1945 and hearing about the bitter fighting in Manila before the Japanese surrendered. From books I found in the library, I learnt that there was already a generation of Filipino writers in English and that several generations had been writing in Spanish. I had heard of the Philippines Revolution at the end of the 19th century but had not read the writings of Jose Rizal. The library had translations of his *Noli de Tangere* and his last farewell, *Mi Ultimo Adios,* and reading them gave me a glimpse of how the new nation of the Philippines saw its origins.

The Rockefeller Foundation's willingness to encourage writing in English was well meaning but premature. English was not widely used in the region. Only Burma and British Malaya taught in English at university level. In 1950, independent Burma had turned against the British Commonwealth and Malaya's university was only a year old. Neither could boast of established poets and novelists writing in English. And although Indonesia was moving away from Dutch and sending students to study in America and Australia, no one wrote in English. Their promising writers were determined that their national literature would be written in their version of Malay, Bahasa Indonesia.

Looking back, as a beginner-poet trying to write in English, I was probably one of very few who needed the workshop's help. The two others invited were from Indonesia: Rosihan Anwar and Usmar Ismail, who both wrote in Malay and it was obvious that they needed no teaching. Rosihan was a journalist who had founded his own publication, *Pedoman*; he was fluent in Dutch and spoke good English but was not the least interested in writing in English. He was known as someone who had translated Jose Rizal's "Last Farewell" from English into Bahasa, and that was an inspiration for young Indonesian nationalists fighting for independence from the Dutch. As for Usmar Ismail, he was already admired for the films in Bahasa that he had directed.

I do not know what they made of the workshop. After a couple of sessions on creative writing, they talked about the Indonesian writers of "Generation '45" (who surfaced during the Japanese occupation), notably about Chairil Anwar whose poems were well known among the Malays in Malaya. When Rosihan found out that I did not know any of the Malay writers who called themselves "Generation '50", he was visibly unimpressed.

He could see that I was not a Chinese who had long settled in Malaya. He might have seen my efforts to write in English as comparable to those among Indonesian Chinese who regretted the end of the Dutch empire.

Most of those who attended were UP students. Stegner was dutiful and told us about his experiences with writing. He was not a poet and said nothing about poetry. What struck me was N.V.M.'s enthusiasm for short story writing. He was a great admirer of Katherine Anne Porter and asked us to do what she did, writing draft after draft until she was satisfied. That did help me appreciate the skills of Guy de Maupassant, W. Somerset Maugham, Edgar Allan Poe, O. Henry and Katherine Mansfield whose stories I had found memorable.

I spent the rest of the week with N.V.M.'s colleague Virginia Moreno. She was interested in poetry and was tasked with nurturing young poets to write in English. She had Malay, Spanish and Chinese ancestry, and getting to know her alerted me to the many cultural layers found in many Southeast Asian communities. That made me more conscious of the interplay of local and cosmopolitan features that shaped the peoples of the region. I made friends among her students with whom I kept in touch for years. None of them went on to be writers just as I was also to turn away from writing poetry. Three became academics while a fourth became a civil servant. Only one of them continued to write, winning short stories prizes on the side while teaching Japanese studies at UP. Two others became historians: an economic historian who became a distinguished university president, and an Indologist who discovered a Maranao version of the *Ramayana*. When I learnt that they too had turned to academia, I felt less badly about giving up being a poet.

However, the excitement of national awakening that I sensed among these friends was years ahead of what was surfacing among the English-educated in Malaya. Listening to them debate their country's future, I was introduced to the writings of Renato Constantino and Teodoro Agoncillo who were challenging the apologists for Spanish and American rule. They also showed sympathy for the Hukbalahap rebels who were allied to the country's communist party; that reminded me of those who argued that the Malayan Communist Party consisted of nationalists and should not be treated as the enemy.

I left Manila with mixed feelings. None of the people I met were committed to writing in English. Some of the older Filipino writers had started by writing in Spanish and only experimented with English after they had had opportunities to study in America. The younger writers who stayed longer in the US did become short story writers and poets, but those who returned were challenged to write in the national language, Tagalog.

⸻◦◈◦⸻

Manila offered other surprises. The YMCA at Ermita where I stayed was close to Rizal Park and I could see several bombsites that were still uncleared. My friends told me the dramatic story of the young poet Homero Chung Veloso who had recently committed suicide in the Y. Knowing I was Chinese, they added that the poet was of Chinese ancestry and wrote in English. They reminded me that people of part-Chinese lineage had been around for centuries. Sixty years later, when writing a foreword to Richard T. Chu's *More Tsinoy than We Admit*, I recalled that event vividly,

> That was the first time I heard someone described with a national identity ascribed to someone whose ancestry was still recognisably Chinese. It provided me with foretaste of things to come. Years later, it became more common to hear of people being called Indonesians and Malaysians of Chinese descent, and there emerged among the Chinese themselves the term huayi, descendants of Chinese....

That story of a poet of part-Chinese descent stayed in my mind to return again and again when I studied the history of the Chinese overseas.

During the workshop, I was introduced to a couple of other UP students with Chinese names. They were curious why, after having studied in China, I was writing in English. I explained that I was simply learning how to write. Afterwards, I realized that my inability to explain what I was doing marked the beginnings of my doubts about the futility of using a foreign language to express a new national identity. My Filipino friends were also doubtful. One of them said that it was ridiculous for them to throw out one colonial language, Spanish after 300 years, merely to exchange it for another that was imposed only 50 years ago.

This raised another question in my mind. Where do the Chinese in the region stand in this ferment for nation building based on indigenous authenticity? As a student of English literature, I thought that was not the right question. My task was to master English so that I could appreciate its literary glories and learn to use it to express what I had to say. It was only later that I realized that the question was central to the future of the millions of overseas Chinese who hoped to adapt themselves as second-class nationals in their adopted homes.

How was I a Malayan?

The Manila workshop led me to find out more about the generations who had been writing their national literature since the beginning of the 20th century. I was attracted to the idea that these writers were helping a new nation to find itself. I also took Rosihan's advice to improve my Malay and read literature in Bahasa Indonesia. He told me to start with Chairil Anwar and Generation '45. That reminded me of the May Fourth Chinese literature that influenced *huaqiao* 华侨 (overseas Chinese) literature in the Nanyang 南洋 (southern ocean). In Malaya, many such writers had been born and educated in China, including a few like Yu Dafu 郁达夫 who had already become famous before coming to Singapore. Many admired the novelist Lao She who had taught briefly in Singapore and wrote a novella about children in the colony, *The Birthday of Xiaobo*.

I had paid little attention to local writings in Chinese before I went to China in 1947. I had simply noted that the writings were inspired by the Baihua 白话 movement. My reading was superficial and I had concluded that their writings were too imitative. After coming to Singapore in 1949 and hearing about the debates among my fellow students about a possible Malayan literature in English, I still did not think of Chinese writings as Malayan. This was also true of what I knew about writings in Malay: I saw them as a branch of the literature of Indonesia and not really "Malayan".

We thought that Malaya would become a very different kind of country, but I wondered if we really understood what that difference entailed. Clearly, the Indonesians already believed in their country's national identity. President Sukarno's speeches spelt that out in passionate language and most Indonesians hailed him as a visionary leader. What was intriguing was that they did not choose the language of the majority Javanese as their national language. Instead, like the Dutch who used Malay as the lingua franca of the archipelago, they accepted that Malay had become the common language of all the port cities. It was the language of business that everyone found useful. How lucky they were to have a common language that all agreed should be the national language.

The Filipinos, with dozens of indigenous languages, had quite a different problem. They were familiar with the power transfers from empire to nation-state in the West, and had moved from Spanish to English after the American occupation. The Americans introduced their public school system to their colony, and urged local universities to switch to English, and a few writers like Jose Garcia Villa did publish in the new language. But the use of Tagalog to write national literature was yet to be settled and I could see that another generation was now being encouraged to write in English. For me, this posed more questions about nationhood. After returning to Singapore, I reviewed what we thought was "Malayan". The poems I wrote could be seen as some kind of response. If Malayan literature was to emerge with a base in English, I should keep on trying. But events moved fast and I soon found myself with two other questions.

How was I a Malayan? Only a few months earlier, I was still a Chinese looking for my place in the sun. Malaya was the place I had left and my return depended on my father's job in one of its Malay states. Learning about Bahasa Indonesia and the demand for Tagalog to be officially recognized, I found myself reminded of my ties to the language of my ancestors. I was not alone. Whether in the Ipoh I knew or the Singapore I was beginning to understand, there were thousands in Chinese schools whose only home was now Malaya. How should we expect them to accept that English should have a part in creating the national language?

Also, what kind of English could serve the country? It could continue to be the language of law and governance and be used to master the business and technical skills that modern societies would need. But surely not the *national* language. Decades later, after Singapore separated from Malaya/Malaysia, there was to be a new twist to the story. Few of us expected that many younger Singaporeans would have English as their mother tongue. In a country called Malaya, we could see that the Malay majority would expect their language to form the basis of nationhood. Fierce debates were going on about which parties should take over when the British finally left, but it was clear that the British accepted the constitutional rights of the Malay rulers and expected Malay leaders to define the core of the new nation.

In short, we were not talking about a *Malayan* literature but about aspiring writers in English finding new ways of expressing a local sensibility. We could certainly try to find new ways to express ourselves; the real issue was whether you wanted to be a writer or not. Using a bit of Malay, Cantonese, Hokkien in our own brand of English, which we called Engmalchin, was legitimate, but that was not itself going to create a Malayan literature. We were aware that only a few people in the country could read English and when my little book of poetry was published, my fellow students hardly noticed. Admittedly, it was not literature. I wrote my poems to show that we did not have to write like Englishmen. Only our English teachers were curious, but I never knew what they really thought.

I have been asked why I did not write in Chinese. If I wanted to write for a Chinese audience, I would have done that. But I was an English literature student wondering if I could find my own voice in that language. I did later try to write a few poems in Chinese and when the Malay Studies Department was established at the university in 1953, I began to study the language in earnest and attended the lectures of our best-known Malay scholar, Zainal Abidin bin Ahmad (Za'ba). By that time, however, I had decided to become a historian and studying Malay was more for reading documents than to keep up with the literary works of Generation '50.

Learning to write in Engmalchin made little sense if a national language had to be based on a language native to the country. The few poems I continued to write only sharpened my doubts. When I finally saw that was not what I wanted to go on doing, I stopped. I have sometimes wondered whether my loss of faith in my poetic skills began with the trip to Manila. Later, when I was in London, I kept up my interest in the work of our poets and particularly admired the work of Edwin Thumboo and Ee Tiang Hong. For years afterwards, I continued to read their work and was delighted to see how they had avoided the road to nowhere that I had taken. I further saw how new generations of poets were finding the voice that we had hoped for. When asked years later to reflect on my earlier experiences, I wrote "Trial and error in Malayan poetry" to warn of the mistakes that we had made. And later, in the 1980s, I reflected on the new trends in an interview with Robert Yeo. By the time I spoke at a forum organized by Philip Holden in 2008, I could say that our Singapore poets could write in English as their mother tongue and could stand with most others in the Anglophone world.

I had continued to follow some of the writers who believed that Malayan literature could be better expressed in other mother tongues like Malay and Chinese. I read some of the collections of poems and short stories published by the Youth Book Company 青年书局 from the 1950s. I also tried to keep up with the Angkatan '50 authors whose writings had been anthologized by Asraf in *Mekar dan Segar: Bunga Ramai, Cherita2 Pendek, Angkatan Baru* (1959). By that time, I had come to appreciate that, apart from Edwin and Tiang Hong, there had appeared another bright star in the poetry firmament. He was Wong Phui Nam, whose best poems were lofty and ambitious. His Victoria Institution schoolmate T. Wignesan asked me to write about writers in Chinese for his *Bunga Emas: Contemporary Malaysian Literature* (1964). I translated a few poems and wrote a short survey of their writings. By that time, Fang Xiu 方修 had produced his three-volume collection 《马华新文学史稿》. It reminded us that Chinese writers had been trying to "write Malayan" long before the Second World War. Together with the literary output of the decades following, it was possible to identify a Malayan creative frame in which the different generations writing in different languages had each picked out their distinctive Singaporean and Malaysian accents.

PART TWO

My New Frame

What is a Nation?

MY FIRST MONTHS at MU had led me to think that literature was one way to look at the idea of nation building. It did little to help me understand how new the idea of a nation was in Asia. The future Malaya was obviously not at all like the nationalist China that we saw losing out to the Chinese Communist Party (CCP) or the Indonesia where the Communist Party of Indonesia (PKI) was a legal party that contested democratic elections. Nor was it anything like Britain the imperial power that was soon to return to more confined borders. Meeting young Filipino and Indonesian writers in Manila alerted me to other imaginaries: both countries comprised innumerable islands each with histories of their own. They seemed to be creating different kinds of post-colonial states. That had warned me off the use of English to produce a national literature but it still left me unclear as to what the Malayan nation would be like.

I knew something about the state of Perak and the people I grew up with. I had also read about the Emergency, the war that was being fought close to Ipoh in the Kinta valley. I consciously set aside the perspective of someone brought up Chinese and educated for China, and tried to imagine the Malaya I would belong to. It was more difficult than I expected. Most books described Malaya as a British colony plus two sets of Malay States, four of them "protected" and five others "advised". Only the most recent official documents sought to construct a broad-framed union or federation. A great deal was left to the many imaginations straining to sketch the kind of nationhood that could satisfy multiple interests.

What I recall of my own understanding was limited to the following. The main protagonists in national development knew that non-Malays made up over 40 per cent of the population on the Peninsula and over 80 per cent in Singapore. If Malaya included Singapore, the Malays were outnumbered. That was why the island city had to be left out of post-war Malaya. In the Federation, the Malay rulers surrendered their powers to the national government in Kuala Lumpur, but retained residual rights spelt out in the constitution. The Conference of Rulers elected the country's head of state, the Yang di-Pertuan Agong, a position that would be rotated every five years.

The Malay leaders made it clear that they wanted the Federation to be a Malay country but were prepared to allow peoples who had settled from other parts of Asia to become the country's citizens. They were especially fearful of the MCP which was led by Chinese who were inspired by revolutions in China and elsewhere. The British were also determined not to allow the communists to win in the context of an ideological Cold War. The residents originating from China and British India had not been keen to accept the British plan to bring the various entities together as a union, but could not stop the Anglo-Malay settlement that followed.

There had never been a country called Malaya and most of the people in the different states, whether Malays or non-Malays, knew little about one another. The Malays were primarily loyal to their respective Sultans. For example, in the state of Perak where I grew up, the Malays were the Sultan's subjects who saw the Chinese and Indians as having come to trade or to work in British and Chinese enterprises.

There were other Malays settled in the Straits Settlements who did not owe allegiance to a Malay ruler. They included those from various parts of the archipelago—notably the Minangkabau of Sumatra and the maritime Bugis from Celebes (Sulawesi)—who were more inclined to respond to the idea of pan-Malay nationalism. There were also those whose Muslim ancestors had come from India and the Arab world who could identify with the indigenous communities. Some felt free to think of a new identity as part of Indonesia Raya, a Greater Indonesia. During the Japanese occupation, this perspective had received encouragement in the context of a Japanese-sponsored Pan-Asianism.

The Federation agreement was negotiated when I was in China, so I knew little about its significance until I returned. When I found that I could become a citizen of the new country, I was unsure what that meant. It was only after I went to MU that I began to think about how this Malaya might be developed. But what I saw in Singapore made me realize that building a new nation would be very complicated. It was assumed that Singapore would become part of Malaya one day, and the hope was that its people would think more or less like the rest of the country. Most of us from the mainland did not give much thought to how Singapore might fit in. We thought that the terms would be negotiated when the time came. In the meantime, the eleven states of the Federation would determine the nature of the new nation-state.

I wanted to study more about the country's immediate problems, especially its economic development. Malaya was important to the British as the world's biggest exporter of rubber, a strategic product. And there was the tin industry, also thought to be the most efficient in the world. The two items were so profitable that many thought that Britain would hang on to Malaya as long as they could and delay the country's independence. This was confirmed when the Korean War started, when even more attention was focused on Malaya's economy.

As for politics, I was quite innocent about what the local Chinese communities wanted. My parents were from the province of Jiangsu while most of the Chinese in Malaya originated from the provinces of Guangdong and Fujian. My father was treated with some respect as an educator but did not belong to any of the dialect, hometown, trade and business organizations that were involved in local and China politics. The long-settled Chinese who identified as Baba or *peranakan* had their own influential institutions. My father was not involved in anything political and never talked about the subject. My mother was interested but was primarily concerned about events in China. Thus, our family remained on the margins of community life.

Some of the local Chinese looked to China and hoped to return some day. The majority, however, saw Malaya as their home and accepted that the Malays would initially have a special position under their sultans. However, together with those Indians who were prepared to be Malayans, they wanted to be treated as equals, and rejected the idea of becoming second-class citizens. What concerned the Chinese most was the future of their language and culture, and especially that of Chinese education. On this matter, my father had strong feelings. By 1954, when he no longer believed in what the government was planning for Chinese schools, he took early retirement.

I also learnt that there was a class problem. At the time, workers in the factories and plantations were largely Chinese and Indian while the rural peasantry was Malay. The two groups did not always see themselves as a working class with common interests. There was a trade union movement to defend workers from being exploited. But the government feared that communists had infiltrated the unions, and their leaders were suspect. Some had come from China and had left-wing connections or sympathies. There had earlier been a Nanyang Branch of the Chinese Communist Party 中国共产党南洋分支会. Later, it was replaced by the Malayan party, the MCP, that focused on independence from British colonialism but sided with the British against the Japanese.

After the Japanese were defeated, the British disarmed the Malayan People's Anti-Japanese Army (MPAJA). But its soldiers, who had fought as partners of the British Operations Executive Force 136, felt that they should have a say in the future of Malaya. They went among the workers and were active in the trade unions. This was clearly against British interests that saw the party being energized by similar parties in China, India, Ceylon, Indonesia and Vietnam.

In addition, racial tensions between Malays and Chinese were also rising. The Malays were afraid that armed Chinese would take over parts of the country. The communists were mostly Chinese with only a few Malays and Indians, while the all-Malay infantry supported the British and Malay constitutional rights. The MCP was banned and the Emergency declared. In this way, the urban communists, including those in Singapore, were driven underground or forced into the jungle.

Most Chinese supported prevailing anti-colonial sentiments and sought equal rights for everyone, but they were opposed to the use of violence. In particular, those in business, whether large or small, wanted peace and order so that they could take advantage of the economic opportunities available. Very few knew or cared what communism meant in this part of the world. Although a few of the English-educated were drawn to socialist anti-imperialism, the majority of those who joined the MCP had studied in local Chinese schools.

This is what I recall I knew when arriving at MU. Nothing there helped me to understand what would have to be done to make Malaya into a nation. We seemed to use the word loosely to refer to the country the

British would soon leave us with. Thereafter, all would have to depend on our leaders. Some names had emerged by the time I got back to Ipoh. The best known among the Malays was that of Dato' Onn bin Jaafar who was the founding president of the United Malay National Organisation (UMNO). The Chinese had yet to decide on their leader but the most active among the English-educated was Tan Cheng Lock, the president of the Malayan Chinese Association (MCA). The communists obviously did not accept his leadership and greeted his election as MCA leader by trying to have him assassinated in Ipoh. I referred to this event in my earlier volume, *Home is not Here*, because my father was a guest at the event at which the bomb went off and Tan Cheng Lock was wounded. My father was badly shaken. What he described was something I brought with me to Singapore later that year.

Colony

THE YEAR 1949 was transformational. For the next two decades, the idea of Malaya and later its extension Malaysia loomed over everything I did: federation, university, encounters with the idea of Malayan literature when I arrived on campus and numerous friends who taught me about the different parts of Malaya where they came from. It was overwhelming. It was months before I realized that, while trying to grasp all that, I actually knew almost nothing about Singapore. That the city was not part of the new Malaya was hard for me to comprehend, like a dark blot on a beautiful painting.

Of course, it was explained to me why. Although effectively the centre of British Malaya since the early 20th century, the colony was not included in the aborted Malayan Union and was then left out of the Federation. I was made to understand how painful that was for the people of the two other siblings of the Straits Settlements, Penang and Malacca, to be separated from their southern brother. But the story usually ended with the assurance that it was only a matter of timing. Singapore was an essential part of Malaya and would soon cease to be a colony when Malaya became truly independent. In the meantime, the city had to put up with the ignominy of being the left-out colony. I found all this difficult to absorb. For years, the contradictory voices demanding a variety of different outcomes for the colony did little to help me understand what was at the heart of the problem.

It was time for me to get to know Singapore. How were its people different from the rest of us who came from the north to study there? What did they think of being colonials? It was unfortunate that I was starting at the wrong end of the city. Our campus was surrounded by the luscious Botanic Gardens and many well-spaced homes for high officials and established executives. To go to the city from the Gardens side of the campus meant walking along shady roads past splendid bungalows to get to the quiet and genteel Orchard Road, in order to catch the bus to town. Even when we used the campus entrance on Bukit Timah Road to take the bus down Rochor Canal Road to Queen Street, it was still lightly populated with many comfortable houses on the way. Nothing on either route could be described as representative of the way most people lived.

In any case, I did not make many trips during my first year. For one thing, I had little money and going out meant eating out. For another, there was so much to do on campus apart from attending classes and holding meetings of one kind or another. We were a small group in the dormitories, the buildings now occupied mainly by the National University's Faculty of Law and the School of Public Policy. It was easy to be involved in campus activities and I found myself joining in many of them, eager to learn from my new friends. I knew it would not be enough to know Singapore by reading books; that would be like scratching a foot itch from outside one's shoes.

Nevertheless, two books did help me learn how the city became the important hub of the British Empire in the east. These were Makepeace, Brooke and Braddell's *One Hundred Years of Singapore,* and Song Ong Siang's *One Hundred Years' History of the Chinese in Singapore.* I confess I never fully digested the information given in them, but they provided me with a glimpse of how different Singapore was from the states of the peninsula. They did make me pause to wonder if it could belong to the Malaya that was being shaped. The books also provided the historical background to what I read in the newspapers each day, and I could soon identify the colony's active leaders and what they stood for. Mainly Chinese and Indian, they acted as future leaders who would in time seek the right to be part of the elites of Malaya after the British left.

I am writing this in the midst of Singapore's 200th anniversary celebrations. It might therefore be surprising to hear that, during my years as a student, very few people mentioned Stamford Raffles. We had on campus the Raffles Society and there were places and institutions named after him but they were for us only names. Years later, when I learnt that my head of department John Bastin, an admirable scholar, would decide to spend his life learning everything there was to know about Raffles, I confess I was very surprised.

I did look out for Singapore friends. There were the freshmen who won scholarships and shared our dormitories, like Hsu Tse Kwang and Sim Kee Boon who both became leading figures among the city's managerial elite. They told me about Chinatown, the east coast beaches, the best places to eat and the areas to avoid. But they often went home after classes and rarely spent any weekends on campus. So I did not learn from them as much as I would have liked. Others were my seniors who were active in literary and other society gatherings. I admired them for the poems they wrote, notably Hedwig Aroozoo, Lim Thean Soo and Augustine Goh. But they did not stay on campus and I did not have many chances to talk to them.

When I became president of the Students' Union, K.R. Chandra and S. Ramdas were on my executive committee and they taught me a great deal. We got to know each other well when they travelled with me to attend an international students conference. They helped me understand other aspects of the rich variety of identities and social customs that flourished in the city. Years later, when they both became senior civil servants, I could see how much they would have helped their colleagues navigate the tribulations of the city-state's early years.

Nothing I learnt that first year, however, prepared me for the riots that took place late in 1950. The Maria Hertogh riots have been carefully studied and the series of TV documentaries about her life after she went to the Netherlands have given us a fuller story of what happened. Here I shall only recall what I understood of the violent outbreak at the time. For me, the several layers of the story highlighted the complex heritage of the colony that I had only superficially grasped. The ingredients of what was to be post-colonialism and transnationalism, of race and religion, of varying ideas of law and justice and the role of the media were suddenly laid bare. In less than a week, all these features of colonial life appeared in sharp relief and, for decades afterwards, they influenced my thinking about Singapore's plural society.

Maria Hertogh's Dutch Catholic father was working in the Netherlands East Indies when the Japanese took Java in 1942 and put him into a prisoner-of-war camp. His Eurasian wife brought her children to live with her mother, but when she too was interned, she left Maria with a Malay woman, who later adopted Maria as her daughter and took her home with her to Trengganu. After the war, Maria's father was determined to get Maria back. Maria's Malay adoptive mother brought her to Singapore and the matter was placed before the courts. The British judge decided that Maria should go back to her Dutch father. Her Malay mother successfully appealed and, on Maria's release, married her to a Malay man. Her Dutch father in turn contested that and eventually the judge awarded him custody.

I had been reading the news and realized that the case had built up emotional reactions among Muslims in several countries. The judge had also ordered Maria to be put in a convent while awaiting the final appeal. The press published sensational stories that displayed Maria learning to be Catholic. The Muslim community became agitated and, on the day of the verdict, large numbers had gathered at the court. When it was decided that Maria would go back to Holland with her father, the riots began. This lasted three days and I learnt later that 18 people were killed and some 170 people injured.

The angry mob beat up any European they could find. We were all taken aback by the intensity of the emotions aroused. Although no Chinese people were involved, my friends and I did wonder if something similar could happen if the Malay and Chinese communities faced a similar issue. Our British teachers told us how shocked they were by the way the issue was handled and regretted the government's poor judgment. One of the British staff at Radio Malaya with whom I had worked described how the taxi he was in was stopped and how the taxi driver saved his life by keeping the doors locked while slowly driving through the crowd.

Overnight, my picture of an orderly Singapore preparing for self-government and full decolonization became clouded. Was this sort of thing inevitable in a "plural society"? I had been introduced to this concept through the work of J.S. Furnivall on the Netherlands East Indies and had begun to think that the concept could well describe the future Malaya. We had read about America being a melting pot for immigrants, and our medical students had light-heartedly called their magazine *The Cauldron* to convey the idea of miscellaneous bits of us thrown into a large boiling pot to make a nation.

I found myself asking if the Hertogh riots could have happened in a Malay state. My thoughts were incoherent but I asked the question, What would have happened if Chinese parents had left their daughter to be brought up by Malays as a Muslim? Would they have appealed to a British judge? Would Christian-based laws have applied to Chinese and Malays? Would there have been any question of sending a Muslim girl to a Buddhist or Daoist temple while awaiting the verdict? There were so many cultural and religious variables involved that I could see how little I knew of the tensions lying below the surface of modern progress. I optimistically hoped that the Hertogh case was unique, but the whole event taught me my first lesson about what a plural society could mean.

The riots helped me lose my innocence about Singapore society. They made me conscious of how difficult the transition from empire to nation was going to be. The focus on fighting communism as an ideological threat to nationalism was forcing us to think what kind of system would emerge when local leaders took over colonial polities and tried to build new nation-states. I believe that we were all made aware of how easily a few insensitive decisions could set the city in flames. To me, Singapore suddenly came alive to leave a clear message that the ethnic underpinnings of nationalism required constant monitoring, not least because joining the rest of Malaya would make the political ingredients even more volatile.

On campus, we were conscious that the British were tightening their control over everything that could enhance or undermine the future nation. The war being fought in the jungle had led to the Briggs Plan, which entailed the rounding up of all Chinese in the rural areas and putting them in "New Villages" that resembled concentration camps. It was done to stop the MCP from recruiting from among some half a million Chinese and also deny its armed forces from accessing food, medicine and other supplies. Most of these rural Chinese were squatters who were unhappy not to be given the right to own the land they cultivated, but they knew little about communism and did not support the violent methods used by the MCP. They were therefore open to alternative ways of improving their living conditions. The MCA sought to win their confidence by providing them with channels to become federal citizens and help them express their grievances. By 1951, the government could see that the Briggs Plan was a winning formula.

Later that year, we were reminded that the MCP was still a potent force with the dramatic news that the high commissioner of the Malayan Federation, Henry Gurney, had been killed on his way up Fraser's Hill. Years later, the MCP leader Chin Peng explained that the killing had been unplanned. The guerrillas had prepared to ambush anyone in British senior officialdom, but did not know that Gurney and his wife were in the car that they attacked. At the time, however, the killing revived fears among local communities that the British were losing their grip. The British also realized that, although they were still in control, their troops were not strong enough to defeat the guerrilla forces spread around the country. Gurney's death led them to appoint one of Britain's most senior generals Gerald Templar to take charge, and they gave him a much larger contingent of battle-hardened troops to make sure that they won this war as soon as possible.

Gurney's killing reminded us that the dangers to the new nation were on the mainland and I looked to fellow students from the Malay States to understand what was really at stake. I had come to know some of my seniors because I had been elected to the Students' Union Council when I was still a freshman. Several were older medical students who impressed me with their maturity and keen sense of public service: notable examples were Mahathir Mohamed, Tan Chee Khoon, Lim Kee Jin and Majid "Coco" Ismail. Mahathir was frankly dismissive of what we were doing in the Union and told us he thought we were *main-main sahaja* (just playing politics), when the real politics was outside among the people. At the time, I did not know he was already active in UMNO and never expected him to be a future prime minister. Chee Khoon taught me how one could be selfless when trying to help the poor, and went on to be a popular opposition member of parliament for Batu in KL. He was also to influence my academic career when he became a council member of the University of Malaya. As for Kee Jin and "Coco" Majid, they both became distinguished doctors in their respective states of Johor and Selangor, and played major roles in raising the status of their profession. All of them thought Singapore was vital to an independent Malaya and would soon be part of the federation. They were also among the first to make me feel what it might be like to have great faith in the new nation.

Political Education

MEETING NEW FRIENDS was probably the most important part of my education as a Malayan. Beda Lim had introduced me to the literary crowd, but he also introduced me to James Puthucheary, the honorary secretary of the first Student Council. James was someone who had been in the trenches fighting in the Indian National Army (INA) for the freedom of India during the war. Even before I left for China, I had learnt of the INA as a cause that some Indian friends in Ipoh had supported. At least one of my teacher's daughters had joined and gone to Burma, as James had done, and I recalled that another daughter had married an Indian army officer who also wanted the British to leave India as soon as possible. We were all a little in awe of those who had such rich war experiences.

When James learnt that I had been in China as a student on the eve of communist victory, he was curious about where I stood between the Nationalists and the Communists. I assured him that I wanted to steer clear of the local protagonists of both the Republic of China (Taiwan) and the People's Republic of China (PRC). The governments of both were competing for the support and remittances of the *huaqiao*, and this had led to considerable confusion within the community and even greater distrust among the Malay leaders. I believed that it was not in their long-term interests for Malayan Chinese to side with nationalists of another country or with a China that the MCP looked to for support.

My equivocal answers seemed to have intrigued James. How could that be? He did not believe me and was curious as to what I really thought. And if I were really innocent of politics, he would educate me to understand the great struggles that were going on and set me right. He seemed to have seen political possibilities in the poems I wrote and decided that I was a progressive at heart. When he was forced to resign from the Student

Council after being defeated at an extraordinary general meeting, he was partly responsible for putting me up as one of the freshmen representatives on the new Council. He himself continued to be active on and off campus and never ceased to highlight the evils of imperialism and the harsh realities of capitalist exploitation. Early in 1951, the British detained him for supporting the Anti-British League.

This only strengthened James' resolve to carry on as an activist. To some of us, the detention made him more heroic when he was released and rejoined us in 1952. We were roommates in the Dunearn Road Hostels and he was one of my dearest friends. He had told me of his early efforts in 1948 to organize a Malayan Students Party with two other friends. One of them was my classmate at Anderson School, Aminuddin Baki, who was one of the founders of the Gabungan Pelajar-pelajar Melayu Semenanjong (GPMS: Coalition of Peninsular Malay Students) and later to become *bapa pendidikan Malaysia* (father of Malaysian education); the other was Tan Chee Khoon, who later became one of the most endearing parliamentarians in Malayan history. The university did not approve the society's establishment at the time when the Emergency had just been launched, but James persisted and recruited me to support his cause.

We argued that, as the university did not have a politics department, or courses in political thought, we had no training in areas that could have helped us debate our futures with greater confidence. Although some did try to follow the latest writings and commentaries about colonialism and imperialism, most of us learnt by arguing hard among ourselves and picking other people's brains. We also found it fruitful to ask our economics lecturers about the need for political measures to solve social and economic problems. The university, presumably with the agreement of the colonial authorities, eventually agreed to let us form the Socialist Club.

I became convinced that it was political power that determined most things in life, including what economic policies to adopt to create a fairer society. I thus discovered that I was something of a socialist. Observing what the colonial governments were doing to extract wealth with administrative power, I became sceptical of the corrective genius of the hidden hand in capitalist economies. This was re-enforced by the Keynesian economics we were taught. Nonetheless, I studied the classical economists, from Adam Smith to Alfred Marshall, and remember reading John Hicks' *The Social*

Framework with admiration. In addition, I found it illuminating to read Eric Roll's *History of Economic Thought* to supplement my understanding of Bertrand Russell's *History of Western Philosophy*. Although I did not find philosophy appealing, Russell's progressive outlook influenced me more than I was prepared to admit.

I thought I might study economics in my honours year. The subject led to other social science disciplines like politics and sociology that I found stimulating. Influenced by anti-imperial writings, I turned against conservative leaders like Winston Churchill who wanted to keep the Empire under British control as long as possible. Although the Americans showed support for the dismantling of European empires, they became less enthusiastic as the Cold War developed and were alarmed at the spread of communist ideas in post-colonial states. This pointed to the American shift to an aggressive defense of capitalism. The arguments became ideological, and I became convinced that it was capitalism that led to imperialist expansion in the first place.

My economics teachers exhorted us to think critically and to separate Cold War polemics from scholarly studies. I believed that the continued exploitation of former colonies was unacceptable and supported policies that enabled labour unions to check the excesses of capitalist enterprise. At the same time, I was ambivalent about seeking change by violent means: nationalists fighting for independence seemed justified but I rejected the violence used in class struggles. James and other friends were held back by the fierce Emergency regulations in operation, but their idealism did lead me to admire the freedom fighters who were ready to die for their country.

My involvement in the Students' Union convinced me that students should be encouraged to support nationalist causes and learn about nation building. When I became union president, I represented it abroad. I made two trips in 1951, one to Ceylon (now Sri Lanka) and the other to India, both newly-independent countries that I admired.

I was intrigued by Ceylon because several of my primary school teachers had come from that island. I was told of the divide between the Sinhalese majority and the Tamil minority but it was only after I got to Colombo that some of the tensions emerging in the nation-building process were explained to me. The meetings I attended at the university campus turned out not to be a conference so much as a get-to-know-you gathering of student leaders from the British Commonwealth. We spent most of our time listening to talks about local society and history and visiting galleries and museums. My Sinhalese host was a law student who was keen to convince me that, as Malaya shared the same legal system as Ceylon, we should be all right after independence if we stuck with it. His home was south of the university on the way to Mount Lavinia and close to Marina beach where we could look at the vast Indian Ocean and see Galle Face Hotel nearby. It was a quiet and beautiful suburb, nothing to suggest that there were explosive tensions building up around us.

I was still interested in literary happenings and admired the high standard of English among the local students. I heard that Ceylon's best-known poet Tambimuttu was in town. He was the founder of *Poetry London*, an admirer of T.S. Eliot and the publisher of some of Auden's poems. My host arranged a meeting and brought me to Nelson Hotel in the Colombo harbour area. There Tambimuttu introduced me to his favourite *arak*, a drink I took to immediately because I had had my share of toddy during the Japanese occupation in Ipoh. He asked me to write him a poem and, as its literary editor, had it published a few days later in *The Times of Ceylon*.

He invited me to join him to visit his close friends, the de Sarams. There we heard their 12-year-old son Rohan play the cello. Tambimuttu told me he would be a fine cellist one day. He was right. A few years later, I heard Rohan in a chamber music recital in London where he was greeted as a great new find. The evening at the de Sarams helped me to see how deeply European the elites of Sri Lanka were and how little those of us who talked about literature and politics in Malaya really knew about those colonials who were truly steeped in Western education.

I was thus made aware that the English language connected us not only through our common anti-colonial experiences but also enabled us to share an admiration for English literature and ultimately the global literature in English. There were different dimensions of sensibility and such sharing had little to do with the political calls for Malayan literature.

Meeting Tambimuttu reminded me of what I felt in Manila when I first saw the divide between what languages people were using and the idea of national literature. Indeed, not long afterwards, Sinhalese became the national language of Sri Lanka and those Jaffna Tamils who had excellent English lost any advantage they might have had in the country.

We met as representatives of student unions looking at our political futures so I was quickly pulled away from such musings. The gathering turned out to be preparatory for a conference in Delhi later in December 1951. For that conference, organized by the United Nations (UN) Student Association of India, four of our Students' Union executive committee members were elected to go, provided we could find the funding from outside sources. Because it was the first time we were doing this, there was enough support for all four of us to attend. The conference was inspired by the hopes that we all had in the UN. The Indian government backed it by providing facilities like public halls for our meetings and official accommodation.

We were put up in a large apartment in Metcalfe House, normally a hostel for Indian Administrative Service (IAS) trainees. Because of the Christmas-New Year break, the rooms were made available to conference participants like us. We were given what we thought was the IAS Officers treatment. For example, we were woken up at 6.00 a.m. by a tall turbaned Pathan who had come to shave us. We thought it wise to decline. An hour later, two men came with morning tea. We gratefully accepted. Although Metcalfe House was not a five-star hotel, this was royal treatment. Our room overlooked the Jumna River, with a well-kept garden in between. It was winter and the river was no more than a stream far from its banks. Every morning we saw a line of women walk down to the water to do their laundry, an unforgettable sight.

Unlike the meeting I had earlier attended in Colombo, this one was openly political. The UN sent its representative, a young American lawyer named Stephen Schwebel who was one of the founders of the UN Student Association (later he was to become president of the International Court of Justice at The Hague). His idealism was infectious and many of us publicly pledged our support for the UN as the key instrument of world governance. We all believed that this was our best hope for peace.

We were also impressed that Prime Minister Jawarharlal Nehru came to address us one evening. He spoke passionately about his expectations of the young and all of us were deeply moved by a world leader who took time off to talk to a mixed group of students from some thirty countries. Two of my new friends were exceptionally excited. One was a Pakistani girl from the Punjab who was touched by the prime minister's inclusive approach and tearfully told me about her family's losses when they moved to Lahore and her sympathy for those who had been forced to move the opposite way. I had read up about the tragedy of partition before coming to India but this was the first time I heard something from a Pakistani perspective.

The other was an Israeli who called Nehru a great leader. He told me he was born in Egypt and had migrated to Palestine to fight with the Haganah and claimed to have been with the Irgun units that bombed King David Hotel. He said that dealing with explosives had damaged his lungs and this had forced him to abandon a military career and turn to scholarship. Because he was fluent in Arabic and had read the Quran, he was sent to work with some excellent Muslim scholars in Delhi. I had read Arthur Koestler's *Darkness at Noon* and his book about the creation of the state of Israel, *Promise and Fulfilment*. In the context of anti-colonialism and post-war images of the Holocaust, my Israeli friend's story left me with considerable sympathy for the Israeli cause.

However, the person who left the deepest impression on me was the secretary of the host association, Romila Thapar. She was a student of history who told me of her determination to retell India's ancient history and correct the dismissive attitudes among many British historians about the periods before the Mughal Empire. I knew little about the subject except that it was Buddhism that had transmitted brilliant Indian art and ideas across the continent to China and Southeast Asia. She was the first undergraduate student I met who spoke about the study of history with such conviction. Listening to her not only drew attention to an abysmal gap in my knowledge but also made me want to learn more history. Years later, we met again as doctoral students at the School of Oriental and African Studies (SOAS) in London where she went to study with A.L. Basham, one of the few British historians of ancient India.

Rather as my unexpected trip to Manila in 1950 had made me take pause about writing *Malayan* literature, the trip to Delhi ostensibly to understand international affairs actually turned me away from current politics and strengthened my interest in the historian's trade. When I discovered that I could not do research on modern Chinese history at my university, it was Romila's passion for ancient history that gave me the courage to go back more than 2,000 years to China's long recorded past.

The trips to Ceylon and later to Delhi taught me to review regularly what I knew about the region's political developments. In Colombo, I had noted the tensions between Buddhist Sinhalese and Hindu Tamils but was totally surprised when those tensions became so bitter that both sides killed without mercy. I was already alerted, after the Maria Hertogh riots in Singapore, to the fragility of inter-ethnic relations, how quickly they could turn into vicious racial and religious warfare. In Delhi, meeting Prime Minister Nehru led me to read his book *The Discovery of India* with great admiration. But arriving at Delhi airport and driving past miles of refugee camps was a deeply disturbing experience; the camps were filled with the victims of the riots in the Punjab following the separation of India and Pakistan some five years earlier. Learning more about these camps made me even more fearful of religious fanaticism. Ever since, I have become increasingly opposed to ethnic nationalism and any kind of exclusivism that could justify rage and cruelty and turn ordinary people into murderers.

I was totally chastened by my two visits to South Asia. On the one hand, the consequences of colonial rule were apparent. On the other, the uphill task of creating nations out of former colonial states had only just begun and the challenges were formidable. I became more sensitive to the fact that I had been born in Indonesia and brought up as a Chinese who had looked to China as his country from afar. I could try to become Malayan, but if ethnicity became central to national loyalty, would efforts at trying ever be enough?

However, there were takeaways that were positive. My Sinhalese host stressed that there was hope for the future because of our common belief in the rule of law, and Tambimuttu's life pointed to how the literary heritage of the English language could override our differences. Stephen Schwebel's faith in a global humanity was uplifting and all of us at the UN

Students meeting went home feeling optimistic. And Romila Thapar's conviction that understanding our deep roots was invaluable had left me with a deep and enduring respect for the ancient past.

On my return, I reduced my commitments as student leader and began to think about what I should do for my honours year. I turned away from any pretense that I could write Malayan poetry and focused on my examinations as a final year Bachelor of Arts student. I still had to choose between economics and history. I had thought that specializing in economics would make me a more useful citizen. But I was far more interested in political and social changes than in analyzing economic phenomena or working on economic policies. Meeting people with different origins and backgrounds confirmed for me that studying history could be an open-ended pursuit of the human condition over time. However, there remained one more matter that drew me back to student affairs. I have earlier mentioned our efforts to persuade the university to allow us to form political clubs to prepare us for the democracy promised for the new nation. To our pleasant surprise, the university agreed to our proposal in 1953. So we established the Socialist Club and, not being burdened like James Puthucheary with having been detained for left-wing activities, I was elected its first president.

I had by that time started writing my master's thesis in preparation for an academic career and was no longer interested in political participation. I believed that students should have the right to discuss politics openly and that would help them identify with the goals of the new nation. I accepted the position to lead the Club and get it started but soon left it to my younger friends to run the society. I was content that many of our members shared my interest in promoting socialism without any commitment to become politicians, but the club did attract those who were willing to enter the political arena when there was an opportunity to do so.

As it turned out, the government's heavy-handed action in 1954 to arrest the editors of the club's publication *Fajar* had the opposite effect and encouraged several of them to become politically active after graduation. Among the people who had helped them was a young lawyer known for his trade union sympathies, Lee Kuan Yew. His active support for the club members who were outraged by the police action led several to join the People's Action Party (PAP) when it was established later that year.

When I completed my thesis in mid-1954 and headed for London, I was happy to hear that the Club had gained a strong reputation as a centre for those with political ambitions.

PART THREE

Pairing Lives

Meeting Margaret

IN RETROSPECT, MY first three years at MU were mixed with expectation and fun. I managed to keep my uncertainties at bay. I read my share of English literature, listened to classical music, wrote some poems, and made many friends. I was learning about Malaya and involved in student affairs. I watched out for the practical questions people asked about sovereign nation-states.

I still had one strong link with the English Literature Department. She was Margaret Lim Ping Ting 林娉婷, the girl I was wooing. And I soon came to think that knowing her would change my life. Meeting her gave more focus to thinking of my future. While I could see the importance of working in public service, I also realized that I was not suited to that line of work. What attracted me was a life of learning and teaching. And Margaret was encouraging about my becoming an apprentice academic.

It really began at the start of my second year. Literature had done me an unexpected favour. This was when a small group of freshmen met to talk about the Romantics and asked me to lead the discussion. It was mainly about Wordsworth's poetry. This is how Margaret remembers the occasion when she told her story to our children:

> I first noticed Gungwu when he was giving a talk on William Wordsworth and I noticed his name on the notice board advertising his talk. Until today, we have never found anyone else with the same name. The romanization of his name used the most up-to-date system when he was born but that system gave way to another so, as far as we know, no one else has the Chinese character of his name, gung 賡 (now geng, or keng) romanized in the same way. I went along to the talk out of curiosity to hear this man with the unusual name. I found a handsome young man speaking with authority and depth on

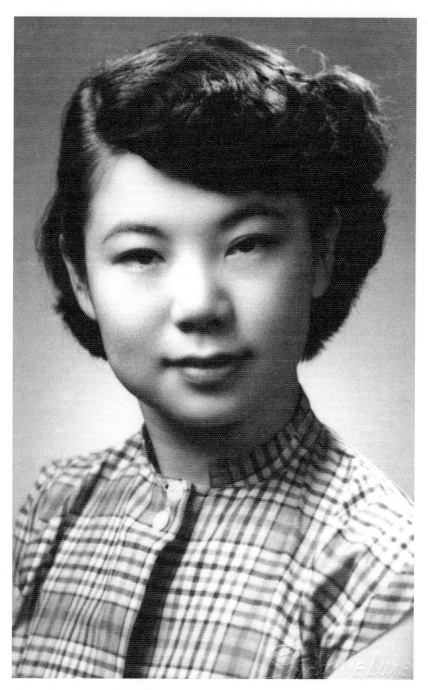

Margaret Lim Ping Ting 林娉婷 at the University of Malaya.

a poet. I was suitably impressed but nothing happened because I was a mere freshman and he didn't notice me then. At that time he had already had a small volume of his poetry published, was editor of the student newspaper and active in student affairs. Later in the year we began to meet and speak to each other. I got elected to the Students' Council for 1951–52 and he became President of the Students' Union the same year.

Actually I *did* notice the lovely girl in the group. I met her again at a student dinner and dance that she helped to organize and again on other social occasions. I recall how quick and sharp she was with her use of words and images. On one occasion, her comments about one of Yeats' poems led me to re-read the poem. I was a year ahead of Margaret. After Beda Lim had launched me as a budding poet, I had gained some fame on campus but I was still struggling to learn what to do. Margaret loved English literature and had a much better command of the language than me. Being three years younger and junior in class, she thought she should just be encouraging. She knew of my Chinese background and was curious as to how I was to re-locate in the new Malaya-to-be.

Beda had, without either of us realizing it at the time, done me another favour. He had decided to teach me about Western symphonic music. During the months after my return to Ipoh in 1949, I had learnt how to play the violin but showed no talent with the instrument. When he showed me his small collection of records, I asked him to play them for me. He chose Sibelius' *Finlandia* and explained its connection with national rejuvenation. He could see that I was new to symphonic music and decided to educate me. I was astonished when he took me through the different sets of instruments like he was conducting the orchestra, pointing to each of them when they came in at various points of the tone poem. That was the beginning. He played *Finlandia* several times so that I could appreciate the harmonic elements that enhanced the melodic lines, and that helped me listen to other music.

Over several weeks, he moved on to Tchaikovsky's Symphony no. 6 (*Pathetique*) and Beethoven's 5th symphony, several times each. He followed the music so closely that I asked if he had trained to be a conductor. He had not; it was simply his good ear for music and his prodigious memory. By the time we had been through his records, he had

soaked me in a part of Western civilization that remained lodged in me
the rest of my life.

Beda was not to know that he had helped me get closer to Margaret. I
had been woefully illiterate about music. My parents cared little for it, none
of my school friends played any instrument and we did nothing musical in
Anderson School. I had only learnt to sing some popular Chinese songs
and other songs at patriotic fund-raising meetings. During the Japanese
occupation, I heard some Japanese war songs and even remembered
their tunes. In 1948, in my second year on the main campus in Nanjing,
I walked past the university's conservatory of music every morning and
heard students with their piano or violin lessons or practising operatic
arias, but I never had the chance to hear them perform in public.

Portrait of a poet, 1950.

By taking me to another level of music appreciation, Beda helped me
to make an impression the following year on a Miss Margaret Lim, then
a freshman who played first violin in the university's orchestra. For that
contribution to my education, I thank Beda from the bottom of my heart.
With his help, when I was wooing Margaret, we had at least two interests

in common: literature and music. One day, she agreed to come with me to see *Macbeth* because it was a film that we thought had it all: Shakespeare and Orson Welles, with a classical composer Jacques Ibert providing dramatic music. I still think of it today as the moment when we became a regular pair on campus.

This was how Margaret remembered the occasion:

In my second year, in October, after a Student Council meeting, Gungwu invited me to see *Macbeth*, at that time being shown in a cinema on Beach Road. This was to prove an interesting outing. Firstly, the film was a "dark" film, with gloom and doom everywhere. It was an Orson Welles film with Orson Welles playing Macbeth. We came out of the cinema feeling somewhat depressed so we decided to have coffee in the shop opposite the cinema. Singapore did not have any huge shopping malls in those days. Everything happened in what we called "coffee shops", or *kopitiam* in Hokkien. At this time, Gungwu had a beard. As you know, most Chinese do not have enough facial hair to have beards but he did. He always claimed jokingly that his beard was inherited from an ancestor who came from some barbarian tribe like the Turks or the Hsiung Nu 匈奴 who had invaded China in the past. It was most unusual for a young Chinese to have a beard, so he was noticed wherever he went.

The reason for the beard was simple, he kept on cutting himself when shaving so decided to keep a beard. The blades used for shaving in those days were not the double-bladed safety razors developed later on, but single blades which cut you badly if you made a wrong move. Anyway, a huge Sikh confronted us when we were drinking our coffee and very aggressively asked whether Gungwu meant to mock the Sikhs with his beard! I was so innocent in those days that I didn't realize that the Sikh was drunk. Fortunately, Gungwu defused the situation by speaking calmly to the man and even invited him to sit with us for a while. I was quite frightened as I was afraid he would hit us. It was certainly an exciting end to a first date! Gungwu told me later that he was afraid I wouldn't go out with him any more!

Margaret was unswerving in her love of literature, but she understood why I decided to turn to history. We had discovered that our backgrounds had more in common than we knew when we first met. She stood out among the female students as the beautiful girl who was keen to discuss Jane Austen and her generation of English poets. She was also the violinist who had studied under the highly-respected teacher Goh Soon Tioe, and played in the Singapore Youth Orchestra. When the university established its own orchestra, she played at the first desk beside the new chemistry lecturer, Rayson Huang, someone who loved playing the violin all his life and who became a dear friend to both of us. None of us could have anticipated that I would one day succeed him as vice-chancellor of the University of Hong Kong. The conductor was Paul Abisheganaden, a dedicated music educationalist whom we both admired. This was serious music and I paid close attention.

During the summer break though, Margaret had a severe illness, something viral called Meniere's Syndrome, after which she totally lost her hearing in her left ear. Here she tells the story in her own words:

Just before the beginning of my second year, a disaster struck me. Suddenly I fell ill and there was a buzzing in my ears, and a few days later, the hearing of my left ear went. The doctors did not know what was wrong with me and I thought I was going to die I suffered so much. I had to lie flat on my bed and couldn't even turn my head as that caused me such extreme dizziness that I vomited. I couldn't keep down any food or water. Finally, I was sent to hospital and got lots of penicillin, a new drug at that time, pumped into me. Fortunately, I was not allergic to it as little was known of penicillin's side effects in those days. I later discovered that I had something called Meniere's Syndrome, a viral disease that usually strikes older people. None of the local doctors knew anything about it and the ear, nose and throat specialist didn't even believe me when I told him I had become deaf in my left ear. He thought I was imagining things!

I was probably on the way to recovery by the time the penicillin was given to me, as that drug would have been of no use at all for a viral disease. But perhaps it helped me not get any other disease in my weakened state. I stayed in hospital for about a week and was ill about three weeks in all. Sadly, I discovered that the hearing in my left ear had indeed been impaired and that my inner ear balance was so affected that for months I couldn't walk a straight line, go downstairs without falling, or walk through a doorway without bumping into the wall beside the doorway. In short, my balance was poor and I couldn't play badminton anymore or even the violin as I could not detect from which direction sound came.

When I was in my first year, I was active in sports, particularly badminton, and was mixed doubles champion with a man called Loporte Khoo. After my illness, I found that I could not hit the shuttlecock and always just missed it! However, I continued to play badminton well enough to be chosen to represent the university for the biennial games with the University of Hong Kong in the summer of 1953. But my hearing problems meant that I no longer could lead the university orchestra as all sound caused my head to ring. It took many years for me to recover and for my right ear to compensate for the left so that it is not obvious I am deaf in one ear. As the nerve is dead, it was not possible for me to wear a hearing aid. I developed the habit of turning my right ear to any person who spoke to me. When a person spoke into my left ear I would not hear anything at all. Fortunately, I never felt sensitive about this and would readily tell the dinner partners on my left that they would have to give me a nudge if I should ignore them when they were speaking to me. Most people have some physical defect and I found an astonishing number of people telling me of their hearing disabilities when I told them mine. Sometimes I even found someone sitting on my left with their right ear deaf so we had to face each other directly in order to converse. I adapted to my disability and do not think about it now.

Mother Tung

MARGARET IS SOMEONE of many talents. After her illness, she turned her attention to other things and quickly regained her sunny view of life. By that time, I had met her mother and heard a story that was uncannily familiar. Ruth Tung Ee Ho 童懿和 spoke of first coming from Shanghai as a young woman to teach adult Chinese in Singapore who wanted to learn to speak *guoyu* 国语 (Mandarin). That was in about 1930, soon after my father had left for Surabaya. She then went back to Shanghai to marry a young scholar at St John's University, Lim Teh Han 林德翰, and it was in the university's hospital that Margaret was born. On the eve of the Sino-Japanese war, the family decided to leave Shanghai when Chung Ling High School in Penang introduced science teaching and offered Mr Lim a job. Thus their daughter Margaret came to the Malay Peninsula, driven by events beyond her control just as my family had come to Ipoh from Java, and just as I returned from Nanjing in 1948.

Margaret tells her mother's story beautifully:

> My mother, Ruth Tung Ee Ho, was from Shaowu 邵武, a town in Fujian province. She spoke a very odd dialect, very different from the main southern dialects in Southeast Asia: Cantonese, Hokkien, Teochew and Hakka. I seldom heard her speaking her dialect except when she was with my aunt so never learnt it. She was a very interesting woman. She led an unconventional life for a Chinese woman of her time. She went on a hunger strike to get her father to allow her to go to university in Shanghai when she was 18 years old. She wanted to go there to study because her older brother was there to study medicine. She was born on 3 June 1910, just before the Chinese Revolution. She avoided having her feet bound and was actually educated at her father's school. Perhaps that was the reason she was

different from a lot of other women of her time. She was very adventurous, doubtless fuelled by her success in getting her way to go to university. My grandfather had been converted to Christianity and became the principal of a congregationalist girls' school in Shaowu.

Her family originally came from the north. The surname Tung is not a southern one. My grandfather was a scholar but I don't know what he did before he became headmaster of the school. He must have been a teacher of some sort. The story goes that my grandmother, who married very young, as was the custom in the old days, had many male children, most of whom died in infancy. My grandfather was being wooed by missionaries to convert to Christianity and said that if his wife bore a girl he would agree to be converted. He did so when my mother was born. My grandmother had five living children after bearing about 16 of them. Public health and hygiene were not what they are today and it was common for babies to die then. My grandmother bore two more girls and one boy after my grandfather's conversion. Probably due to having more experience by that time, the babies all lived. Girls are also known to be tougher in infancy than boys and all the three girls survived. My mother ended up with two brothers and two sisters.

When my mother went to Shanghai, she got a place in the University of Shanghai 沪江大学, an American Baptist missionary university. She knew no English then, and it is a testimony to her spirit that did not deter her. She told me that she spent the first six months in a total fog, not knowing what was going on, until one day, the words made sense. After that, she became very fluent in English, albeit speaking and using it sometimes ungrammatically. I like to think of it as slightly "fractured" but perfectly understandable English. My mother partly supported herself at university by sending Chinese textile goods such as tablecloths, napkins, embroidered blouses and so on to an American friend in California.

During her university years, my mother became interested in propagating Mandarin to all overseas Chinese as she greatly admired Hu Shih, at that time one of the best known scholars and philosophers of China and a prime mover in the effort to propagate Mandarin as a national language.

At that time, in the 1920s, Mandarin was not universally used in China. Nationalism was rising in the face of foreign threats and it was felt that the Chinese should have a common spoken language. They already had a written script that for 2,000 years could be read by any educated Chinese, whichever dialect they spoke. It was now time to have a common spoken language as well, and the northern *guanhua* 官话 (officials' language) used in the court and in Beijing was chosen to be that language. You can imagine how the young must have been inspired to build up a nation that could speak the same language from north to south, east and west. My mother was so inspired. She was convinced that Mandarin was the future for all Chinese and when she graduated, she travelled to Singapore to teach at a Mandarin language school for adults who spoke southern dialects such as Cantonese, Hokkien or Teochew.

I do not know what and who influenced her or even introduced the idea that she should go to the Nanyang. Perhaps this was another manifestation of her adventurous spirit. This is when she was part of the great wave of teachers, journalists and other intellectuals who left China to go to Southeast Asia. The labourers and merchants who went to the region earlier had become relatively prosperous and they were sufficient in numbers to want to build their own Chinese schools for their children. The various colonial powers which ruled over most of the region did not spend much money on education. The British, for example, usually set up one boy's and one girl's school in each town. These schools used English as the medium of instruction. They needed clerks and low-level administrators to staff the government offices and help with the colonial administration and these schools met those needs. There was a tertiary level college for the humanities and science, Raffles College, and one King Edward VII Medical College, but the number of students in these institutions was very small. Some brilliant or wealthy students managed to go to England for higher education but their numbers, again, were very small. The missionaries and various charitable organizations also got into the act and began to found more English primary and secondary schools for the children. To their credit, they built schools for the girls as well as for the boys.

The Chinese community, wishing to preserve their language and culture and tradition of learning also began to start private schools that used Mandarin as the medium of instruction. This was why Gungwu's parents and my parents came to the region. Gungwu's father, for example, was recruited first to teach in Malaya and then became a principal in the late 1920s of the first Chinese high school in Surabaya, Indonesia. Later, in 1937, my father was one of the first science teachers to be recruited by the Chung Ling High School (for boys) in Penang which was one of the most advanced schools in the region at that time (and still is an excellent school). To most Chinese at that time, these jobs overseas were only temporary, and they would go back to China when things improved in the country. Little did they know that great historical events would prevent that and that most Chinese in Southeast Asia would never go back to live in China again.

To go back to my mother, although she went to Singapore when the Great Depression was affecting the economies of the whole world, she never spoke about it as having affected her. The school she helped to found, Kuoyu Chiangshi Shueshiao 国语讲习学校 (of the same name as the one she later established in Penang), did not seem to have had a problem attracting students. The school had quite a large staff and over a hundred students, all of them keen to learn Mandarin. They were mostly adults so classes were held in the evenings. The children were taught during the day. Unlike the other staff, she could speak English so could mix freely with the English-educated dialect-speaking Chinese. She met many prominent Chinese of the time, such as Sir Han Ho Lim. They were all keen to learn Mandarin and she kept up these friendships so that when our family went to live in Singapore in 1942, we were not totally without friends.

The Japanese war came to Southeast Asia in 1941. The effect on Margaret's family was more dramatic than mine. Before the Japanese reached Penang, the family caught one of the last trains to Singapore, not expecting the invading forces to overwhelm the British in Malaya within a couple of months. In Singapore, it was Margaret's mother who provided safety for the family through her friendship with some of the *peranakan* notables whom she had taught the first time she was here. She had had a Christian upbringing and had links with the Methodist church so the church community was a great help. She could not resume teaching Chinese under the circumstances and therefore began to develop entrepreneurial skills to keep the family alive.

Margaret remembers the hard times but also the fun she had growing up with children of well-settled families in Singapore who had gone to English schools. Although her parents were active in Chinese education, both could speak and write English. In fact, Margaret was to discover her father's stack of books of 19th-century English fiction and read them during the occupation years. Compared to what I read from the education department library in Ipoh about the same time, which was mostly popular fiction, the novels she read were several notches higher up the literary ladder.

We had other common stories. Like me, she did not go to school during the Japanese occupation years. At the Methodist Girls' School that she got into after the war, it was her ability to write good English that helped her move up quickly to the higher classes; what was more, it was also a brilliant mathematics teacher, Ruth Wong, later professor of education at the University of Malaya, who enabled her to sail through the Cambridge School Leaving Examinations. In my case, Mr Ung Khek Cheow in Anderson School had rescued me in a similar way a few years earlier, but my mathematical skills were decidedly inferior to Margaret's.

However, one story was totally different from mine. Her parents might have chosen each other before they married, but it was not a happy marriage. Their different temperaments finally led them to separate when her father had to return to his home in Taiwan when the island was returned to China after the war. Margaret, her sister and three brothers remained in Singapore, and their mother became the sole breadwinner of the family. By the time I met Mrs Lim, she had become highly respected as the Chinese teacher who had opened a private afternoon school using the premises of Victoria School. She was in great demand because many families who sent their children to English schools wanted their children to learn Chinese and take the Chinese paper in the School Leaving Examinations. It was hard work doing almost everything on her own, but the school earned her the income that she needed to support her five children.

As her oldest child, Margaret played her part in her mother's work and helped in the demonstrations of Chinese art, music and opera that her mother wanted her students to appreciate. This she continued to do even after entering university. I recall her operatic part as Hua Mulan 花木兰, the legendary woman warrior who took her father's place in the army and fought heroically on the frontier; I still treasure the two photographs of her in that "male" role on the school stage.

But Margaret and I did not build our friendship on anything to do with things Chinese. That was not what the University of Malaya was about:

a last-ditch effort to educate a generation of graduates to appreciate what it meant to be part of a global imperial enterprise. For Margaret and me, that meant that English language and literature was its starting point. Since we admired the literature, there was no reason to resist. But we also realized that we needed to know our fellow students coming from different parts of "British Malaya". Margaret had her local classmates and other Singapore friends but she was curious about those who came from the various mainland states. As for me, I knew very little about any state other than Perak. In addition, I was seriously handicapped by my ignorance about Singapore. Before I met Margaret, I did explore the city with others like me who had come from the Malay states, but it was Margaret and her friends who introduced me to corners of the island that I would not have discovered on my own.

Margaret and her mother.

Father Lim

IMMIGRANTS USUALLY HAVE interesting stories to tell. I thought mine was pretty odd, but Margaret's was much more interesting. I admired her mother for her ability to deal with sudden changes in her life, but only learnt about her father after she returned from a trip to Taiwan to see him. The story she told after her return left a deep impression. It not only made her family more intriguing and something I remain fascinated by, but also touched on the complex relations between China and Taiwan that are relevant to the present day. Here is how Margaret tells her father's story:

My father came from a prominent Taiwan/Amoy 厦门 business family. I don't know much about them but did meet my eldest uncle in Taiwan in 1954 when I visited my father, someone who was later to be the first non-Kuomintang 国民党 (KMT) mayor of Keelung 基隆, a port in the northern part of Taiwan Island. But I mustn't get too far ahead in my story. My father went to the Anglo-Chinese School in Gulangyu in Amoy, an island which was like a foreign concession and filled with beautiful Western-style buildings. He had a few classmates whom I got to know later, notably a world famous archaeologist, Prof. Cheng Te-kun 郑德坤, who worked in Cambridge University. Another who met him at university was Prof. Robert Lin (the best man at his wedding in Beijing and a physiologist like himself), who ended up in the University of Malaya in the 1950s, thereby proving that chance has a strange way of linking people together.

From all accounts from people who knew my father and from my own observations, he was highly intelligent and was capable of better things than his ambitions made him reach for. He was also very charming when he wanted to be. My mother told me that while in Yenching University in Peking he got a Rockefeller scholarship to do a PhD in the United States but he had no desire to be an academic or to engage in research. He had the peculiar idea that such learning was "useless and backward", little knowing of the explosion in education that was to take place in the second half of the 20th century. Instead, possibly because of his family background, which was almost entirely in business, he admired entrepreneurs like Henry Ford, who famously said "history is bunk". In other words he wished to be an entrepreneur himself. However, he was one of the least business-like men I ever met and he had no idea that he was totally unsuited to being a businessman. For one thing, he was too trusting and was constantly being cheated by his business partners. He continued to trust people in spite of evidence to the contrary. He also did not have the dedication to moneymaking and success that all successful businessmen have, so he was totally without the skills that could make him succeed in business. Ironically, this can be attributed to his family again.

My grandfather had three wives, each of whom produced a son. My father was the youngest son, the son of the third wife. He was very spoilt by his mother, in the way Chinese families spoil their sons, and never learnt that only from dedication and hard work could you really succeed in life. His failures he attributed to the scheming of other people, never seeing that he was easily taken in himself. His eldest brother was involved in the family business early on, and from what I remember, nothing was ever said about my father learning anything about the family's various enterprises. He was known to be academically bright so was sent to the Anglo-Chinese Boys' School in Amoy when he was very young, at about 11, so he was removed from the family business environment.

So coming from a business or merchant family does not necessarily mean that you know about business. Families are also wise enough to know which son has the skills to continue with the business and you certainly wouldn't want to entrust your fortunes to a son who was more academic than shrewd! Even if you inherit a fortune, you still have to know how to safeguard it or you will lose it. My mother was the opposite of my father as she learnt early on that you could only get what you want if you fight and work for it. You can see that a marriage between a practical down-to-earth and enterprising woman and a dreamer with a quick temper who never exerted himself in a meaningful way would not be very successful. It is no wonder that the marriage foundered from its early days. Never were two people so unsuited to each other!

The mismatch was made worse in a way because my mother always earned more than my father. He was used to being pampered and not having to exert himself; even his studies came easily as he was so intelligent. She was used to being enterprising and hardworking. When I asked her why she remained married to him when she was independent financially, she said that in her day divorce was a disgrace and one simply didn't do so. She remained for more than 13 years in this unhappy marriage with a man who had ambitions that he couldn't fulfill for himself, until great events intervened on her behalf.

I had heard some bits of the story before Margaret went to Taiwan to meet her father in 1953, eight years after they parted. Up to that point, I had simply thought in terms of an enforced family separation. What she told me after her return made her tale part of a larger story that has kept me enthralled for seven decades.

I had kept up a desultory correspondence with my father. To my surprise, he asked me to visit him in Taipei and offered to pay my fare from Hong Kong to Taipei return, and my mother offered to pay my fare to Hong Kong as a graduation gift. This visit was quite an adventure as it was exciting for me to travel for the first time on my own to Hong Kong and beyond.

At that time, Taiwan was in a state of war with China, the Kuomintang had only occupied the island for eight years. The Taiwanese had been colonized by the Japanese for about 50 years. The Japanese got Taiwan as a spoil of war when they defeated the Chinese in the Sino-Japanese war of 1895. It was not that the Taiwanese did not want to be part of China again; it was that the Kuomintang were no better than the Japanese as they treated the locals like colonial subjects who had no say in anything about their own fates. About a million mainlanders (largely officials and soldiers) came and were like invaders keeping the best jobs for themselves. The legacy of the Kuomintang was that the locals did not like the mainland Chinese and today they are in the ascendant in their desire for independence from the mainland.

Hong Kong was an eye-opener for me. There were so many people! I was unused to this and was particularly upset by the hordes of children who followed me around begging for money. The people from Guangdong province particularly were the ones to stream into Hong Kong. There was no housing for them so they lived in makeshift huts dotted along the hillsides. During the typhoon season many of these dwellings would be destroyed and people killed. Hong Kong was desperately trying to house and feed these people, but in 1953 the Hong Kong government hadn't gotten itself organized to do this yet. In addition, there was now the Cold War, and Hong Kong was the centre for spying activities among the various powers that wanted to find out what the Chinese were up to. So security was tight and everyone was careful.

Finally, my visa came through and I flew to Taipei to visit my father. The city was drab, there were banners everywhere, strung across the streets, exhorting the people to fight back to regain the mainland, to defeat the bandits who were now ruining, and not running, China.

Margaret and her father.

I found that my father was not much changed even though I had not seen him for about eight years. I found that he had formed another family with a local woman and now had a 5-year-old daughter. I was quite shocked and he was probably right not to tell me in advance as I might not have visited him. I was young and much less tolerant in those days than I am today! When this daughter grew up, I wrote to her occasionally, and she turned out to be very nice and a fine young woman. She became a doctor, finally fulfilling my father's ambition to have a daughter as a doctor.

To continue with my visit. It was not a great success because immediately after I arrived, he took me to the immigration department to get me an exit visa. I was questioned about my reasons for being in Taiwan and asked why I wanted to leave since I was a Chinese citizen. I was shocked as I never considered that the government would think of me as a Chinese citizen. This was because of a law passed in 1909 which proclaimed anyone born of a Chinese father to be a Chinese citizen no matter where he or she was born. So the question asked of me, why did I want to leave Taiwan and not live with my father, was a pertinent one and gave me a real fright.

My mother later told me, after I had returned to Singapore, that she would not have allowed me to visit my father if I had been a boy. Then, as a Chinese, I would have to do national service in the army and they would have forced me to stay! However, I did get my exit visa and returned home safely. The Taiwanese no longer have this policy and have sensibly realized that a lot of Chinese would not go to Taiwan in case they enforced this old policy. My brothers visited our father years later without any trouble. Gungwu and I refused to go there for more than three decades until the government no longer treated the overseas Chinese who visited the island as people who supported their government against the PRC.

Anyway, this incident gave me such a fright that I never wanted to visit Taiwan again! Apart from this, I didn't have a happy time because I was once again faced with a father who constantly criticized my mother. I would defend her and get angry so he didn't have a good visit with me either. However, when it was time to leave, I did feel sad, because I felt that I would probably never see him again, and indeed I never did. I continued to write to him through the years and was glad to know that his daughter, my half-sister, made him happy. She married another doctor and was doing well in her profession when tragedy befell them all. Sadly for him, she got cancer while carrying her first baby, and soon after her baby was born she died. Although I didn't have much affection for my father, I was very sorry for him. He did not have a successful life, not only in a material sense, but also in the feeling that he had not achieved anything worthwhile in his life. His one great success could be said to be his Taiwan daughter, but she died and left him bereft. It was a sad episode towards the end of his life.

Decades later, after the Maoist and Chiang eras had ended, we felt free to visit Taiwan. Margaret had lost touch with her father's family but we were curious about the Lim family history. The main link was her uncle Lin Fanwang 林番王 whom Margaret had met in 1953 when he owned a photography shop in Keelung. The Lim ancestors had moved from Xiamen to Yilan 宜兰 in northeastern Taiwan in the early 19th century before moving to Keelung. Margaret's grandfather was a very successful businessman who sent his sons to study in the best Chinese schools in Fuzhou, where her uncle Fanwang was sent, and Xiamen, where her father went to the Anglo-Chinese School. There were many other members of the Lim family who studied in Japan, and several were prominent in Taiwan's medical profession, to which Margaret's father wanted his own family to belong.

We learnt that Lin Fanwang was elected mayor of Keelung in 1960. Although his private life was a public disaster, he was re-elected in 1964. He was respected for building many schools and good roads and improving the city's harbour facilities. When he died in office a year later, he was buried in the Chiang Kai-shek Public Park. When we visited his tomb in 2010, we found it well kept and were surprised to learn that it was the only grave in the park. Local anti-Kuomintang sentiments had kept the tomb in place but, during the bitter election campaign in 2014, pro-blue Kuomintang supporters were thought to have defaced the tombstone. When our family saw the tomb again in 2018, we noted a feeble attempt to repair it. Later that year, however, the new pro-green mayor had the tomb tidied up and put new photographs of the site on the web. They stand as a symbolic reminder of Taiwan's complex politics since 1945.

Learn to Share

MARGARET COULD SEE that my interest in a Malayan literature and my desultory verse writing had led me away from the serious study of English literature. I was still reading the poets and novelists, and continued to be interested in their French and Russian counterparts, but I was also attracted to social science writings that were more relevant to the future that Malayans would have to face. I did keep up my literary interests through Margaret and, without being conscious of it at the time, had also read what was later to be recognized as Commonwealth literature, the writings of R.K. Narayan, his *The English Teacher* and *Malgudi Days*. I thought they were comparable to E.M. Forster's *A Passage to India*, George Orwell's *Burmese Days* and Leonard Woolf's *A Village in the Jungle*. A few years later came V.S. Naipaul's *A House for Mr Biswas* and Chinua Achebe's *Things Fall Apart*, and I began to notice the work of South African and Australian writers and learnt to appreciate what white colonials thought of imperial rule. It was somewhat ironic that we began to appreciate some of the literary products of the British Empire only after the empire had begun to decline. With that, the more we read of what others were writing, the more we could see the common elements in what the British were doing in their colonies.

It was because of Margaret that I came to realize that I was encountering something called love that I had not given much thought to in the past. Like many others my age, I knew many songs about love and had toyed recklessly with the word. I was never sure how to use it or what its use entailed. Meeting Margaret led me to learn that the word could describe what I felt. How that happened was and still is a mystery. I imagine that something like love could grow silently; it no longer matters whether my mind could comprehend it or not. What I know is that it has a lot to do with time, home and freedom.

It was the English word that I found difficult. In the Chinese that I spoke at home and what I was taught to read in classical Chinese, the word *ai* 爱 (love) was commonly used in a Confucian context of mothers loving their sons. My parents never used the word about the way they cared for each other. My friends who went to Chinese schools more frequently used *ai* to describe loving one's country. At public rallies to support efforts to raise funds for China's defence against the Japanese invasion, I would hear loud calls for *aiguo huaqiao*, patriotic overseas Chinese, to donate money or volunteer to fight in China. And most people responded willingly.

Had I gone to a Chinese school and read modern stories and poetry, I would have known how far ideas of love had transformed the lives of the post-May Fourth generation in China. In the 1910s–30s, thousands of essays and poems were written to celebrate the coming out of the word *ai* from ancient convention. These were accompanied by cries of rebellion against the cruel and decadent extended family system and expressions of hope for new nuclear homes. When I went to Nanjing and visited Shanghai in 1947–48, there had already been many failed marital experiments and the word's shine was somewhat worn.

In my year and a half in China, I found the word *ai* rather muted in both home and politics. Even in songs popular among the students, the word was used repeatedly but with little feeling, certainly with none of the consuming passion expressed when first used at the beginning of the 20th century. In class at National Central University, I can only recall seeing the word "love" in English in romantic poetry and some novels, and noted how inadequate the word *ai* was when used to translate love.

I do not recall ever using the word in school, and I did not speak any English during the Japanese occupation years. It may have first come to me from reading romantic poems in my father's copy of Palgrave's *Golden Treasury*. I certainly came across it often in the popular novels I read just before the war ended, but none of that registered in my mind. It was not something I had any experience of apart from the way my mother loved me.

Two images of the word did leave a mark. In my last year in school, Shakespeare's *As You Like It* was one of our Cambridge examination texts, and our teacher, Mr Dempsey, showed us how much fun one could have with the word. Indeed, I enjoyed the comic aspects of its many manifestations. Outside school, the British film *Brief Encounter* came to mind. The story impressed me by the different levels at which love could affect the lives of two mature people who first met by chance. How they managed that and returned to their respective spouses remained in my mind for years. I still remember the picture of pain and doubt that the two people experienced, but I don't think I understood how a single word could possibly convey the range of emotions they went through.

I later read novels and saw films where love seemed to be everywhere and the word was freely dispensed. It seemed to have been something that was at the heart of all Western creative work. Was that why I "loved" literature? Certainly, Mr Dempsey made sure we did not mistake the frothy displays of love for the real thing by taking us carefully through Shakespeare's great sonnet, "Shall I compare thee to a summer's day?"

When I arrived at the university, I told Beda Lim that I loved literature and used the word when historian Brian Harrison asked me why English literature was my first choice for studies. Both Beda and Mr Harrison nodded with approval. The word was used casually and just to express my preference for poetry and fiction. It became clear soon after that the word had a serious side and I would have to try to fathom what a chameleon it had become in common speech. It was not till my third year, after I met Margaret, that the word gained a focus, and thereafter I became shy about using it. I almost stopped using it except as a light-hearted substitute for "enjoy". I was not conscious that the change had anything to do with meeting Margaret and only became aware much later that knowing her had started me on an experience that would become very important to my life. We met in early 1951, married at the end of 1955, and the word took clearer shape in our lives through the years. I no longer hesitate to say that I have loved and know how I have been loved, but I must admit that the word still creates some turbulence in me from time to time. I now know that meeting Margaret in the university in Singapore was when this awareness began its long journey from what was often a literary cliché to an enduring personal experience.

We enjoyed having fun together. Nothing much was said about how we felt. Margaret observed what I was doing, in her words:

I'm afraid both Gungwu and I were not "good" students, in the sense of attending classes religiously and working hard. Instead, because there was no final examination in the second year, most of us goofed off and instead spent our time joining societies, putting on plays and concerts and generally enjoying university life. It is sad that this is no longer possible today. High marks seem to be so important now and students are very competitive. Gungwu was notorious for not attending classes and for handing in late essays. However, he worked hard at student politics, in the sense that he took part in many activities on the campus. He earned extra money by tutoring other students, especially in English. He was already showing his abilities as a teacher at that time.

There were many stories about him as he was such an unconventional student. One of our friends, a Chinese called Thiagarajan (he was brought up in an Indian family) once complained to me that because Gungwu had not attended many of his economics classes, he asked Thiag to give him a short summary of what he had missed. The next day at the test, Gungwu got 60 marks while Thiag got only 40! As you can imagine, Thiag was not happy about this but made a joke and a story about it. Another story concerned a literature test in which Gungwu got only 7 marks. Why 7 marks? Everyone thought it was impossible for him to get only 7 marks. After all he gave lectures to other students on literature! The lecturer explained that instead of answering the questions, Gungwu had just written a poem, so he decided not to give him zero as that would have made him a martyr. Seven marks would show he had not done well! I think Gungwu learnt his lesson and never did that again. So you can see that we thoroughly enjoyed ourselves while at university. Gungwu had many friends with whom he spent evenings discussing the future of an independent Malaya, which national language would be used, what kind of literature was possible in such a country and all the hopes of a young generation waiting to run their own country.

Margaret wanted our children to know more about the environment in which we began our studies at MU. She put down what she thought in this way:

Gungwu's other friends had more political interests. Some of them might have been actual communists. You must remember that then communism was not the failure we regard it as today. There were Cambridge University graduates in England who sympathized with the Russians and spied for them. Burgess and McLean the British diplomats who spied for the Russians for years, were yet to be exposed. The Special Branch in Malaya, the intelligence unit looking out for subversive elements in society, kept an eye on MU's left-wing students. Chinese nationalism was often thought to be the same as support for communism. Chinese school students were very militant. When Mao and his armies took over in China, he said "the Chinese can now stand up". This was a very significant statement as the Chinese had endured more than 100 years of humiliation by the West, when Chinese were discriminated everywhere. The sense of pride among Chinese that China finally had a government which would not bow before the West was very great, no matter what their political beliefs.

The Special Branch in Singapore in the 1950s was headed by a British intelligence officer called Richard Corridan. For some reason (probably because of a mutual interest in modern English poetry), he took a liking to Gungwu and realized he was not a communist although many of his friends were. These friends were the most interesting people around, and Gungwu discussed politics and drank beer with them. But he never took part in any of their activities in their secret cells. Corridan had lent books to Gungwu and discussed literature with him and concluded that he was just a friend and not a co-conspirator of these communists. His life would have been totally changed if he had been arrested with them just before I entered university. Another lot was arrested during my third year. They were members of the Socialist Club, which had as its founding president who else but—Wang Gungwu! They ran a journal called *Fajar* which was considered to be subversive. Gungwu by then had decided to be an historian so he was no longer playing such a big role in student affairs any more.

In part four, I shall talk about what happened when I took my first steps towards trying to become a historian. Here I shall simply touch on how my decision helped me to know Margaret better.

I cannot remember whether I ever asked Margaret what she thought of my following an academic career. We both knew that if I wanted to do a higher degree after graduating from our colonial university, the best way was to get a scholarship to a British university. My professor bluntly told me that it did not matter much what topic I chose to do my research on. As long as it was at a British university, I would get the best training for a career in the University of Malaya.

Margaret's unusual background added new dimensions to the girl I first met. The more I knew about her, the more I marveled that we should have met in Singapore the way we did. When I chose not to get a job after my honours degree but to go on studying, Margaret gave me every encouragement. And when that prospect was more or less understood and her mother met my parents, it was all smooth sailing. Everyone agreed that, should I be awarded the scholarship to continue with my doctoral studies in London, we should get engaged.

Let me turn to her account of what that meant for her, how she felt about coming to Europe, and how our generation of colonials saw post-war Britain easing out of its imperial burdens, and how our stay there gave us a taste of the freedom that we have valued all our lives, something we have sought to make sure that we would never lose.

Why did we go to England? Partly because American degrees were not valued and partly because England or Britain was the "mother country". This was an attitude peculiar to those who went to English schools. The Chinese in China mostly looked towards America because they were accustomed to the institutions in China set up by American missionaries. To these Chinese, America was the Mecca. But to Malayans and Singapore, it was natural to go to Britain for our studies.

At that time, there were not so many people migrating to England as to cause alarm among the British. Anyone who was a British subject could go to Britain and live there. There were no visas and no restrictions, so long as you had the right passport as a British subject or British Protected Person. The curriculum in our schools was such that we knew more about each county in England than we did about Malaya. We knew next to nothing about the neighbouring countries in Southeast Asia. This is particularly true of the English-educated. This was so true that when independence was being discussed, some social leaders of Penang sent a petition to Queen Elizabeth not to give independence but for Britain to continue as the ruling power. The

Chinese-educated had China, a much larger country, to concentrate on. But they were equally ignorant about Southeast Asia and the rest of the world as their focus was on China.

So it was natural that when we thought of higher studies we would think of Oxford and Cambridge and the University of London. Some went further north to Manchester and Edinburgh, but the three former universities mentioned were the most common. It was not easy to get accepted by these universities, but University of Malaya degrees were recognized and as most of us did well, our degrees were well regarded.

By deciding to become an academic, Gungwu was dedicating himself to years of extra study with very little money. At a time when most students did not even do an honours degree, thereby finishing in three years after which they looked for jobs, Gungwu went on to do a master's degree, which took another year, and then had to go to Britain for three years before he could start earning any real money.

Here again, Margaret's account of our separation and reunion tells it better than I can.

Our courtship continued for four years. There was no thought of marrying before either of us had finished university and got a job. We decided to get engaged before he left to do his PhD, on my 21st birthday. I would follow a year later after I had saved up enough money to go to England. My brothers were finishing school and it was their turn to go to university. I could not expect my mother to continue to support me.

When Gungwu got his MA in history, he planned to go to the School of Oriental and African Studies to do a PhD in some aspect of Southeast Asian or Chinese history. Unusually among the local students, he knew enough Chinese to do research in that language and was also fluent in English so that he could write in the language. In fact, by the time he was 23, he had produced a volume of poetry, a thesis on Sun Yat-sen (which would provide him with the basis for years of writing and lectures on that subject) and his thesis on the Nanhai trade. He did all this work without supervision as there was no one in the History Department of the University of Malaya who knew Chinese and could supervise him!

One of the conundrums of my life was whether to seek a new home in Malaya or choose to study China and its history and be ready to move wherever I could do that most effectively. It was a bit like the choice between writing like native tropical Englishmen or finding local voices to describe what we saw and experienced. As my friends put it at the time, more orchids and no more daffodils. But other voices turned out to be more compelling. My decision to go on studying actually steered me back to the land of daffodils.

Margaret also found this ironic and somewhat amusing. But she always had a realistic frame from which she saw me for most of my life—both encouraging and spurring to me to do better! Looking back, that was an excellent foundation for that elusive something called love.

PART FOUR

Double Vision

World of Learning

BACK IN 1949, and during my first three years at the University of Malaya, I was uncertain what I was going to do with my life. After toying with the idea of Malayan literature in English, I was content to be among the anti-colonials who admired the socialist opposition to the capitalism behind imperialist aggression. Taking part in student union affairs was instructive and taught me to think carefully about the world around me. But I realized that what really interested me were the conditions that governed the lives of people and how events unfolded in response to changes over time. I saw that I had in fact been asking historical questions from the day I arrived on campus, when I found myself horribly ignorant of the country that I hoped to identify with. With the new friends I met, I was curious where they came from, who they thought they were and what they wanted to see in the future Malaya. One question would lead to another, and there seemed to be no end to what I could learn from each of them. Many of the answers went back in time; most had to do with what the British and the Dutch had done to the Malay states, India, China and the rest of our region.

I could not forget that I was not local-born and had just returned from a China that had turned communist. With the local Emergency at its height, and with news of China's alliance with the Soviet Union reported every day in the newspapers and its massive intervention in the Korean War, it was clearly wise for me to stay out of political activities. In trying to understand what was happening, I looked out for books that could teach me about Malaya and its history. Our history courses only dealt with larger questions like the rise of the West and its successful domination over Asia. The microcosm of small states like those on the Malay Peninsula or any of the three Straits Settlements featured only marginally on that canvas.

It was not until my third year that I discovered that this approach through empires actually provided a valuable background to help me understand what happened locally. For example, what led to the end of the Malacca and Johor empires, what was the relationship between Francis Light's Penang and the Sultan of Kedah? How did Anglo-Dutch rivalries relate to the rise of Singapore? Also what happened in Perak before and after the Treaty of Pangkor? My reading was sketchy, but coming at these events from the European perspectives of long-distance trade and expansion had its advantages. It was instructive to see forces from afar overwhelm even the most powerful local interests. These stories of outside interventions provided my first glimpse of the fragility of Southeast Asian states in the face of concentrated and hostile naval power. They raised questions of what motives drove the empire-builders to do what they did, how the various local peoples responded, and why their traditions inhibited them from dealing successfully with unexpected changes.

But I must admit that it was not these stories alone that led me to decide to study history. I had enjoyed the world history course taught by Brian Harrison and learnt a great deal from Ian Macgregor's lectures on the pioneering Portuguese and their Dutch rivals. Although I was less interested in Eric Stokes' rich accounts of what the British did to justify their advances into the Indian sub-continent, the way he introduced the effects of Jeremy Bentham's and John Stuart Mill's ideas on British policies in India was inspiring. It taught me not to neglect the place of political thought in history and prepared me for the course on political thought that our professor of history Cyril Northcote Parkinson was to teach in my honours year.

The public lectures by Parkinson were a decisive factor in my choice. I was interested in his descriptions of the way people, individuals, made the difference in the unfolding of events. He was especially convincing on how capable leaders could shape the ideas and institutions that changed the course of history. I was also impressed by his frequent references to the role of the past in contemporary affairs. Although I knew that he was an imperialist at heart, I found him open-minded, and this was confirmed when he commented on some of my provocative views in the essays I wrote for him during the honours year.

Looking back, I believe that it was the combination of my personal inclinations and the experience of learning about the new Malayan environment that led me to choose history. I wrote about this in 2004 in my essay for Goh Beng Lan where I described a time when the idea of *Arts* consisted of "pre-imperial knowledge" and "pre-social science". For me, history encapsulated that idea. It was an open window to a wider canvas that covered everything that had a past that could be relevant to the present. And when I was training to be a historian, I kept being drawn to the origins of a variety of peoples and events whose connections and interactions illuminated the present for me.

I might also have been attracted to the academic life during my second year. When staying in Singapore during the vacations with a part-time job at Radio Malaya, my young colleagues from England taught me a great deal about communication, contemporary affairs and the arts. The job paid me enough to stay close to the university and use its library. For more than two months, and during every vacation period in the years that followed, I found the campus and its resources invaluable. It occurred to me that, for someone with a minimal background to belonging to a pluralistic country that was so multi-varied, a university campus could be the ideal place where I could get my share of freedom.

Choosing to study history also made me realize how much the past had influenced various parts of my life. As described in my book, *Home is not Here*, my mother's stories of her life and of our family origins were reinforced by my father's determination to start my language learning with classical Chinese literature. Whether through prose or poetry, it was legendary heroes, wise rulers, loyal ministers and the lyrics and morality of early agrarian life that were real to me. In school, my teachers also reflected a quiet resistance to British rule, whether they had come from Jaffna, Kalinga, the Hooghly or Lahore, although the local teacher who was an early graduate of Raffles College in Singapore, read us British Empire history out of J.A. Williamson's textbook and nearly put us off the subject for good. For me, Britain's history imbibed through reading English literature was more interesting.

My first-year history had taken us back to Egypt and Babylon, Mohenjo-daro, Jerusalem, Athens and Rome, Chang-an, Karakorum and Samarkand. That was followed in my second year with a global history forged by Portuguese and Spanish sailors that brought the modern West to our region. What was new was the logic of linear chronology that sharpened the sense of cause and effect in the unfolding of events. Although the linear approach was no less man-made, it was a refreshing supplement to the cyclical perspectives in Chinese history that I was familiar with. When we were brought to the 19th and 20th centuries in our third year, the effects of the industrial revolution and capitalist economics helped me understand why it was probably inevitable that India would be transformed by the British belief in progress.

In the end, these courses readied me to learn from Parkinson. He taught the ten of us in the class how to use primary sources for the 10,000-word "academic exercise" that we had to write. He encouraged us to use archival documents supplemented by secondary and oral sources to write local history. The Raffles Museum and the university library both had microfilms of Colonial Office papers and most official reports. There were almost complete sets of locally-published magazines and newspapers, and we were warned to read them critically as secondary sources.

I had read about the activities of Chinese reformers and revolutionaries in the Straits Settlements at the turn of the century and began to look for colonial documents that reported on their movements. There were many published materials about Sun Yat-sen and his rebellious followers in the Nanyang and elsewhere. I asked to write on this subject and outlined what I would need to do. Parkinson was most encouraging and offered to pay my expenses to seek more records in Hong Kong. I gratefully accepted. I like to think that was what kicked off the academic life that I was thereafter to lead.

The course on documents was based on Parkinson's own use of colonial records for the book he was writing, *British Intervention in Malaya, 1867–1877*. It was fascinating to see him test us with documents that he was examining and talk about what he knew about the colonial officials who wrote or commented on them in the files. As I mentioned earlier, he also taught a course on political thought. He made no secret of the fact that he was conservative and proud of the empire, but he portrayed its contributions with humour and also came across as a defender of liberalism as represented by John Locke and John Stuart Mill. I still remember how he picked on an essay I wrote on equality and liberty and tried to persuade me that I was less socialist than I thought and was arguing like a liberal. He was certainly liberal where I was concerned, not only sending me to Hong Kong but also helping me obtain the British Council scholarship to study for my doctorate in London.

⸺◈⸺

The four weeks spent in Hong Kong taught me a great deal and also drew me back to bits of China's recent revolutionary past. The city was a hub of Chinese political activity both nationalist and communist. It displayed a different variety of colonialism and attracted many well-known Chinese scholars who did not want to live either in Chiang Kai-shek's Taiwan or Mao's mainland China. There was so much history made and being made in that city that I did not have a moment to spare trying to read what was available and contacting people with memories of Kang Youwei and Sun Yat-sen.

I was especially keen to learn about Kang Youwei about whom less had been written, and find out more about his years of exile after 1898. Fortunately, I found one of his disciples, Wu Xianzi 伍宪子 (Wu Hsien-tze) who was willing to meet me. Kang Youwei had been derided as an archconservative and monarchist by the Nationalists who supported the more charismatic Sun Yat-sen. Hence material on Sun was plentiful, while almost no one paid attention to Kang's life. Meeting Wu Xianzi was especially fruitful because he offered to write down what he knew about Kang in Singapore and Penang and I was able to use that to fill the gaps in our knowledge of his movements between 1900 and 1911. This original account was translated and included as an appendix to my thesis.

I also tried to find descendants of Sun Yat-sen's earliest comrades, the other three of the notorious "Four Rebels" (四大寇) of his youth, especially of You Lie 尤烈 who was with Sun in Singapore and was active in secret society activities there for many years. But I was not successful. (It was not till years later that his descendants sent me a copy of a short biography that confirmed his role as Sun's major secret society contact.) Instead, I met the son of Tse Tsan-tai (Xie Zantai 谢赞泰), an Australian-born Chinese who was one of the founders of the *South China Morning Post* and the author of *The Chinese Republic: Secret History of the Revolution* (1924). His son led me to read the book, and that gave me a different view of Sun Yat-sen's early years as rebel leader in Hong Kong. To the Tse family, Sun's followers were so determined to promote his image as "father of the republic" that they refused to give any credit to the first president and leader of the Revive China Society 兴中会 (Xingzhonghui) in Hong Kong, Yang Quyun 杨衢云, after he was assassinated by Qing agents in 1901. Although I could see the partisanship in the different accounts, it was a timely reminder that there had been fierce rivalries among the rebel groups. This alerted me not to be too carried away by the fulsome praise given to Sun Yat-sen's every word and move.

Apart from chasing old records, there were other gains. The most memorable was the chance to meet the historian Qian Mu 钱穆 (Ch'ien Mu), whose majestic *General History of China* 《国史大纲》 I admired. It was far superior to the history textbook by Miao Fenglin 缪凤林 that I had used in Nanjing in 1947. Also, I had just read Qian Mu's new book on the strengths and weaknesses of dynastic governance and was delighted to meet him and ask him questions about why he judged the post-Song emperors so harshly. We met at the New Asia College that he had recently founded. He had a room that served as his office, sitting room and bedroom, with a corner kitchenette. In his Wuxi-accented Mandarin that I struggled to understand, he surveyed the history of China and pointed to its governance failures in the past and in modern times. Although I was in no way a historian of China, he earnestly encouraged me to study Chinese history from an outside point of view. I also had my first glimpse of how a traditional historian could engage modern Western scholarship and what it meant to be one of the many Chinese professors who chose the life of displacement when politics and ideology dominated their world of learning.

I also had the bonus of staying at May Hall at the University of Hong Kong, where the Master G.B. Endacott was also a historian. He learnt of me through Brian Harrison who had recently joined HKU and through C.N. Parkinson, who had asked him to help me. Endacott described for me a different kind of colony, where most of its residents saw themselves as Chinese nationals and were readily involved in China's politics. Staying at HKU was not only convenient but also made me very envious of its excellent library of Chinese books. I also found the hillside campus site very beautiful. It was to attract me back many more times and I eventually became its vice-chancellor in 1986.

As with my earlier trips to the Philippines, Ceylon and India, the trip to Hong Kong had long-term effects on my thinking and my career. In the first three trips, I saw the deep Catholic effects on native Filipino culture and the dilemmas of an American hybridity; I was reminded of the wide dispersal of Buddhism out of India and its survival in Ceylon; and my Delhi friends overwhelmed me with their inspirational "discovery of India" that was to shape their country. Where Hong Kong was concerned, it was no less than my re-entry into the life of Chinese who had no sense of national borders and would always see China as theirs to respect and criticize. Although my stay was brief, only four weeks, the chance to meet various types of Chinese using the city as their base for every activity on the mainland was an unforgettable experience. It was one that was to draw me back to the study of the civilization-state that produced these people. Then there was the additional dimension of being on the frontline in a global ideological Cold War, one that made some of the politics intriguing, if not downright sinister.

My two uncles who moved to Hong Kong after "liberation" reflected some common experiences. My father's first cousin (my grandaunt's only son), Hsu Bo-chiao 徐伯郊 had abandoned his stocks and shares business in Shanghai and was now someone who was helping to evaluate art objects brought out of China and, at the same time, also helping the authorities on the Mainland to buy up as much of the best art pieces in order to have them returned to China. He was well placed to do this because his father, Hsu Sen-yu 徐森玉, was an art historian who became the director of the Shanghai Museum.

My father's younger brother, my uncle Huwen 琥文, worked for a national import-export company that was divided into three parts: one in Taiwan, another in Hong Kong, but with its nominal headquarters still in Shanghai. From what I learnt, the three divisions were somehow in touch, and trading whatever and wherever they could. The situation was still fluid in 1952, even as the governments in Taiwan and the PRC were both cracking down on all freedoms, and tackling their on-going civil war in the midst of the larger Cold War.

The new China was becoming increasingly involved in many developments in the region. The Korean War had been going on for almost two years and a deadly series of negotiations were still going on. Chinese military commitments in the northeast had reduced the pressure on both Taiwan and Hong Kong and gave political and psychological space for hundreds of thousands of Chinese to make the necessary adjustments. At the same time, the Hong Kong economy like that of Malaya (including Singapore) was greatly boosted by the commodity demands of the Korean War. And, in contrast to what was etched in my mind when I arrived in Shanghai and Nanjing in 1947 in the middle of the civil war, when I was confronted by images of desperate uncertainty, the faces of those streaming in large numbers into Hong Kong seemed to be filled with hope and expectation. I could see how the different images were making me more sensitive to the way the past was connected with current developments. I certainly thought that turning to history would enable me to better understand what was going on.

On my return to Singapore I sought help to locate some of the people there who had known Sun Yat-sen, including the descendants of those who worked for him when he was in Singapore between 1900 and 1911. He had visited the city at least seven times. In particular, I hoped to meet Chen Chunan 陈楚南 and Zhang Yongfu 张永福, who in their twenties had both been loyal supporters of Sun Yat-sen when he came to Singapore. I was unsuccessful but later realized that I had not tried hard enough. In the case of Zhang Yongfu, I sensed that people were hesitant to talk about him, but did not then fully understand why. It was much later before I learnt that there were still sensitivities about his having once been a supporter of Wang Jingwei 汪精卫, the leader of the left-wing of the Kuomintang against Chiang Kai-shek, who had turned to support the Japanese during the war. It was a pity I never had the chance to talk to the two men because they knew Sun Yat-sen very well. Fortunately, Zhang Yongfu wrote an account of that period 《南洋与创立民国》 (*Nanyang and the Establishment of the Republic*) that helped me to complete my academic exercise.

Distant History

I HAVE BEEN hard put to explain to my friends and colleagues why, for my master's thesis in 1953, I moved from the first decade of the 20th century to write about the growth of China's interest in the Nanhai 南海 (South China Sea) trade that began some 2,000 years earlier. Also, why did I write a thesis that covered more than a thousand years of history?

After I was appointed a tutor in the department and looked around for a thesis topic, I discovered that I did not have access to archival records in any part of China. If I were to do research on modern history, I would have to depend largely on Western and Japanese primary sources. That did not seem right; the idea of working primarily from non-Chinese sources did not appeal to me. But I was still keen to do research on Chinese history, so I began to look at topics in pre-modern periods for which Chinese sources were plentiful.

After reading various studies by Chinese historians past and present and some European journals, I learnt how early Chinese records had provided modern scholars with materials that helped them to reconstruct key parts of early Southeast Asian history. At the same time, European scholars using archaeological, architectural and epigraphic sources could illuminate the cultures of those parts of the region that were deeply influenced by ancient Indian ideas. What was fascinating was the contrasting picture of the aesthetic remains originating from the Indian Ocean mingled with trade products from the China trade. I thought that this would not only enable me to learn how to deal with many kinds of historical documents but would also teach me more about the region in which the Malay Peninsula had a prominent place. The thought that this would educate me further about the country that was to be my home made the subject particularly attractive.

Some of the Chinese historical records that were relevant to this early Nanhai trade were familiar from the classical texts my father had taught me as well as the readings for the Chinese literature and history courses that I did in Nanjing. Most of them consisted of pre-selected and published documents quite unlike the primary sources of modern history that I had learnt to use under Parkinson. The scholarly articles I read about early Southeast Asia showed how these pre-modern sources called for different methods of textual verification, and I was very conscious that I had no training in using such documents. But reading what the European, Chinese and Japanese scholars were able to do with such sources was instructive. I felt confident that I could learn from them if I read their writings carefully. I examined how they used isolated fragments of information that were found nowhere else to throw light on many aspects of China's relations with the polities around the Nanhai. In some cases, identifying some place names and the lists of products that had made commerce profitable for the Indian and Southeast Asian merchants who travelled to China proved to be very helpful and the scholars were able to construct credible accounts of what happened.

In the midst of this reading about the history of trade, I had a moment of enlightenment. This was when I found another strand to the Nanhai story. I read Fa Xian's 法显 *Record of Buddhist Kingdoms* and realized how extraordinary it was for him to have travelled early in the 5th century all over India and also Sri Lanka. After two years' stay there, he embarked on a merchant ship sailing to a port in Sumatra or Java; there he changed to another ship bound for Guangzhou that was diverted by a storm to land way past the mouth of the Yangzi river, coming ashore in the vicinity of Qingdao in Shandong province. That introduction to Buddhist pilgrimage led me to read about Xuanzang's 玄奘 remarkable journey about 250 years later to India and back via Central Asia, and also Yijing's 义净 accounts of the monks who travelled back and forth by sea between India and China. Of particular interest was the fact that they regularly stopped at Sri Vijaya (Sumatra) to learn Sanskrit and Pali at the Buddhist centres there, in preparation for their sutra studies in Nalanda and other holy sites in India. Although not directly linked to trade, these maritime travels over several centuries by monks from China, Korea and what later became Vietnam confirmed the importance of merchant shipping in connecting the countries of Southeast Asia with southern China. They also provided me with a glimpse of the spiritual and intellectual dimensions that accompanied the risk-taking enterprises of long-distance trade.

I was hooked and told Parkinson, who was officially my supervisor, that this trade was going to be my topic. I planned to go back to the beginning of the story and take it as far forward as I could in the one year that I had available for me to write my thesis. He did not blink an eyelid and seemed to think that this was something I could do more or less by myself. He did not claim to know anything about the subject and assumed that I knew what I was doing. All he did was to remind me that I had to finish in time and to travel to London for the new academic year in October 1954. When I finally completed the thesis in August that year, he was on leave and left word that he did not need to see it before submission. That was how simple it was in those days. By the time my thesis was examined and passed, it was too late for the 1954 convocation and my degree was awarded in absentia in 1955.

—◦◦◦◦—

It had never occurred to me that the field of sinology, as developed in Europe in the 19th century, would ever be relevant to my own work. As far as Parkinson was concerned, I was learning to be a historian of ancient China and writing about its maritime trade with its southern neighbours. I shall in the next part of this chapter write about my experiences discovering what sinology entailed after I got to the School of Oriental and African Studies (SOAS) and encountered the idea of orientalism. Here I shall only describe how I entered the portals of that field by depending on the scholarly work I was reading. I quickly realized that, for me to tell the story of this early trade, I needed to know much more than what my study of history had taught me.

China's Nanhai trade originated when, at the end of the 3rd century BCE, the Qin emperor Shihuangdi sent his armies down to conquer the Luoyue 骆越 chiefdoms (now southern Guangxi and northern Vietnam). The armies seized the key ports and pushed further south to the borders of what was later known as the state of Linyi 林邑 and kingdom of

Champa 占成 (now central Vietnam). Another part of the Qin forces went down the West River and captured the capital of the Nanyue 南越 kingdom (today's Guangzhou) and took control of the Pearl River delta. After the Qin empire fell, the military officers it had left at these southern ports revived the Nanyue kingdom, the first Chinese polity that flourished by encouraging maritime trade. A century later, Emperor Han Wudi conquered Nanyue and took control of all the ports that were trading with the Nanhai states and beyond to the Indian Ocean. That trade continued to expand, with many ups and downs through the centuries, until it became what it is today, a development essential to modern China's continued economic growth.

What contributed most to its early growth was the rise in the Han population on the southern coasts. The numerous wars in the north led many of their families to move south and, for different reasons later, the southward movement of peoples continued to be significant from the fall of the Han dynasty onwards. I had not paid attention to where the borders of ancient China were, so it was chastening to learn that it was the Qin-Han empires that extended those borders south of the Yangzi River. What was more, it was the conquest dynasties ruled by nomadic tribes from the steppes after the 3rd century that forced waves of Han peoples to migrate southwards. Over time, the immigrant clans assimilated the indigenous Yue peoples and the more entrepreneurial among them acquired the maritime skills that enabled them to compete with the merchants who came from lands across the South China Sea. In that way, these southern Chinese were eventually to become integral to the economic development of Southeast Asia.

I had to unpick several more strands of war, trade, religion and migration. These involved the rise of independent southern kingdoms from the Wu 吴 and Eastern Jin 东晋 to the Song 宋, Qi 齐, Liang 梁 and Chen 陈 dynasties established by the powerful Han clans that had sought refuge in the south during the three centuries when the north was ruled by a succession of nomadic rulers. All the southern states took a keen interest in the polities of the South China Sea and several expeditions were sent to assess their significance for their economic needs. Their records were particularly important in providing information about ancient places that kept no records of their own.

Our library had sets of several key journals, notably *Bulletin d'Ecole francaise de l'Extreme-Orient*; *T'oung Pao*; *Journal asiatique*; *Asia Major*; *Journal of the American Oriental Society* and the journals of various branches of the Royal Asiatic Society. Fortunately for me, it also had the translations into Chinese by Zhang Xinglang 张星烺 and Feng Chengjun 冯承钧; and the translations into Chinese of works by several Japanese scholars on China's relations with Southeast Asia, notably those of Kuwabara Jitsuro 桑原 隲藏, Fujita Toyohachi 藤田 豊八 and Ishida Mikinosuke 石田干之助. These enabled me to understand the depth of scholarship involved. It also made clear to me that I was not ready to do the kind of research that required knowledge of local Southeast Asian languages as well as several classical languages like Greek, Latin, Sanskrit, Pali, Persian and Arabic. I could only handle writings in Chinese, English, French and some basic Japanese. There was no question of doing the kind of original research that I was reading, but I thought I could still tell the story of China's Nanhai trade as it developed from the 3rd century BCE to the 10th century.

Looking back, the two scholars whose work inspired me most were Paul Pelliot and Feng Chengjun. Pelliot started his life as a sinologist in the École française de l'Extrême-Orient (EFEO) in Hanoi. His extraordinarily learned study, "Deux itineraires de Chine en Inde a la fin du VIIIe siècle" published in the EFEO *Bulletin* (1904) opened my eyes to what could be done to fully explicate a text that was 1,200 years old. It was a kind of scholarship that I had not encountered before. Feng Chengjun, who had studied with Pelliot at the Sorbonne, followed his footsteps and also translated a large number of European studies of the peoples and regions in neighbouring China. His own work on China-Nanyang relations 《中国南洋交通史》 (1937) was fascinating and most helpful. It directed me to put together a storyline that assisted my reading of the large number of Standard Histories 正史 and the ten great compendia inspired by Du You 杜佑 (十通、会要) as well as Sima Guang's *Mirror for Government* 司马光 《资治通鉴》. Not least, I was able to dovetail the stories of the learned monks Faxian, Yijing and the many others who travelled to India with the growth in Chinese trading interest in the scented woods so plentiful in the region.

Locally, two scholars were a great help, the respective editors of the *Journal of the Malayan Branch of the Royal Asiatic Society* and the *Nanyang xuebao* 南洋学报, Carl Gibson-Hill and Hsu Yun-ts'iao 许云樵. Both gave me valuable advice about how to deal with a variety of pre-modern printed sources. Also helpful was Tan Yeok Siong 陈育崧, who was not only a publisher but also a collector of Chinese books. He allowed me to use his private collection before the university established the Department of Chinese Studies, when He Guangzhong 贺光中, its first head, swiftly built up a fine library of classical texts in time for me to consult.

All this time, I was approaching the source materials as a historian, but I soon realized that I was stepping into a different arena. This was called Hanxue 汉学 (Sinology) and referred to methods of research that combined the traditions of classical Chinese and Japanese learning with European scholarship that had drawn from their own classical and biblical studies. It could also be traced to the work of Jesuit missionaries from the late 16th to 18th centuries. Following growing interest in China in the 18th century by Enlightenment scholars like Voltaire and Leibniz, French and German scholars began to broaden the philological beginnings of Sinology to cover the whole range of literary and historical studies; by the 20th century, the field was steadily advancing to also cover some of the social sciences.

In China, Wang Guowei 王国维 and others were quick to appreciate the value of this sinology by foreign scholars, and persuaded a whole generation in China that the work of European and Japanese scholars had much to offer and could provide fresh insights on early Chinese history. Two men, Chen Yuan 陈垣 and Chen Yinke 陈寅恪 were outstanding. In 1953, I was still new to the field and had not grasped the depth of scholarship that their work entailed. Nevertheless, I recognized that their skills would enhance my history writing and I should try to emulate them one day.

I also discovered that Jinan University in Shanghai had become very interested in all things Southeast Asian. Some of their scholars had moved to Singapore before the war, notably Zhang Liqian 张礼千 and Yao Nan 姚楠. Together, they founded the South Seas Society (Nanyang Xuehui 南洋学会) and published the *Nanyang xuebao* just before the Japanese occupation, the journal that was revived under Hsu Yun-ch'iao's editorship after the war. There were also strong links with Xiamen University's Nanyang Research Centre 南洋研究所. The writings of this pioneering group made me more confident that I could handle the period from the Qin-Han dynasties to the Tang and the Five Dynasties.

All the same, I did realize that I was handicapped by my lack of background in the field of *Hanxue*/sinology. What my father had taught me of Chinese classical prose and poetry was drawn from his own love of Chinese philology, but he did not train me in that field. What I learnt from him as well as from my teachers in Nanjing in 1947–48 was mainly confined to literature, with bits of relevant history thrown in. The little I knew about historical methodology came from my British teachers, who were primarily concerned with modern history and made no reference to Chinese historical knowledge. So here was I applying skills learnt from Western European history to try to use Chinese texts without fully understanding their provenance nor how documents were selected and organized in the large sets of official collections that I depended on.

Nevertheless, my self-taught "apprenticeship" had begun. Almost everything was new and, although I had an exciting year of learning, it was most demanding and I endured many moments of doubt about whether I could finish the thesis on time. I shall write more about having Margaret around to encourage me, and indeed she helped to keep me focused as I struggled to get ready to take up my scholarship to study in London. I also had to convince her and her mother that I was worthy of her and to get everyone to agree that we should get engaged before I set off in August 1954.

Fortunately, Parkinson thought I had promise and commended me on my ability to adjust to all the inadequacies of the academic system I was working in. It was he who encouraged me to continue my studies in England. My parents could not afford to send me there. So he strongly supported me for a two-year British Council scholarship. The PhD degree needed a minimum of three years to complete, but he thought that, once in London, there would be other opportunities for getting an extension. British universities did not require any coursework; it was assumed that anyone accepted into a PhD course would have learnt to do research through a master's degree, and that such a person would have been capable of doing the doctoral thesis by themselves. Bearing that in mind, he got me the scholarship and I readied myself to travel to England.

Why 10th Century

WHEN I APPLIED to the School of Oriental and African Studies, I thought I would go on with my writing on Chinese activities in the South China Sea. As I was finishing my thesis on the Nanhai trade, I learnt that Paul Wheatley, the historical geographer in our Geography Department had started to study the commodities that were traded between China and Southeast Asia during the Song dynasty. He was concentrating on the many lists of such trading items that could be found in the surviving texts of the great Song Compendium of Documents 《宋会要辑稿》. I thought that I should turn to a later period, when maritime trade made notable advances after the Mongol Yuan dynasty conquered Song China. During the early Ming dynasty, under Emperor Yongle, Zheng He's 郑和 navies made seven expeditions to the Indian Ocean and led to the rise of the Malacca Empire. From those expeditions, the relations between China and all the coastal kingdoms of the region were brought to new heights.

I had found out that Otto van der Sprenkel was teaching at SOAS. He had been a professor of economics at Nankai University 南开大学 in Tianjin for many years and specialized in Ming economic history. When I learnt that he had worked on Ming history with some of the best scholars in China, I was keen to study with him. Unfortunately, by the time I arrived, he was heading in the opposite direction and just about to leave to go to the Australian National University (ANU).

I was enrolled in the History Department at SOAS headed by Cyril Philips, who had made his name writing a history of the East India Company. Coming with a scholarship from Malaya, I was registered with the professor of Southeast Asian history, D.G.E. Hall. Hall said he would be happy to be my supervisor and, where I needed help with Chinese sources, there were experts at the school I could turn to. The library had an excellent collection of Chinese books and journals, and the head of the Department of Chinese was a famous Chinese and Tibetan philologist, Walter Simon, the epitome of the European sinologist.

Among the first friends I made in London was Jerome Chen 陈志让 who had completed his PhD on the economic policies of the Qing dynasty during the 19th century. He had done this with Otto van der Sprenkel and was waiting to be examined while working for the Chinese section of the BBC. He told me that he had waited for a year after sending his manuscript to van der Sprenkel to read. It was only when his supervisor was about to leave for Canberra that he told Jerome that the thesis could be submitted. Jerome thought he should tell me about his experience as a cautionary tale about the British system of graduate supervision.

He then told me that he was now working on Yuan Shikai under whose presidency of the Republic of China (1912–16) the warlord era had begun. I was still interested in 20th-century China, particularly in the early years of the republic that was dominated by warlords. Having seen for myself in 1947–48 the tragedy of the civil war in China, I wanted to know how China became so divided and why every warlord claimed to be a patriot who fought only to enable China to be united again. Most of all, I was keen to understand why, often at great cost to its peoples, China had always become one again and again. Also, it would seem that whoever was able to reunify China was seen as a great man, no matter how tyrannical or cruel he was. I envied Jerome's courage to take on the man who took the republic away from Sun Yat-sen and then tried to turn the clock back to monarchical rule.

By that time, I had set my mind to continue with the history of dynastic China. I had just come from writing the last chapter of my Nanhai trade thesis, which ended in 960, conventionally taken to be the end of the most divided period of Chinese history, that of the Five Dynasties and the Ten Kingdoms 五代十国 (907–960). In short, my previous work stopped on the eve of a partial reunification. I knew how deeply divided China was from the 870s to the 970s and the divisions were remarkably like those of the early 20th century. Being reminded of the warlords made me think that this was an opportunity for me to leave a peripheral subject like trade in the Nanhai to work on a theme that was much more central to Chinese history.

◦─◦⟨◦✕◦⟩─◦

The question in my mind was encapsulated in the famous opening line of the *Romance of the Three Kingdoms* 三国演义, "What was long divided was bound to be united; what was long united was bound to be divided" (分久必合，合久必分). That was a generalization that could be traced back centuries to the fall of the Han dynasty, when the Three Kingdoms divided the empire for over half a century. Each of the three rulers sought to reunify the empire and eventually it was the Western Jin 晋 dynasty that almost succeeded in doing so. But that partial unity did not last for long. By the year 318, north China under the Jin was overwhelmed by a slew of nomadic invaders from the north, northwest and west, by armies from areas later called Manchuria, Mongolia, "Turkestan" and Tibet. For the next three centuries, the struggles continued, often in the name of the unified empire ideal. When the dynastic founders of the Sui in 589 and the Tang in 618 finally succeeded, the idea that all contestants for power should see reunification as a sacred duty had taken root in the popular imagination. If this was so important a tradition in Chinese political culture, I thought that studying the aspirations of 10th-century "warlords" was a good way to get to the heart of Chinese history.

There were two further reasons why I was now attracted to this subject. Everything I had done in Singapore had to do with China's relations with its southern neighbours and much of what I had written about concerned only the Han peoples who had migrated to southern China between the 3rd and 10th centuries. As a result, I did not feel that I knew enough about what really mattered in the northern heartlands of political power. Secondly, I had noticed how the north had always prevailed in conflicts between northern and southern China, right down to the Communist victory in 1949. Although all military leaders claimed that they sought to end divisiveness and make China one again, it was invariably those in the north that succeeded. Why was that? Why were the Three Kingdoms reunited under the Western Jin in the north, yet the Eastern Jin that rebuilt its power in the south was unable to bring an end to the fragmentation and chaos brought about by the "Uprisings of Five Barbarians" 五胡乱华? At its most divided for about 120 years, that "China" saw at least sixteen very unstable kingdoms. Eventually, order was restored when the north was united and the following period became one of North-South division (420–581). And it was the Sui and Tang imperial founders of northern dynasties who reunited China.

Ever since that time, Chinese people were taught to believe that division was a tragedy and unification the ideal that everybody should work to achieve and preserve. Following this line of thinking, I decided that, if I could not work on the 20th-century warlords, I would study those of the 10th century. I would seek to understand how the Tang Empire was broken up by a group of regional governors with their own armies that defied the imperial centre and fought one another instead. These autonomous *fanzhen* 藩镇 brought the Tang dynasty to an end and cleared the way for various groups of Han and non-Han contestants to keep the empire divided for over a century. In particular, I would try to understand what were the factors that made it possible after 960 for one of those groups in north China under the founder of the Song dynasty to succeed.

Nobody in London at the time knew much about the subject or was interested. I found that the Five Dynasties was a subject totally neglected in Western literature. Only one Western scholar, the German sinologist and sociologist Wolfram Eberhard teaching at the University of California Berkeley, had devoted a whole book to the subject. He had published his *Conquerors and Rulers* in 1952. I found the book interesting but thought that he was more concerned with the Shato 沙陀 Turk conquerors who established three of the five dynasties than with the reunification questions I was asking. His interest in the Turkic dynasties had come from his decade as professor of Chinese history in Ankara and, while that perspective was important, it did not help me understand the division and unity tradition that obsessed most Chinese political leaders. There was therefore an important but neglected story to tell and I was now keen to try to understand what happened.

Meeting Sinology Halfway

I SPENT MY first months at SOAS deciding what to do if I did not pursue my original plan to work on Ming relations with Southeast Asia. Jerome Chen's example reminded me that I could do research on modern China as a historian but, if I continued to work on pre-modern China, those in Europe who worked on historical topics were invariably sinologists.

I had been aware of the difference in Singapore when I was reading the work of Paul Pelliot. In comparison, Chinese scholars like Qian Mu and Chen Yinke were historians who were deeply steeped in Chinese classical philology. And the Japanese scholars who specialized in China's history were similarly well trained in classical philology. I had wanted to be a modern historian but now I was venturing into 10th-century China in a British university where the historians of China were sinologists. I was in the curious position of being a student planning to do a doctoral degree in Chinese history without any training in sinology or in Chinese history. Reading Eberhard's book made me aware that a sinologist could become a famous folklorist and ethnographer who could teach history in Ankara and sociology in Berkeley. But I did not know any historian who was recognized as a famous sinologist.

Fortunately, two scholars in England helped me square the circle at a critical moment. Edwin (Ted) Pulleyblank and Denis Twitchett had both been inducted to Japanese language studies during the war when they worked on cryptography listening to Japanese radio communications and went on to study classical Chinese and sinology after the war. Ted Pulleyblank also had an excellent background in European classical studies and this was to draw him back to philological and linguistic studies, although his PhD at SOAS was in Tang history after receiving sinology training under Walter Simon. I found his thesis in the SOAS library and was inspired by his work on the An Lushan 安禄山 rebellion. It was a valuable introduction to the divisive conditions that followed the rebellion, eventually the major reasons for the dynasty's decline. His thesis suggested that it might be possible for me to write post-Tang history even without formal training in sinology. But I missed learning directly from him. By the time I arrived in London, he had been appointed to the chair of Chinese at Cambridge University.

I was fortunate to have Denis Twitchett at SOAS. He had just returned from Japan and Professor Hall asked him to help me. He had done his training in Oriental Studies at Cambridge, under the Czech sinologist Gustav Haloun, and then spent years working with Japanese scholars of Tang China. He advised me to read the research of Niida Noboru 仁井田陞, Kato Shigeshi 加藤繁 and Yudo Yoshiyuki 周道吉之, all of whom reinvigorated Tang-Song history with their original insights. Although they did not focus on the question that most interested me—what happened that made it possible for China to be reunited under the Song dynasty—their work was very helpful to my understanding of that period of division. Theirs was the "modern Japanese sinology" that had evolved from traditional Chinese scholarship, but also drew on the best of European oriental studies. I took Denis' advice and set out to hone my reading skills in Japanese. Thus I was able to make good use of the work of many Japanese scholars, writings that enabled me to approach the major Chinese sources with confidence. I began to feel that I might be able to harness relevant bits of sinology to help me become a historian.

———◈———

One fortunate event gave me further encouragement. I was invited as a graduate student to attend the Jeunes Sinologues (Young Sinologists) conference in Paris in September 1956. This enabled me to meet a large group of European *sinologues* whose names I had heard of and some of whose writings I had read. This was an opportunity to hear them present their papers and meet and talk to some of them. What was special about this meeting was that the PRC authorities had accepted the invitation to send four of their most senior historians to the West, to report on some of their recent work. They were led by Jian Bozan 翦伯赞 who was the head of the History Department of Peking University and one of the university's deputy presidents. His was seen as the official view of Chinese historiography. I was fascinated to hear several European scholars challenge his Marxist interpretation of ancient history, claiming that his efforts to categorize Chinese "slave" and "feudal" societies in the Xia, Shang and Zhou dynasties were quite unconvincing. He was accompanied by Xia Nai 夏鼐 who had studied Egyptology in London and was now China's leading archaeologist. Everyone paid close attention to his reports on recent discoveries in northern China. Two other historians were Zhou Yiliang 周一良 and Zhang Zhilian 张芝联. Zhou spent years at Harvard and made his name researching the period between the Han and Tang dynasties. Zhang studied at Yale and Oxford; he specialized in European history and became China's expert on French history. Zhou Yiliang was especially interesting because his work was relevant to mine on the 9th and 10th centuries.

It was only after the meeting that I realized that this was an exceptional moment for scholars in China. The four scholars had been sent to Paris on the eve of Mao Zedong's speech about "letting a hundred flowers bloom and letting a hundred schools contend". A few months later, the "anti-rightist" campaign was launched and scholars who did not conform to orthodox Leninist ideology stopped writing altogether and were lucky if they were not incarcerated or punished.

At the Paris meeting, there were also three scholars from Hong Kong who updated us on the research being done there. They were Luo Xianglin 罗香林 of the University of Hong Kong and He Guangzhong 贺光中 and Rao Zongyi 饶宗颐 both then at the new Chinese Studies Department of the University of Malaya in Singapore. They spoke for the traditional Chinese scholarship now established in Hong Kong and represented in my eyes by Qian Mu, the founder of New Asia College whom I had the privilege of meeting a couple of years earlier. Unfortunately for them, the presence of the PRC scholars stole the show because the Europeans were more interested in what was happening to scholars on the mainland. I sensed the frustration of the Hong Kong group, but could understand the intense curiosity about the Maoist onslaught on all forms of pre-Marxist China studies.

European sinologists from the major centres in France, Germany and the Netherlands were there and I could see what a long tradition of China studies they represented. I met one scholar from America, Benjamin Schwarz from Harvard. His presence was a surprise. I had read his book *Chinese Communism and the Rise of Mao* and wondered how he was also a sinologist. Actually, he was deeply read in ancient Chinese philosophy and showed great curiosity in my work on the late Tang and Five Dynasties, a period that he thought was a turning point for Confucian thought. His presence assured me that there were different roads to sinology and my marginal position was not hopeless.

I felt privileged to be the only graduate student of Chinese descent attending and was both humbled and inspired by the quality of the discussions that I heard. At the same time, I recall feeling how poorly prepared I was for the research that I was doing and wondering what kind of academic career I could be good for. It was my first taste of the borderless nature of good scholarship and an experience that I have valued ever since.

D.G.E. Hall had another student using Chinese sources to study early Southeast Asia, Michael Blackmore, and would have been happy to have me join him. Michael was a friend I met in Singapore who was trained in sinology in Cambridge. Unlike me, he was coming from that classical training to learn to use historical and anthropological methods to study a very controversial topic to do with Yunnan and the land borders of Southeast Asia, that is whether the Nanzhao kingdom's ruling elites were Tibeto-Burman or Thai. We were good friends and he was my best man when Margaret and I were married. Hall would have preferred for me to study with Michael and keep up my interest in Southeast Asia. He was disappointed that I moved away from Southeast Asia to be a historian of China, but remained my supervisor. Denis Twitchett, who was asked to help me, was a new lecturer in the Department of Chinese and about to complete his own PhD and therefore could not be officially appointed to supervise me. As it happened, I spent eight months away in Cambridge in 1955–56 when Denis was in London and, when I returned to London for my final year in 1956–57, Denis had left to join Ted Pulleyblank in Cambridge. Nevertheless, he took good care of me, gave me excellent advice and paved the way for me to write Chinese history without the full sinologist training.

In the History Department, the professor of Far Eastern history was William Beasley, a historian of modern Japan. He was also master of my residential hall and tried as much as possible to help. When I wanted to learn more Japanese, he introduced me to Ronald Dore, who had used his language skills to become an outstanding sociologist of modern Japan. Dore tutored us and it was in his class that I met Philip Kuhn. As we picked up some fine points of the language together, Philip became one of my best friends. He demonstrated in his career that the modern historian with social science skills could use sinology to deepen his understanding of the more archaic traditions. That was another dimension of sinology that I began to appreciate.

The head of the department, Cyril Philips, was keen that I remain primarily a historian. He was professor of South Asian history and, unlike the Far East, South Asia had the well-known indologist A.L. Basham as reader. Basham had several students in ancient history. One of them was Romila Thapar, whom I first met at the United Nations Students conference in Delhi. Unlike me, however, she was trained as an indologist before she chose to specialize in history. For her, there was no uncertainty about being an indologist-historian. I envied her ability to move so successfully between indology and history.

Philips knew Parkinson's work and encouraged me to keep up with modern historiography even if I continued with early Chinese history. I told him that I admired historians like R.H. Tawney, E.H. Carr, Pieter Geyl, Henri Pirenne and Steven Runciman, and had recently read A.J.P. Taylor's *The Struggle for Mastery in Europe, 1848–1918*, and Lewis Namier's *The Structure of Politics at the Accession of George III*. He was happy to learn that I was keeping up with some of the best historians in Europe and then encouraged me to read more *medieval* history. I did not at the time understand why. Only when I was submitting my thesis in 1957 did I realize that, as a student of history, I could not be awarded a degree in Chinese but, since I had worked on 10th-century China, my doctorate would be one in medieval history. By that time, it did not really matter. I never thought that China had its own Middle Ages. In any case, I never saw myself as a medieval historian, only a Chinese historian.

EngLit England

DURING MY FIRST year in London, I found that I had not shaken off my literary interests. London's streets were surprisingly familiar. Staying in the shadow of the University Senate House meant that I was walking distance from Bloomsbury and the British Museum, from Soho and Piccadilly Circus, and the secondhand bookshops on Tottenham Court Road. The British Council made sure that its scholars from all over the empire were given every opportunity to follow their literary and musical interests. For me, that was irresistible, especially when it was one way that, at a long distance from Singapore, I could still share something with Margaret that we both enjoyed.

The Council subsidized trips both in and out of London every weekend, and I took every opportunity to visit literary sites, historic cathedrals and museums and the major musical events. It was a pleasurable way to enhance my cultural education, from Hardy's "Wessex", Stonehenge, the Lake District and Stratford-upon-Avon to walking the streets of London. When I described my trips to Margaret, she could sense my excitement about those places and people that she knew well through her own reading. She did not complain but must have wondered whether there would be much left for us to do together when she joined me the next year.

I loved the new Royal Festival Hall and wished I could go to all the performances there. I could afford to be up with the "gods" for a few concerts; for the rest, I had to be content to read about the orchestras, their conductors and some of the talented soloists who performed there. The one great treat was when the Council offered me a ticket to the premiere of William Walton's opera, *Troilus and Cressida*. I had admired the music that Walton had provided for Lawrence Olivier's *Henry V* and *Hamlet*, films that I had thought awesome when I saw them in Ipoh and Singapore. So I felt really privileged to have had the chance to see his first opera. It was my first exposure to opera and frankly I was unable to appreciate much of it. It was only after going back to the best of Mozart, Verdi and Puccini over several years that I learnt to love opera as a wonderful musical experience. Even then, it never displaced my preference for the great symphonies.

I was fortunate in other ways. From Connaught Hall, just beside SOAS, I was able to visit the British Museum regularly. There, through the volume and variety of the artifacts displayed, I was able to see the imperial outlook on those parts of the world that Britain traded with and sought to dominate. While I could not share the pride its people felt about their past, it gave me another perspective of their global reach. What surprised me was how my excursions in English literary history had led me to set aside some of my harsher views against imperialism. Connecting poems and novels to people and places had helped me to see the softer face of English culture. In particular, I remembered Lytton Strachey's *Eminent Victorians* that my Chinese professor of English in Nanjing was so fond of. That had introduced me to the Bloomsbury Group. In Singapore, I had read novels by other members of the group, like Virginia Woolf and E.M. Forster. And when I became an admirer of John Maynard Keynes through my economics classes and my interest in a liberal socialism, I was surprised to learn that he was also a member of that group.

Bloomsbury had become flesh for me a couple of years earlier when Margaret and I met an Englishman doing his national service in Singapore. He was looking after the grounds at Flagstaff House on Kheam Hock Road, a few hundred yards from Margaret's home. I cannot remember how we met but we became good friends. It turned out that the young man, Adrian Goodman, was the grandson of Lady Ottoline Morrell, whose home in Bloomsbury was the regular meeting place of Keynes, Strachey, Woolf and Forster before and after the First World War. It happened that Connaught Hall at Russell Square was but a couple of streets away from the Morrell house and garden. Adrian had arranged for me to call on his mother, Lady Ottoline's daughter, when in London and I did. His mother invited me to tea and let me look at the hundreds of first editions of books signed by some of the best-known authors of that generation.

It was there among the first editions that I discovered that Arthur Waley was also a member. I still do not know why I had not noticed when I was in Singapore that he belonged to that group. We had read his translations of Chinese poetry, including *The Book of Poetry*, and were struck by the view that some of them were admired as *English* poetry. I had been very impressed by his *Three Ways of Thought in Ancient China*, by his pithy comments on Confucian thought and his judgment that the legalists 法家 had nothing to do with the law but were really a bunch of hard-headed realists. And, in particular, I enjoyed reading *Monkey*, his version of Xuanzang and Sun Wukong's *Journey to the West*《西游记》.

And, although T.S. Eliot and Ezra Pound were not members, Eliot was well known to the group and his office was nearby, and Pound had translated some Chinese and Japanese poetry and commented critically on Waley's versions. What that confirmed for me was how close the English literary coterie was. I need hardly say that this British literary and musical culture did put pressure on my efforts to train to be a historian of China. Margaret noticed that I seemed to enjoy the distractions more than my efforts to decide on my research topic, and might have wondered if they were the cause of the delay in making up my mind. I did not think it interesting to explain how I found myself positioned in between what the British called "medieval history", for which I was totally untrained, and a field of learning the Europeans called "sinology" that covered almost all studies of China before the 19th century. Had she known, she would have been alarmed. Perhaps unconsciously, that was why I told her more about my literary adventures and avoided describing my struggles with my thesis subject.

In fact, my indulgence in British culture did not affect my efforts to explore the mysteries of sinology. I was fascinated to discover that Arthur Waley had become a sort of icon in that field without being trained. I had no ambition in that direction, but perhaps I also could make a historical contribution without *Hanxue* training. My own mentor, Denis Twitchett, took a generous view of my hopes. I sensed that he did when I attended his inaugural lecture in 1961 as professor of Chinese at SOAS and heard him praise Arthur Waley by suggesting that he had carved out his own slice of sinology. Was that why Denis remained so indulgent of the way my academic career was later to develop?

I was not lost to London's other blandishments. My regular visits to the British Museum enabled me to know the bookshops nearby, including the communist publishing house of Lawrence & Wishart, where the latest periodicals and magazines from the PRC could be found. About the time I arrived in London, it published the first English edition of Mao Zedong's *Selected Works* that became a talking point among my fellow Afro-Asian students at SOAS. And when I visited Malaya Hall some weekends to pick up the latest news, I met Malayans who were familiar with Mao's writings. I later learned that some had travelled to eastern Europe and a few had actually visited the PRC.

This made me curious how China was beginning to transform radically its social structures and cultural values, but I found myself more concerned about the political developments in Malaya. My friends updated me about the communists there being pushed deeper into the jungle, and it was clear that their insurgency was losing. In Singapore, however, civic resistance against colonial power was growing and unionists and students were more active in the streets. At the same time, parties using labels like "Labour" and "Socialist", with new leaders like Lim Yew Hock and David Marshall were regrouping. I was not clear how the trade unions were being divided but heard stories about the small People's Action Party under Lee Kuan Yew gaining the support of left-wing unions. What intrigued me was to learn that my university friends—James Puthucheary, Jamit Singh and Sydney Woodhull and some other members of the Socialist Club—were actively assisting the party.

I had kept Margaret informed about the literary sites I had visited and promised to leave some key places for us to see together when she joined me. Margaret in turn wrote to tell me how much she was enjoying being a Sixth Form English teacher at St Andrew's Secondary School. She included side comments about the unrest in the trade unions and some of the Chinese high schools. In particular, she kept me up-to-date about the new Nanyang University that was being enthusiastically supported by the Chinese community both in Singapore and in the Federation. The man who led the campaign was Tan Lark Sye 陈六使 who made his fortune in the rubber industry and dreamt of building a great university like his kinsman Tan Kah Kee 陈嘉庚 had built in Xiamen. The Hokkien Association donated a large piece of land in Jurong and registered the university as a private institution. Margaret told me that the university had appointed the famous writer Lin Yutang 林语堂 as its first vice-chancellor and that key professorial appointments had already been made. I knew some of the people involved and followed developments with great interest. The idea of another university for all those students who were unable to go to universities in China was most welcome. I certainly looked forward to being associated with it on my return. Little did I know that one day I would be entangled in the explosive politics surrounding what was seen as the university's "sacred" mandate.

When Margaret eventually learnt that I had decided to change my research topic from China's relations with Southeast Asia to the study of the Five Dynasties, she was troubled enough to ask if I knew what I was doing. I explained why I had done that and she assured me that she still believed in me. Her faith in my claims to know what I was doing was often tested in our lives, and I am fortunate that it survived the seven times we had to move our homes during the first 12 years of our marriage.

PART FIVE

Make a Family

Reunion and Marriage

THE SCHOLARSHIP THAT the British Council awarded was only for two years. It was barely enough to pay for my travel to London and my living expenses. There was no provision for a spouse. Neither of us had the money to enable Margaret to come with me. It would have been years of separation while I trained to climb the academic ladder. She, however, was resourceful. She knew that the only way she could have joined me was to work and save her own money for the trip. Looking back, I am chagrined to think that my lack of initiative and inability to help had put Margaret through such a tough year. Because it was her determination that made it possible for us to be together again a little over a year later, I can do no better than let her tell her story of our reunion.

In September 1955, I joined Gungwu. I still remember how excited I was to travel to England. I had arranged to travel with my friend, Ivy Soh. We booked places on an Italian ship that dropped us in Naples. From Naples, a train would take us right to London, going via Paris. Gungwu had done the same on another Italian ship and had enjoyed the trip across the continent of Europe.

When I got to Victoria Station, there was Gungwu to meet me. It was wonderful to see him again as I had missed him so much in our year's separation. While he was seeing new sights and meeting new friends, I was living in the same place and living a very restricted life. However, we had a wonderful reunion as he had planned a busy programme of activities for me during the time I was to be in London. He was then living in Connaught Hall, a hostel next to SOAS. He had arranged for me to stay in a women's hostel near his for the two weeks I was to be in London before I went to Homerton College in Cambridge.

Kew Gardens, 1955.

Why was I going to Cambridge when Gungwu was in London? That was due partly to Gungwu and partly to my English lecturer, John Copley and his wife Kate. They had encouraged Ivy and me to go to Homerton College when they heard I was thinking of doing a post-graduate diploma in education, and when I mentioned this to Gungwu in a letter, he also encouraged me to go to Cambridge as he was visiting Cambridge at that time, trying to gather some material for his thesis. He told me he could remain in Cambridge, and so we would be together.

But Gungwu had made a miscalculation. London University had a rule which stipulated that a candidate for a degree had to be in London for at least six terms of nine. As Gungwu had already been in Cambridge for one term, we had to recalculate our options.

However, we were at least in the same country, and we made the best of our time in London after I arrived. Gungwu and I had a wonderful two weeks, seeing plays and concerts and even an opera. It was a Wagner opera and all I remember of it is of a large woman, probably a famous singer (except that I wasn't interested in opera in those days), who was dressed in a suit of armour stamping up and down the stage! We also went to visit Professor R.E. Holttum, former director of the Singapore Botanic Gardens and recently retired as our professor of Botany, who had an office at Kew Gardens. He was pleased to see someone from Singapore and, with his advice, we enjoyed the gardens very much.

Connaught Hall was very convenient; however, it had some of the worst institutional food you could ever imagine. I had a few meals there and never wanted to eat there again! Every cliché you have ever read about English institutional food could be applied to the meals there. As a result, Gungwu learnt to cook some simple meals. He knew how to cook rice (which is more than I did at that time), and his favourite pork dish, soya sauce belly pork. There was a pantry with a few burners in it on every floor and most students had a few pots for their own cooking. There were no refrigerators, however, so Gungwu put his small pots of rice and meat on the ledge running along the outside of his bedroom window. It was so cold outside most of the year that this kept the food quite fresh and refrigerated. So during my two weeks in London, I had a few meals cooked by him.

Finally, my time in London was up and Gungwu escorted Ivy and me to Cambridge. We travelled by train, the first of many journeys I would be making on that route.

Homerton College was not part of Cambridge University at that time, although our degree was awarded by the university. It has since become one of the Cambridge colleges that award graduate and post-graduate degrees. At the time, it was actually a teachers' training college. Kate Copley knew the principal of the college well and thought highly of the institution. It had a two-year diploma course for post-secondary school graduates. However, in 1955, it decided to add a Postgraduate Certificate in Education for university graduates. The Certificate would be a Cambridge University qualification and the examination monitored by the university. I had originally applied for and obtained a place in the University of London Institute of Education but changed my mind as I thought living in Cambridge would be much more pleasant. However, I was later to regret my decision as the course I took was rather undemanding and I didn't learn as much as I would have in London.

Homerton College was my first experience of college life. It is hard to imagine the restrictions placed on students in those days. All the colleges in Cambridge had restricted times for being out at night. All ten of my classmates, being graduates already, found the restrictions rather absurd. We had to be in by 10 p.m. but special allowance was made for us and we could stay out until 11 p.m.! It was a women's college and I was introduced to a steady diet of English food: meals of sausages and mashed potatoes, overcooked vegetables and heavy puddings for dessert. I hardly had any Asian meals in the first term. Cambridge didn't have any Chinese restaurants to speak of and Chinese restaurants in London were expensive. The most irritating thing about them was charging anything from sixpence to one shilling for a small bowl of rice. This was expensive in those days as we usually never paid more than ten shillings for a whole meal in a restaurant. We found Indian restaurants better value as the rice served was in larger portions. Cambridge was cold and we were young and so had larger appetites.

Gungwu and I communicated by mail. In those days there were two deliveries of mail a day and sometimes, I would receive two letters a day from Gungwu. I was certainly the envy of the other girls for getting so much mail! We also saw each other every weekend. Either he or I would travel, Gungwu to Cambridge, and I to London. We would catch the early morning train on Saturday and return late on Sunday. Mostly, I went to London as there was much more to do there. We couldn't afford good seats but found our way to theatre seats high up in the upper circle with the "gods", as the saying went. We didn't mind that in the least because we were able to hear some of the best musicians and see the best actors that London could offer.

Eventually, we got tired of all that travelling so Gungwu suggested that we marry so we could live together. He had found out that his supervisor was willing to turn a blind eye to his living in Cambridge for another two terms, the first had almost gone and there were only two terms left of the academic year. Up to that time, there was no thought in my mind of getting married in England. My mother had asked me not to and to wait until we returned to Singapore so that she could have a big wedding for her oldest child. But by that time, Gungwu's parents were staying in London for a post-retirement break, so they could be the official hosts for our wedding reception.

I wrote to my mother to ask her permission to marry and gave her our reasons. She agreed, much to my relief, the only stipulation being that we should marry in a Methodist church. Gungwu's mother was given the task of choosing the "right" date to get married. We decided on the end of the year after the first term was over. For all her non-religious and non-superstitious nature, Gungwu's mother consulted various Chinese texts, like the Yi Ching 易经, taking our birthdays into account, and selected the 21st of December. I guess she was right, as we have been happily married for 64 years now and look set for the rest of our lives!

We had not planned to get married in England and did not talk about that possibility the whole year we were apart. But once the decision was made, Margaret again proved to be the one to get everything done with the minimum of fuss. Let her describe what had to be done.

My classmates were very excited to hear I was getting married. I asked Ivy to be my bridesmaid and I decided that I would wear a cheongsam 长衫 as a wedding gown. In order to do that I had to sew my own, which I proceeded to do on a borrowed sewing machine at the college. Ivy also sewed her own cheongsam, in a pale blue which complemented my ivory-coloured cheongsam. I paid for her costume and headdress, of course, and was pleased that she could sew her own cheongsam. Most of us had to learn to sew as ready-made clothes were not as easily available as they are today. We then put together a list of people from Singapore/Malaya who were in London and also some English friends.

I must tell you of the man who gave me away at the wedding. When Gungwu's parents arrived in London, his father found an old school friend from Taizhou, Mr Chien Tsun-tien 钱存典 who was at that time the owner of a Chinese restaurant. He had been a senior diplomat with the Kuomintang government, and when the PRC was established decided not to go back to China but to remain in England. He then married a Chinese woman who was involved with the restaurant business. His restaurant was quite popular and successful so we asked him to cater for our wedding lunch. I think there were about 30 guests in all.

I know you must think me very remiss in being so vague about my own wedding! My excuse must be that we have moved house so often that my papers are in a mess. I didn't keep a wedding album as I should have. I was orchestrating a London wedding from Cambridge and had to leave a lot to Gungwu. He found the church for us and organized the invitation cards and so on. You must also realize that we had so little money that we couldn't afford a photographer at our wedding. We just went to a studio on the way to our reception to have some photos taken. These we have today. The photo taken of me alone was so successful that it was displayed in the studio's Oxford Street window for months, and many of our friends commented on this.

I remember that we had a lovely service in Hinde Street Methodist Church, which was a church many London university students and staff went to, and then a delicious lunch reception with our friends. Many years later, in 1975, Gungwu and I happened on the church while all three of our children were with us and we went into the church, spoke to the pastor and he found the church record which showed our wedding date and details!

For this, probably the biggest decision of our lives, I must add to Margaret's story by saying how much I respected the pastor of Hinde Street Church, the Methodist Church for the University of London. I called on him and told him that I had no religious beliefs but was familiar with certain aspects of Christianity; it was my fiancee's wish that we be married in church. He invited me to his room to talk further. He was very gentle and thoughtful in explaining the key tenets of a Christian marriage. I assured him of my respect for the faith and our shared belief that marriage was for life. He then invited both of us to see him together and was delighted to learn how familiar Margaret was with church affairs and was satisfied that Margaret knew what she was doing marrying a non-believer. I had never talked so intimately with any religious leader in my life and was most grateful for his kindness towards me.

Gungwu has teased me for years about not remembering the name of the hotel in Torquay where we spent our one-week honeymoon. But neither does he remember! We tried years later, in the 1990s, on a driving holiday to Torquay to find that hotel but the town had changed so much and the buildings were so different that we couldn't find it.

To give you an idea of costs in 1955, the hotel charged us £7 for the two of us for a week. This included breakfast and dinner but not lunch. Also, because it was during Christmas week, we had a grand dinner and ball at which we were supposed to wear costumes. During the day, we wandered around, took buses to the nearby towns where we shopped and visited antique shops.

Gungwu and I discovered that many of the families who were at the hotel had gone there year after year for their Christmas holidays and enjoyed meeting the same people every year. Perhaps it was our youth. We just couldn't imagine going to the same place every year. The world was, after all, a very big place and one visit in Torquay was really quite enough! However, everyone guessed quite rightly that we were on our honeymoon and treated us very indulgently and kindly. They had probably never met a Chinese couple before this!

We were regularly met with the total ignorance of the average Briton about the country's own colonies. We were often asked how we could have learnt English so well after such a short stay in England. Or which part of India we lived in. A few months later, on the ferry back across the English Channel from France, I was spoken to in pidgin English by an English woman living in Jamaica, who just assumed that "natives" could not understand standard English. By that time, I was no longer surprised that the British, with their widespread empire, knew less about us than we knew about them.

Cambridge and London

CAMBRIDGE WAS OUR first home. Although we had no more than seven months there, it was a lovely place to start our married life. We could finally be together in our own flat—no more railway stations and hurried partings!

And exploring Cambridge could be done systematically, allowing us time to savour the ancient courtyards of the great colleges and the historic museums. We now had the kind of routine that married life provides: Margaret bicycling to Homerton or the Chesterton Boys' School and me walking every morning to the university's library. Unlike SOAS library, which was dispersed across London in several storage places (we had to wait an average of three days to get the books we wanted to borrow), here I could find everything I wanted in one place. By coincidence, the librarian in charge of the East Asian collection was Dorothea Scott who had been in charge of the British Council Library in Nanjing that I had frequented in 1948. She readily shared her China stories and was very solicitous, thus enabling me to use the collection efficiently.

Two regulars in the library were A.R. (Bertie) Davis and his student John Frodsham. Both were literary scholars: Bertie on a number of Six Dynasties and Tang poets and John on the poetry of Xie Lingyun 谢灵运. I recall reading some of their translations and being impressed by the scholarship that explained each poem. I was soon to discover that the world of sinologists was a small one. Bertie was shortly to leave to take up the chair in Oriental Studies in the University of Sydney; John later came to join me in the History Department of the University of Malaya. Later, when I was at the Australian National University and John joined me there, all three of us were again to share common interests not too far apart.

At the time Margaret and I were in awe of Joseph Needham. He had just published the first two volumes of his *Science and Civilisation in China* and announced several others, to cover the whole range of scientific work in China. I was bowled over by what could be done with the wide range of Chinese texts if one had the imagination and scientific skills that Needham had. We had met him on a couple of social occasions on campus and I called on him at his college. He asked me what I was doing. When I told him about my Nanhai trade research, he showed great knowledge of the tropical plants in Chinese *materia medica*. I recall being elated when he suggested that I should have my study published. It was the kind of encouragement that any academic apprentice would give his eyeteeth for.

As for the early months of our married life, Margaret recalls the time vividly.

Before we left Cambridge to go to London for our wedding, we had already found a flat to live in. It was the ground floor of a two-storey terrace house in Orchard Street, by Christ's Pieces. Opposite our row of terraces, was a row of charming thatched roof cottages. Alas, the thatched roofs have been converted to tiles now. Of course, this is sensible as apart from there being ever fewer people who know how to thatch roofs, such roofs are fire hazards and thus have high insurance premiums. Our landlady converted the ground floor two rooms and kitchen into a flat, with the former living room becoming the bedroom, the dining room becoming the living room and kitchen, and an extension at the end for the very cold bathroom. We paid £4 a week, which was standard for that sort of accommodation.

My main memories of that year, apart from adjusting to married life, were of learning how to shop for food, cook and the "joys" of domestic work; doing my practice teaching at the Chesterton Secondary Modern Boys' School and of watching first-class cricket. I learnt to cook from a cookbook illustrated by Chiang Yee 蔣彞, famous as The Silent Traveller, whom we later got to know in Canberra, thereby proving once again that the world is a very small one.

All teachers in training have to do a period of practice teaching. This is to give them hands-on experience of the classroom. It can be a tremendous shock to a young teacher to face 40 pupils all at once. You have to get to know the faces and the personalities behind the faces, you have to memorize their names and you have to impart some knowledge to them in 45 minutes. You also learn that most of them don't want to be there and have no desire to read Shakespeare or know that Alexander swept across to India from Macedonia!

British secondary modern schools were established to help pupils who were not so academic to acquire an education. They would learn more practical subjects and later go on to learn some skills for jobs in the real world. The most hated examination in Britain for many years was the eleven-plus. This was taken at the end of primary school to see where a child would go next: Would they be academic enough to go to a grammar school, or would they be pronounced a "failure" by getting only enough marks for a secondary modern school? The general feeling was that the latter school was for the not-so-bright. It was no wonder that both teachers and pupils felt that being in such a school was a measure of their second-class status.

Anyway, when I first stepped into Chesterton Boys' Secondary School I found myself surprised that education was not valued by the boys. Most of them were looking forward to leaving and earning money. The school had every class move from their classrooms at the end of each period, thereby clogging the corridors and causing pandemonium before they settled down. Boys six-foot-tall would be rushing into a class and fight over places where they would sit. Tables and chairs were sometimes damaged and it took at least ten minutes before everyone settled down. I found this very difficult because it took away precious time for teaching. I also found that all textbooks and exercise books were free, so the boys did not value them and threw them around. There was hardly a textbook that did not have its cover torn or defaced. Having come from Asia where it was a privilege to go to school and where education was so highly valued, I just couldn't understand the boys' attitude.

This experience so disillusioned me that I almost gave up teaching altogether! The pupils didn't like the teachers and most of the teachers seemed to dislike the pupils in return. It was also the reason why I didn't look too hard for a job as a teacher when Gungwu and I went to live in London after I finished my course. Fortunately, I had curiosity value in the school, being the first Chinese woman the boys had ever seen. To interest the boys I would talk about Singapore and Malaya and Chinese customs. I even dressed in a cheongsam and brought along chopsticks and rice bowls to show them how Chinese people ate. Anyway, I survived my teaching practice and went back to college with a feeling of relief.

Our first six months of marriage passed very agreeably. Gungwu worked during the day at his research in the library and wrote at night in our flat. Cambridge was very cold, suffering from winds blowing across East Anglia, winds that came from the continent, as far away as Russia. In the spring, though, the air cleared and the students would start punting along the river. We sometimes did this too and punted down to Grantchester to have tea. The Backs, as it is called, is the area where the colleges back on to the River Cam and is one of the most beautiful parts of Cambridge. We would walk along there, visit the various college chapels, listen to the singing by the wonderful boys' choirs at certain services and generally enjoy Cambridge student life. We made some friends, entertained at home and we began to feel like a married couple! Occasionally, we would go to London to visit Gungwu's parents as well as to take in some plays or concerts.

On such occasions, we normally spent the day with my parents and, if we also went to a play or concert, took the late train back to Cambridge. I learnt that my father spent most of his time in the library at the British Museum reading some of the latest scholarly writings on philology. This was hard on my mother who, not speaking English, was alone in their flat. She sometimes had Malayan friends visit her but the only one she saw on a regular basis was Huang Yifan 黄逸梵, someone introduced by Xing Guangsheng 邢广生, a close friend in KL who was Huang's former colleague. Huang was some ten years older than my mother. My mother told me about her distinguished and wealthy family background and how she left her opium-smoking husband and spent decades in Europe. After the Sino-Japanese war, she lost most of her possessions in China and had since been struggling to make a living. I met her on several occasions and, just before we left London in August 1957, was asked by my mother to bring her some gifts. I saw her briefly but did not know that she was very ill.

I soon forgot about that last meeting in 1957. I had not realized that her daughter was the novelist Zhang Ailing 张爱玲, whose writings I did not begin to read until a few years later. However, when the last letters that Huang wrote to Xing Guangsheng were published in early 2019, I realized that Huang died only a couple of months after I last saw her. Only then did I know what a remarkable life she had led, trying to be a modern woman before Chinese society was ready. In my mother's memoirs, she commented sadly on how the descendants of many powerful Chinese families had been destroyed by wars and revolutions. It was her way of warning us not to take a good and lucky life for granted.

During our visits, we would try to catch up on news of the family in China. There was not much to tell about our Wang and Ding relatives but my mother did expand on what she had heard about the PRC, if only to remind us how quickly Mao Zedong had betrayed his promise of "New Democracy". She was clearly content never to return as long as the CCP was using the Soviet model to transform the country beyond recognition. She also told us that my father had been offered a job at the Malayan Teachers' College at Brinsford Lodge in Wolverhampton, but alerted us to the fact that my father's health was not good and they planned to return to Malaya during the summer. She knew that Margaret would complete her course in Homerton and we would be moving to London soon but explained that she really did not think they could stay for another winter. As it turned out, the Suez crisis delayed their trip and their ship had to travel via the Cape of Good Hope. After we sent them off, we went to Paris to attend my first sinologist conference which I detailed in an earlier chapter. Margaret describes what followed.

> On one of our visits to London, towards the end of our stay in Cambridge, we found a flat in Hammersmith, in the western part of the city. We would go to Paris first for a conference after leaving Cambridge and would move in after our return from Paris. This flat was again a converted one in a three-storey house, with the owners occupying the ground floor with one room, and a first and second floor flat, each with a large sitting/dining room, bedroom and kitchen. We found the landlord and his wife very pleasant. He was from Poland, a refugee, and had married an English woman after he made his way to England. His name was Kaminsky. He and his wife worked and they kept only the front room and the kitchen at the back for themselves.
>
> That summer, Gungwu and I went to the Jeunes Sinologues conference. This was my first visit to Paris as I had gone to England from Italy without stopping in Paris. This would be the first of many conferences we would attend together but there was something special about this one. The PRC were sending some delegates and everyone was very excited about this.

The French pulled out all stops to make this conference a memorable one. They certainly succeeded. Although we stayed in a student hostel, a rather spartan one, we had good French food every meal. The conference was interesting, and many young scholars who were later to become famous attended. We were also given a wonderful tour of the Loire Valley, ending at the Chateau de Beauregard for dinner. We were greeted with a phalanx of trumpeters who sounded their trumpets as we entered the grand dining hall. The food was wonderful and the evening was a great ending to a most successful conference.

However, I began to feel quite unwell when travelling in the Paris Metro and suffered from intermittent bouts of dizziness. I thought I was getting influenza or something like that or even that the French water had upset me. But I realized after we returned to London that I was pregnant! We had taken no particular precautions against pregnancy. Those were pre-pill times and most of us who married young had children fairly soon. In Singapore/Malaya that would be understandable as it was possible to have servants and all my women friends continued working after childbirth. We did not delay having children because of careers because it was not necessary to do so. Actually, most of us never even thought that not having children was an option! There were also our mothers-in-law breathing down our necks, waiting for us to produce the first grandson!

I was fortunate because I never suffered from any bad bouts of morning sickness with any of my four pregnancies. I just didn't feel well some days. I was accepted as a patient at Hammersmith Hospital and went there for antenatal care as well. This was when I discovered one of the disadvantages of the National Health Service—long waiting lines. We would be given 2 p.m. appointments to see a doctor, only to find ourselves waiting for three hours before we could see him. When I asked why we couldn't be given appointments closer to the time the doctor could see us, I was looked at with surprise that I should voice an opinion about this.

On the whole, I had no complaints about the system, especially when I discovered that there was absolutely nothing to pay when I took our first baby, Ming, home after ten days at the hospital.

While I was pregnant, Gungwu was working away at his thesis. He had figured out a way of explaining this period of chaos in China in the 9th and 10th centuries. He would meet Denis Twitchett at a pub when Denis came down to London and discuss his work with him. I don't think Denis actually ever saw the whole thesis! During this period, Gungwu also began to cough and sneeze every morning before he commenced writing. Sometimes, he would sneeze 20 times in a row. There were no computers then and he wrote every single word of his thesis by hand. Sometimes he would be so exhausted by his sneezing that he couldn't work at all. I thought he was suffering from a psychosomatic illness, that is, he couldn't face working on his thesis and so sneezed as a way out of working at it. However, we soon began to suspect that he had an allergy, most probably due to the paper he was using. We went to a specialist to discover what he was allergic to. Gungwu had all sorts of tests which confirmed that he suffered from hay fever, but not what caused the allergy. Antihistamines in those days were not sophisticated and would cause drowsiness so he couldn't take them during the day. However, he struggled on and continued his work.

Birth of a Baby

MARRIED LIFE HAD its own momentum in the 1950s. We had made no plans to have a family, certainly not while I was still studying and when neither of us had a job. When Margaret told me she was pregnant and the baby was due in April 1957, I was startled and not at all ready for fatherhood. She was untroubled and assured me that she was set to learn what was necessary. Actually I knew she did not have a clue what it meant to be a mother in a foreign land far away from other members of her family. Her idea of preparing for the happy day was to buy a book and read up on it. It has always amazed me how cool she was and how quickly she learnt. We moved to London and she scouted our neighbourhood to find out where to buy what she needed and what facilities were being provided. All that time I struggled to finish my thesis with a growing sense of urgency that I had better get it right if I hoped to start a job when my scholarship ran out in August that year.

This very significant event in our lives was marked by a great deal of ignorance. Gungwu's parents had returned to Singapore in July 1956, and I knew little of the social services provided in London for pregnant women like me. Neither Gungwu nor I knew anything about babies and as I was quite healthy throughout my pregnancy and didn't put on much weight, I did little but read one book on how to deal with babies. As we would be returning to Singapore in a few months, we bought a carrycot for the baby and a rather grand English pram to wheel him around.

My pains started early on the morning of 9 April 1957. We called the ambulance to take me to Hammersmith Hospital. That was the practice then. Gungwu came with me but was soon asked to leave as I was prepared for the birth. He was not allowed to see me the whole day. He spent the day with some of our friends, waiting to hear about the baby. He was allowed to visit me at visiting hours in the evening, at about 5 p.m. but the baby was still waiting to be born. I didn't have too bad a time but just had to wait a long time. Eventually, at about 3 a.m., Ming was born.

My ordeal was not over. This was a time when there was no such thing as patients' rights. We were told what to do by very strict and starchy staff nurses and we were expected to follow the rules. Fathers were not allowed in the wards except at visiting hours so Gungwu didn't even know how I was as the hospital had no policy of informing the father when birth had taken place. Ming was taken away from me almost immediately after he was born. His colour was bad, a "blue baby", they said, a condition caused by the cord being round his neck during birth. The nurse took him to a private nursery to watch him. At about 4 a.m., I was wheeled into a ward with 24 beds, and at the foot of each bed, there was a cot with a baby in it. I was the only one without a baby!

I was so exhausted by the long labour that I tried to sleep, but the ward was woken up at 5.30 a.m. so I didn't get much rest at all. All the mothers woke up and started to breastfeed their babies. I was the only exception. I felt terrible because every mother there looked at me with pity thinking my baby had died as there was no cot at the foot of my bed. Also, the nurses refused to tell me anything about my baby, and kept on saying that the doctor would speak to me, which he did, at about lunch time when he came on a quick round. He just said that the baby needed watching and when I asked whether I could see the baby, he said I couldn't. That wasn't very reassuring but I didn't want to make a fuss so didn't insist, as most women today would have.

I was the only Chinese in the ward but the nurses could not have thought I couldn't understand them as it would have been obvious after speaking to me for a few minutes that I could speak English as well as they did. Gungwu was not allowed to see me until 5 p.m. that day, and by the time he came, I was in tears, and he was too when he didn't see a baby with me. We both really thought something terrible had happened to Ming. However, after Gungwu left, at about 8 p.m., Ming was brought to my ward and handed to me. It was wonderful to hold him and to see him properly for the first time! He was large for a first child, weighing 7 lb 6 ounces and was most precious to us especially when I later realized he could have been brain-damaged from the cord. The trauma surrounding Ming's birth has remained with me to this day.

Today, hospitals are much better and do not treat their patients as though they are all idiots and ignorant. Husbands are allowed to be with their wives and even if the babies have to be put into a nursery, the mother would be allowed to monitor the baby instead of remaining in ignorance and fear.

Our baby, Ming, was a source of great joy. He was a wonderful textbook baby and did everything the books said babies should. We put him in a carrycot by an open window for the fresh air, protecting his head with the cot cover and he slept happily in the sitting room with music playing while Gungwu worked and I typed what he had written. It would have cost us about £25 to have the thesis typed so I decided that I should type it to save that money. I still remember my fright while I was typing his thesis that he may have been wrong in the way he dealt with the subject and with the thesis that he was expounding. It was too late, of course, to be worried about whether the thesis was on the right track as we were down to our last £200 and he simply had to finish so that we could return to Singapore to start earning some money.

Margaret and Ming, 1957.

We did not work all the time. We took Ming for walks and we had friends who were kind enough to baby-sit when we wanted to go to the cinema or to a play. We made quite a few friends in London. Unlike in Cambridge, where there were relatively few Asians, London had lots more. I'm not sure how many of us there were from Malaya, but there must have been hundreds. Students used to meet in Malaya Hall, a couple of townhouses in Bryanston Square bought by the government to cater to its overseas students. There would be occasional meals of Southeast Asian food. In those days, you couldn't get home style food easily and the greatest treats would be to be invited to a home where some Asian food would be served.

When I think back on those years in London, I am shocked at how little the British system catered for postgraduates. You were fortunate if your supervisor bothered to read your writing. It was thought that you should know what to do and how to go about your research. The supervisor was there merely to guide you if you should need it. The American system was and is quite different. The universities set up proper courses to help you with your research and the supervisors helped you along at each stage. The chances of failure were therefore not so great. We knew of some students who had failed their PhDs in Britain because of inadequate advice or supervision. It was a shocking waste of a person's time and reduced their chance of a decent career. It was still not common for people to get PhDs. It was thought to be an American disease and many famous professors in Britain had only an honours degree. However, by the 1960s more and more graduates were doing PhDs as competition was getting greater.

After Gungwu submitted his thesis some time in June 1957, his sneezing stopped. We started to prepare for our return to Singapore. He applied for a job in the History Department of the University of Malaya and was accepted as an assistant lecturer. We were so happy as that meant we had something to return to. Gungwu was also offered a job teaching Chinese at SOAS at a salary of £700 a year, but we weren't in the least tempted and wanted very much to return to Singapore. Denis knew that it was a matter of some urgency for Gungwu's thesis to be examined as we would run out of money very soon so he arranged for it to be examined very quickly. In August, Gungwu was asked to appear for an oral exam or *viva voce*. He came home feeling quite optimistic.

The next morning, a parcel came for him addressed to Dr Wang Gungwu, with an article in it sent by one of his examiners. This man was Edwin (Ted) Pulleyblank, professor of Chinese at the University of Cambridge and a fine scholar. It was an act of great kindness. This was his way of telling us quickly that Gungwu had got his PhD, as the official result would not come for some time yet. I have never forgotten this kindness and realized that it would be so easy for people in power to be kind or to help those in need by such small acts, which would result in much happiness. We have both tried in turn always to be helpful to our colleagues, our students and anyone who needed our help. Good deeds do go round, and make us happier as a result.

We had very little money left by the end of August when we had to return home. Gungwu had his fare paid for by the British Council, but we had to borrow mine from his father. We borrowed $1,700 from him for our return by ship to Singapore. The trip home was pleasant and we made many friends, ate too much, went sightseeing whenever we could, and the three-and-a-half-week trip from Southampton to Singapore passed pleasantly.

PART SIX

Great Place to Work

Closer to Home

ON 31 AUGUST 1957, when we were still at sea, the Federation of Malaya attained its independence. I was now someone from a sovereign state in the family of nations. We were reminded how much had happened in British Malaya while we were away. For two years, I had been immersed in getting my thesis finished and learning how to be a husband and father, but I did try to keep up with the country's progress towards independence. I had noted the failure of the Baling talks when the MCP rejected Tunku Abdul Rahman's amnesty offer and then his demand for their surrender. At that point, Malaya was ready for Merdeka (freedom). We remembered Tunku's visit to Cambridge in 1956 when he confidently told the students there to get ready to serve the country. When we docked in Singapore, he and his triumphant coalition of the United Malay National Organisation-Malayan Chinese Association-Malayan Indian Congress (UMNO-MCA-MIC; the Alliance Party) had already celebrated the moment when the new flag went up as the Union Jack came down. I recall feeling, without really understanding why, an indescribable pride.

Singapore politics had a different hue. The Labour Front government led by David Marshall had sought independence but disagreement about which authority, Britain, Malaya or Singapore, should have the final say on security matters had prevented progress and Marshall resigned. We learnt that his successor Lim Yew Hock was willing to accept colonial orders to arrest left-wing union leaders and keep them in detention without trial. Among them were friends from the University Socialist Club, including James Puthucheary and Sydney Woodhull who were also members of the People's Action Party (PAP). Also, I saw that the majority of our MU alumni had become civil servants and schoolteachers in either the Federation or Singapore. A few had chosen to be political activists while yet others (notably doctors and scientists) preferred an academic career with MU. It was now a city buzzing with political changes and high expectations for eventual independence.

I had not followed the colony's politics as closely as that in Malaya and, with several activist friends detained, had to seek out others to find out what was happening. Two leaders whom I had previously met found time to talk to me. Goh Keng Swee and I were doing our PhD in London at the same time, and we had discussed Singapore's future in Malaya. He now took the trouble to explain what self-governing might mean as a stage towards joining the federation. I had known S. Rajaratnam as a journalist and found him willing to discuss the City Council elections later that year. But I am not sure I grasped the full implications of what they told me about the fully elected legislative elections promised for 1959.

The university, however, seemed much the same. In the History Department, Professor Parkinson, now famous for his Parkinson's Law, was about to embark on his international career as management guru and public intellectual. My former teachers Eric Stokes and Ian Macgregor had both left. Stokes had gone to Rhodesia and was head of the History Department in the new university in Salisbury, while Macgregor had gone to teach in West Africa where, I was sad to learn, he died soon afterwards. Among my new colleagues was Ken Tregonning who had joined just before I left for London. I was sorry to miss Emily Sadka who had left to go to Australia. Succeeding her was Eunice Thio whom I knew well as my senior. All three worked on Malayan history and added strength to the research projects that Parkinson had initiated. Two others arrived just before I returned. They were Leonord Young, who had completed a major study of British diplomacy in China, and Alastair Lamb, whose range of historical interest was the most ambitious, ranging from British India's plans in Central Asia and Tibet and stretching across the deserts and steppes to reach Peking. All of them focused on the second half of the 19th century. As the only one who worked on ancient (medieval?) history, I was the odd man out.

Parkinson asked me to teach what was called the "early modern" period, 1500–1800, focusing on the history of the "Far East". This period was several centuries later than the 10th-century China that I had just finished writing about, but periodizing any Chinese history before the Opium

War had always been a problem. The common view was that Imperial China remained more or less the same for the 2,000 years after the Qin unification. Modern Chinese historians did not accept that judgment but traditional historiography that was centred on the standard histories and the several great compendia done in the Song, Ming and Qing dynasties could easily be seen to have supported the idea of "unchanging China". Therefore, in the eyes of many, the 10th-century Tang-Song transition years could not have been very different from the mid-Ming China of the 16th century.

I knew otherwise and realized from the start that I had a lot more learning to do to stay ahead of my students. Fortunately, Parkinson gave me time to get prepared and I spent the next couple of months reading up everything I could find in the library on the three centuries of Chinese and Japanese history, as well as the coming of the Portuguese and Spanish, followed by the Dutch and English East India Companies. As it turned out, I was more ready to teach about the European adventurers. I could still remember Ian Macgregor's lectures but only wished I had taken detailed notes and followed up more of the readings that he had recommended. As for the Ming-Qing transition of the 17th century and the dramatic end to the Senkoku era with the rise of the Tokugawa in Japan, I was conscious of huge gaps in my knowledge. Where China was concerned, I could read the primary sources as well as the work of modern scholars in Chinese. For Japan, however, I had to depend mostly on books in English. I explained that imbalance to my students, that I was only able to use a limited range of books and articles on Japan. All the same, the reading I did gave me great satisfaction. Learning about that 300-year period enabled me to extend my understanding of northern China and beyond, to Manchuria, Korea and Japan, and made me more aware of the underlying differences between East Asia and the region now called Southeast Asia.

Fortunately, I was not alone in being interested in the ancient past. I discovered that Alastair Lamb was someone with insatiable curiosity. He was keen to pursue the extent of Hindu and Buddhist influences on the Malay Peninsula, and that had led him to bring a team of students to do archaeological excavations in Kedah. I asked to join them because I was attracted by the chance to return to my work on the early Nanhai trade, which had reached past the Straits of Malacca to the Bay of Bengal. Thus within months of being back, I went on the first set of excavations in the Bujang district of Kedah. I shall say more about this later.

Margaret started teaching again at St Andrew's School and enjoyed getting to know the very bright students who expected her to keep them interested in the world around them. In Margaret's own words,

> As for me, St Andrew's School had written to me while I was in London to ask me to return there as an English teacher. I would be in charge of 6th Form English. I accepted because we both needed jobs and some income for our new life in Singapore.
>
> Some of the students whom I had taught before had now gone up to the sixth form, so I taught them again. I enjoyed my time at the school very much. Little did I know that I would be there for less than two years.
>
> Although we had a lot to buy in the first few months, we paid off the loan from Gungwu's father within three months and were not in debt again until we built our house in Petaling Jaya and got a mortgage in 1963. By and large, we had a good income, which increased steadily and which we spent without much thought as we were still young and didn't feel we needed to be too careful with our money.

Malaya's independence also meant that the Tunku, as prime minister, could not see why the university carrying the country's name should be in Singapore. I was not aware of the negotiations that had been going on before my return. But it became clear that there would be a MU campus in Kuala Lumpur, and it was agreed that the freshman class of 1958 would actually start their studies there, before the KL campus took in their own first cohort. Thus, within months of my return, I was asked to help Alastair Lamb, who had volunteered to teach that first class in KL, by flying there for two days every fortnight during term and teaching in a borrowed building in the technical college. It was a strenuous assignment, and my frequent absences made Margaret's home-making duties heavier than they already were. She never complained. She could see how excited I was to see a new campus being built and readily supported me when the time came—at the end of 1958—to decide whether or not to volunteer to move to KL to what some of us thought would become the national university of the country.

However, in September 1957, our main challenge was to settle down to our first local home. During our months in Cambridge, I had begun to appreciate Margaret's talent for making our lives comfortable, and really admired the efficient way she organized our flat in London in preparation for our first child, as captured in her own words in the previous chapter. More severe tests were to come, as the university housed us in the medical faculty accommodation in Tiong Bahru, now within the Singapore General Hospital. That was miles away from both Margaret's school and my office in Bukit Timah. We managed to adjust to all that travel every day, but it was soon clear what a great strain it was for Margaret. Her account, written for our children, describes our first year in Singapore.

We were assigned a two-bedroom flat in Macalister Road, within the medical faculty grounds. The block of flats was only three stories high but it didn't have any lifts. We were given a third floor flat so had to walk two long flights of steps with baby stroller, shopping bags and so on to get to our flat. It was not at all convenient because of our baby. The flat was quite spacious but it didn't have a study. It did have a large balcony shared by the two bedrooms, which were side by side. So we turned the second bedroom into a study and put Ming's cot in the balcony and protected it with bamboo blinds which were lined with thick cotton to prevent the rain from coming in. This sufficed for a while.

I found returning to Singapore and setting up our new home very stressful. I not only started work within a few days of our arrival, I had to train a new maid to take over the care of our baby. She was one of those who wore black trousers and white tops and considered domestic work to be a profession, so she soon took over the baby without too much trouble. Ming was adorable, good natured and healthy, and everyone fell in love with him.

After we found a maid, I turned my attention to our new home. I had to buy practically everything, from teaspoons and chopsticks to pots and pans, as we had nothing but a set of bedsheets which we were given as a wedding present. Because we married in England, we didn't have many wedding presents. As we didn't have a grand wedding reception in Singapore we didn't get the customary *hongbao* (red packets) either, so we had to pay for everything from our own funds. We were really strapped for money and had to be very careful with our funds. I had to do all this shopping in between work. We arrived in Singapore on a Wednesday and I started work the next Monday. I should have taken one more week, but the school was desperate for me to start work and we really needed the money so I had to fit everything in in the first few weeks.

Eventually, we had enough to meet our initial needs. We had hardly any suitable clothes either as we had to stock up on tropical clothes. It was easier for Gungwu as all he had to do was buy more shirts and get a tailor to make some pairs of trousers for him. I bought a sewing machine and began to sew a lot as it was still not common to buy ready-made clothes. In any case, I was always fussy about what I wore and preferred to sew my own.

We also had to buy a car. The university had an interest free car loan, but because Gungwu was only an assistant lecturer, we could borrow only $4,000, which was only enough for a small car. We bought a small Renault for that price, but it was not a good buy and the car gave us a lot of trouble over the years. On top of that, my school was quite a long way away and in a different direction from the university. It usually took me about 30 minutes to get there. I had to start from home before 7 a.m. as school started at 7.30 a.m. It finished at about 1.30, after which everyone would go home for lunch.

I was a conscientious mother, and after work, would arrive home at about 1.45 p.m., have lunch with Gungwu and then play with Ming in the afternoon while our servant took a nap! I also had papers to mark in the evenings so was kept very busy. We also entertained quite a bit and had an active social life. I would prepare cakes for tea for Gungwu's students and give dinners to friends. As a result, I was down to 98 lbs in weight from all the work and running up and down the stairs. I was also anxious to have another baby as I thought it would be nice to have the children about two years apart.

Ming walked on the day he turned one, but he also developed a bout of diarrhea, which turned him from a plump baby into a thin one. This was partly because he was teething. I went through a lot of anxiety about this as we couldn't seem to stop it and I was afraid he would become dehydrated. The doctors were not very helpful, regarding mothers as something of a nuisance and being hysterical about their children. If a child has diarrhea for six months that should be of vast concern, it seems to me! He never regained the weight he lost and until today remains lean, not a bad thing as obesity is the problem rather than leanness.

I duly got pregnant again but sadly lost the baby after three months. I'm sure all the stress and work as well as anxiety about Ming were the cause of this miscarriage. I soon recovered and we tried again soon afterwards. However, Gungwu insisted that the university give us housing on the ground floor and because of my miscarriage the university agreed and allocated a house just opposite the university in Dunearn Road. This house was part of a complex of buildings that served both as a student hostel and as staff housing. This place was much more convenient for Gungwu and also nearer to my mother who was down the road from us.

After settling into our new home at Dunearn Road, we tried again to have another child. This time, we succeeded and I got pregnant with our daughter Mei. However, she was not born till July, after we moved to Kuala Lumpur in May 1959. You can understand why I associated moves with babies in the early years of our marriage!

A few months after our return to Singapore, the PAP had won control of the City Council and Ong Eng Guan became the city's mayor. He began introducing some radical changes to the way the city was run and dramatic results were expected in the elections that were due in 1959. I had not followed the city's politics except to attend student meetings at which various party leaders were invited to speak on their respective programmes. Teaching in two cities, starting our homes twice in two parts of Singapore and preparing to move to KL had kept us busy. In addition, on the basis of my earlier work on Kang Youwei and Sun Yat-sen—what might be called the "prehistory" of the Kuomintang in Malaya—I was also invited to give public lectures and to edit the *Nanyang xuebao* and make it into a bilingual journal.

What was totally unexpected, but was to add another dimension to my future research interests, was the invitation from Radio Sarawak to give a series of eight talks on the history of the Nanyang Chinese. I was not working on the subject and not sure why I was asked but agreed to accept the challenge because it would give me a chance to learn more about the Chinese communities that had developed all over the region for several centuries. I had grown up among some of the Chinese merchants and workers and was conscious of the large numbers of Chinese sojourners who later settled and established sizable local communities. After all, I had, without planning to do so, become a member of one of these Malayan Chinese communities.

I was also aware that the newly-independent governments in Southeast Asia were increasingly concerned that the PRC Mainland and the ROC Taiwan were competing for the hearts and minds of the Nanyang Chinese, seeking their remittances to support their plans for development, as well as drawing them into the Cold War between the US and Soviet blocs. In particular, the rivalries among the Chinese in Indonesia were in the open and were seen as interfering in the political struggles between President Sukarno and his PKI supporters and their right-wing nationalist opponents. Such contestations had also been observed in Malaya but the British had been able to keep both the pro-PRC and pro-ROC forces under control. It was in that context that I recalled what I had learnt about the Chinese in the Philippines when I visited Manila in 1950 and also read the available studies about the Chinese in Thailand, Indochina and Burma. It was for me a timely opportunity to understand the situation better, and I was particularly concerned to explain the historical background of Chinese relationships and migrations in the region.

There was another reason for my interest. Just before leaving London, I had read about Mao Zedong's extraordinary slogan of "let a hundred flowers bloom and a hundred schools contend". I saw that it had something to do with the PRC sending four of their top scholars to the Jeunes Sinologues Paris conference. But that "liberal" moment did not last long. By the middle of 1957, Mao had declared that he had succeeded in drawing the Rightist snakes out of their holes and launched a campaign to rid the country of these pests. I wondered how the various groups of overseas Chinese were reacting to the way so many well-known intellectuals and artists were singled out for punishment. Again, would a better understanding of *huaqiao* history help?

When I began to prepare these talks, I found myself on a steep learning curve. I recall, after a long day of teaching Chinese and Japanese history, reading late into the early hours of the morning everything I could find on the history of the overseas Chinese, notably texts written before the Second World War in Chinese and translated from the Japanese, and making piles of notes that I had to turn into the eight talks I was asked to give. It was a fateful decision because the talks were well received and were soon published as *A Short History of the Nanyang Chinese*. For what really was a very small book it drew a great deal of attention, and the encouragement that I received led me to begin researching into the dilemmas that overseas Chinese communities were now facing in the post-colonial nation states that were being built all over Southeast Asia.

I should also mention that one of the reasons I agreed to give the lectures was because I had met Maurice Freedman and found his work most illuminating about Chinese society in the Nanyang. He had done fieldwork on the Chinese in Singapore and written two famous reports, one of which, on Chinese family and marriage, had just been published. He told me about his new work on lineage organizations in southern China and I was struck by how he was able to do this from published sources, mainly those by foreign officials, travellers and missionaries who had lived in Fujian and Guangdong. He was a student of Raymond Firth, the professor of anthropology at the London School of Economics (LSE) who had written a classic study of the east coast Malay fishermen.

He told me about T'ien Ju-kang 田汝康 from China who was also a student at the LSE and whose work on the Chinese in Sarawak had also been published. He also introduced me to Marjorie Topley, another of Firth's students, who was working on Chinese religious institutions in Singapore. As I began to read the historical literature on the *huaqiao*, I realized that Maurice's work demonstrated how much the methods of anthropology could help the work of historians. Those methods had helped several other scholars to produce studies of the Chinese in Southeast Asia that complemented the pioneering work of Victor Purcell. After I went to KL, I found that their books had added new dimensions to the study of *huaqiao* and their current plight, and were most helpful to me. Many years later, when Maurice was professor of anthropology at Oxford and organized a seminar series on Chinese society, he invited me to a year-long visiting fellowship at All Souls College. I was struck that the other participants in the series were anthropologists and sociologists and I was comfortable working closely with them.

Preparing the set of Radio Sarawak talks, however, did mean that I was getting further away from any work that was linked to sinology. I realized that I was not keeping up with the research I had been doing at SOAS. I wanted to teach well, I needed time to prepare my thesis for publication, but I also felt obliged to serve the community by giving public talks outside of the campus. Friends and families, colleagues and students in turn made me feel that something interesting was happening each day. The way the horizon was brightly lit by nation-building activities was distracting. Before long, I noticed how much Malaya's success in beating back the communist insurgency had attracted the attention of the Cold War protagonists, the US and its allies and the internationalist partners of the USSR.

In particular, what struck me as new was how much the Americans had assumed leadership in the region's affairs now that the European empires were dismantled. American scholars and journalists were regularly visiting the campus. They were mainly of two groups: some were China scholars who had left the PRC and now studied all things Chinese in our region, while others were keenly interested in nation-building problems, especially those in countries facing communist challenges. For the first group, Maurice introduced me to G. William (Bill) Skinner who had just published his work on the Chinese in Thailand, and to Donald Willmott who studied those in Indonesia. Both were anthropologists and I was intrigued by the way they approached their research. The other group, among whom Robert Scalapino from the University of California Berkeley was best known, was mostly looking out for threats flowing from the extension of the Cold War. Many were visiting Singapore and Malaya to see how the British were winning the war against the communists. But there was also keen interest in the role of the Chinese in Southeast Asia as agents for Communist China, best represented by Robert Elegant's *The Dragon's Seed: Peking and the Overseas Chinese*. Elegant gave up journalism soon afterwards and turned to writing fiction. That was his real talent.

There were a few outliers. One of them was a historian, Stanley Spector who worked on the high mandarins of mid-19th-century Qing China, in particular, Li Hongzhang 李鸿章 who was to become the last of the Han Chinese whom the Manchu court could count on to save the dynasty. Stanley was unusual in having first come to Singapore to teach in a Chinese high school. When I met him, he was on a Social Science Research Council Fellowship studying how the Chinese were dealing with the end of British rule in the colony. He was interested in Chinese nationalism overseas and how that could help local Chinese resist the siren calls to support communist New China. He piqued my interest when he told me that he knew Chuang Chu Lin 庄竹林, the US-educated principal of Chung Cheng High School 中正中学 who was briefly detained by the Special Branch just before I returned from London. Chuang was a remarkable educationist who later served as vice-chancellor of Nanyang University. I recall being very moved when Stanley told me how much he respected Chuang Chu Lin's dedication to education. Stanley became a good friend. Two years later when I made my first visit to the US, I called on him at Washington University in St Louis and he invited me to stay at his home. I shall write more about that trip in another chapter.

Move to Kuala Lumpur

WE LIVED IN Singapore all of 20 months. Margaret made us two successive homes, in neither of which we stayed more than a year. Perhaps that was an early warning about the way our peripatetic lives would unfold. But Margaret seemed to have taken it all in her stride. She was so efficient that she could be wife, mother and household manager, dutiful daughter and daughter-in-law, full-time teacher to batches of lively sixth form boys, and still had the energy to host my students for tea and our friends for dinner.

We had not expected to move to KL when we returned to Singapore. Singapore had been Margaret's home since December 1941 and she had looked forward to making a home for us there. Although I did not identify with the city the way she did, I had grown to see it as a vital part of the country I hoped to belong to. If it was only a matter of time before Singapore and the Federation were to become one, why leave for KL now?

The choice was mine: the attraction of being in the country's capital, the idea of helping build a new campus that could shape the new nation differently from that in a port city, KL's access to a vast hinterland, all added up to irresistible appeal. It had something to do with my early life in Ipoh to think of KL as familiar, but simply larger and more central. But the fact that my career as a historian seemed to dovetail well with the new nation's need to forge a new historical identity may have also helped me decide to go. Although I was ready to teach Chinese history, I had two experiences that added other dimensions to what I thought going to KL would enable me to do.

The first had occurred earlier in 1954 while I was working on the Nanhai trade. As a history tutor, I had accompanied a group of MU students who volunteered to help the director of the National Museum in KL, Gale

Sieveking, excavate the site of Kota Batu, the original site of the capital of the Johor Empire, Johor Lama. It was my first taste of archaeological research and it made me realize what could be done to unravel the history of the ancient trade between China and the region. The glimpses of Malay resistance to Portuguese domination for some 200 years after the fall of Malacca opened my eyes to how much more we needed to know. That had led me to write my first piece on Malayan history, "Johor Lama", published in the MU History Society's *Malayan Historical Journal* before I left for London.

The second took place in 1958 when, as mentioned earlier, I assisted Alastair Lamb to lead a batch of MU students to excavate sites in the Bujang area of Kedah that H.G. Quaritch-Wales had reported on before the war but had not had the chance to excavate. The National Museum in 1955 invited the university's History Department to help with a series of excavations. There were so many sites in that part of Kedah that we needed to know which sites would help us most to unlock the story of ancient Indian influences. Not least because some Chinese ceramic shards had been found, we also looked out for further evidence of maritime activities from the east. A bonus for me was that my first brief report of our excavations was published in the *Journal of the Malayan Branch of the Royal Asiatic Society* that year.

The two expeditions whetted my appetite for a historical hinterland that could be linked with the ancient China trade that I had earlier worked on. I also felt that, in contrast to complete dependence on literate evidence, on philology and fragments of texts, this kind of study led you to tread the land on which history was made and that would bring me closer to a better understanding of my adopted country.

I cannot now recall what the decisive factor was in my desire to move our small family again. What was critical was how Margaret felt about leaving Singapore. She was very fond of St Andrew's and enjoyed having her students question the way the new nations of the region were seeking to be free from colonial hang-ups. The new developments for a post-colonial Singapore offered her many new career opportunities. Furthermore, in our new home at Dunearn Road, she was closer to her school, her mother lived nearby and my parents were not too far away. Had she shown reluctance to move, what would I have done?

She did not hesitate. To her, my career choice came first. If going to
KL was good for my work, she would go with me. It did not occur to me
then that this was only the beginning. I thought I was making a lifelong
commitment to Malaya and she made clear that she was willing to share
that with me. Nothing at the time even hinted that this was to be the
first of many other moves to come and that she would have to give up
her career again and again so that I could pursue mine. What was more,
hers was such a positive outlook of our future together that she never once
expressed any regret for what we did. She later wrote about this move for
our children and captured the changes in our lives as follows.

> Given a choice, Gungwu wanted to go to Petaling Jaya and take part in the
> building of a new university. It was an exciting prospect and although I was
> well settled in my job and had been offered a new one running the Singapore
> Cultural Centre, I agreed that a move to KL was the thing to do. I was about
> seven months pregnant but was very healthy and so set to packing up once
> again for another move. This time, we had more books and some household
> goods. The university would pay for our move and for our fares so it didn't
> cost us much except for another upheaval in our lives. By this time, we
> had two cars. Gungwu had bought a Peugeot with the number BB1 from
> a British friend of ours, John Bottoms, who was leaving for a lectureship at
> SOAS. So I drove the Renault with Ming in the backseat, and Gungwu the
> Peugeot, packed to the gills with various household goods, and we made
> our way to KL. A lorry followed behind us with our other household goods
> and our books and papers. This was our fifth move of house. For the first few
> days, we stayed at the railway station hotel in KL, a most beautiful baroque
> building with old fashioned but spacious rooms.
>
> Our social life in KL was very busy. We found that everyone welcomed the
> coming of the university. All the diplomats were in KL, and some of them
> told me that they found few people they could talk to before academics
> began arriving! We were invited to all sorts of diplomatic functions and got
> to know ambassadors, other diplomats, foreign business people and local
> dignitaries.
>
> We went to so many cocktail parties that I began to get tired of it all. I
> don't drink any alcohol so found it tedious to stand around holding a tepid
> glass of orange juice while my feet would start to ache. Eventually, Gungwu

and I decided to cut down on them to only a few given by interesting friends. The trouble with going to diplomatic parties is that you no sooner start making friends with a diplomatic couple when they get transferred and you have to start all over again with their successors.

That was Margaret's way of making light of what was really a major change in our lifestyle. We were young and energetic and events were moving so fast we had little time to reflect on their longer-term significance.

When the time came for us to leave for KL, we saw it simply as moving to another city in the same country. As we saw it, Singapore would soon be free of colonial rule and would demonstrate to the rest of the country how efficient a modern government could be. Campaigning for the elections to a fully democratic Legislative Assembly was fierce. When we left for KL in the middle of May 1959, most of us thought that Lee Kuan Yew's PAP would win the elections. We even heard that many expatriates in the business world were so fearful of a pro-communist PAP that they were preparing to leave Singapore if the party won. Two weeks later, the party won a landslide victory. My friends were enthusiastic, especially when Lee Kuan Yew as prime minister refused to take office unless his main PAP comrades were released from detention. This was the kind of independence we expected from the new leaders. We looked forward to the day when there would be one country and the national university would have two campuses.

In KL, we arrived in the midst of state elections that were followed by national elections to the country's first parliament. Although no one doubted that the Alliance Party (a coalition of UMNO, MCA and MIC) would win, I was interested to learn that the socialist opposition (Labour Party and Parti Ra'ayat) was popular in some urban constituencies. I was new to national politics and listened carefully to my friends who were actively involved. Together with settling our family into a new home and helping to build a new campus, I did not have the time to learn enough to know what to expect of the country's first taste of nationwide democracy. The fact that it went smoothly and both the Alliance and opposition leaders behaved with civility was very encouraging. There was good reason to believe that the country was off to a great start and I was closer to home.

Whose Region?

MALAYA WAS INDEPENDENT. Singapore was getting ready to become self-governing. During the three years I had been away, I noted events like the Malayan constitutional talks in London; the Anglo-French Suez fiasco; the Geneva conference on the fate of Indochina; the Bandung conference in Indonesia; and the Hundred Flowers campaigns in China that marked the end of liberal illusions about Mao Zedong's CCP. I was conscious that the region called Southeast Asia was taking shape.

What was less clear was how Malaya stood in the region called Southeast Asia, still largely a British effort to make the "Far East" more manageable while the American victors in the Second World War were redefining the Pacific. My earlier visits to Nanjing, Hong Kong and Manila had awakened me to the fact that there was very little understanding about what kind of region Southeast Asia was to be. It was obvious that the United States was the biggest player. After my visits to Colombo and Delhi, it appeared that Britain's influence in the region was now confined to Malaya and the colonies in North Borneo. The Thai military regime clearly looked to the US while Sukarno's Indonesia had ambitions to unite the larger anti-imperial world of Afro-Asia against American dominance.

Where then was the Southeast Asia that I was taught to see as the region in which Malaya belonged? I now tried to find time to learn what was happening. The biggest change since 1954 was the emergence of America as the power that sought to fight against Soviet communism in Europe, and its Chinese partner in what was still seen as "the Far East". Its success in Western Europe, especially with the North Atlantic Treaty Organization (NATO), had inspired a parallel Southeast Asia version (SEATO) now based in Bangkok. Only two of SEATO's members were in the region: Philippines and Thailand. French Indochina stayed out, and Indonesia and Burma were openly suspicious of its "neo-colonial" features. I now realized that almost all those who wrote books and learned articles about Southeast Asia as a significant region separate from China and India were Europeans, Americans and Japanese. Those within the region were busy studying the developments in their respective countries and this was particularly true among historians. This remained so for several decades. It was the main reason the Association of Southeast Asian Nations (ASEAN), established in 1967, meant little within the region and why it was scholars from outside the region who did serious research on its history.

While in London, I had followed some of the debates in the US about American fellow travellers who had "lost China" to the CCP; my friend Philip Kuhn had given me a lively account of the McCarthy hearings that had tried to ferret out communist sympathizers in the state department. I also read about the defeat of France at Dien Bien Phu and the Geneva conference, and learnt a great deal from listening to SOAS teachers who specialized in Indochina and Thai affairs. I was not clear if Malaya would try to take an independent position or simply join one side or the other while the two superpowers carved out their respective spheres. What was clear, however, was that Malaya was now central to what was left of the British Empire in Asia, and a vital link with Australasia. Total independence under the circumstances seemed impossible. It was the British who defeated the communist insurgency in Malaya. A communist China supporting similar movements in the region, notably in Indochina and Indonesia, could threaten the fragile peace on the peninsula. For the federation of nine Malay states and two, and possibly three, former British colonies, dependence on Commonwealth forces would appear unavoidable for a while.

My five years studying in MU and three years in British universities had taught me the value of academic objectivity. They also led me to be sceptical of political parties seeking to win power, not because I thought that was wrong but because I was personally not inclined to political partisanship. I have explained why I chose to go to KL. Malaya needed a new university and the prospect of doing something for higher education in my country was appealing. But one other link was relevant. I was becoming a regular commentator on world affairs on radio and being in

KL would help me acquire a national perspective. I had also done a series of talks on the history of the Nanyang Chinese; that made me sensitive to the fate of the millions of Chinese in the region who chose to become citizens of new nations. Being at the capital would give me a better idea how to understand their future in the country.

I had resumed my study of Malay; and the expeditions to Kedah also helped me to get a better perspective of the rise of other riverine states, like Perak and Selangor. I was also fortunate to have a friend like Asraf at the Oxford University Press who was willing to spend time in guiding me in my reading of Malay literature as well as the local Malay press. He also encouraged me to study Jawi to read *Utusan Melayu*, the newspaper established by Malay leaders. Reading Malay writings enabled me to follow the work of those among my colleagues who chose to write regularly in Malay. When Sutan Takdir Alisjahbana became head of the Malay Studies Department, he and my friends Syed Hussein Alatas and Syed Husin Ali encouraged me to understand Malay society from within in order to correct the bias in Western writings. This education drew me away from the radical writings of Ishak Haji Muhammad, Burhanuddin Al-Helmy and Ahmad Boestaman that I had been reading earlier on. In a multi-communal (ethnicity-based) Malaya, I became less sceptical of the monarchical system and more appreciative of Prime Minister Tunku Abdul Rahman's open-minded approach to ethnic differences.

The larger question concerning the future of Malayan politics in a Cold War between powerful ideologies remained unclear. The region we had been taught to call Southeast Asia was clearly divided. Before I left for KL, a group of us were invited to meet then Vice-President Richard Nixon who was going around the region to explain why the US would not make "the mistake of Munich" and allow North Vietnam to take over the south. In effect, he said that America must take over France's imperial burdens in Indochina and we must expect a hot war to begin soon.

I had made brief visits to KL when my father was federal inspector of Chinese schools in 1952–55, but did not really know the city. In 1958, I went there to give lectures but had little time to venture beyond the familiar places. Now our new home was located on the Petaling Jaya edge of the new campus, and a short walking distance from the Faculty of Arts where I had my office. The new buildings were coming up fast; there was so much to do to get our courses started that I hardly went anywhere else. Margaret had to travel further to her school in the middle of the city and organized all the shopping for our household needs.

In Margaret's words to our children:

The university had just built a few houses at that time to house their staff at Jalan University. We moved into a very new and nice two-storey house with three bedrooms and a maid's room. We engaged two maids, a Malay maid for the children and also so that they would learn Malay, and a Chinese for general housework and cooking.

Petaling Jaya was sparsely populated then and the developments were mainly along one side of the Federal Highway. The university site was mostly red laterite and we felt excited at the thought of helping to build a new campus. As the buildings went up one by one, the campus began to take shape.

As for me, again I had to quickly settle into a new home and get back to work. I used to wonder why I was always rushing around! When we were still in Singapore, a friend had told me about a vacancy at St John's Institution, another boys' school in Kuala Lumpur. I wrote to the principal and was offered the job immediately. Again, it was to teach Sixth Form English. This school was a Catholic school run by the La Salle Brothers. They knew that I was pregnant and would be going on maternity leave soon after I joined the school, but they were so desperate to have an English teacher that they appointed me anyway.

Most of KL had the kind of tropical shophouses found in other towns in this part of the world. However, there were notable differences in the architecture of some of the government buildings, which made them very striking. The railway station was the grandest of them all, being baroque in the Arabian style, with domes and other architectural features that make it very whimsical and charming—especially for a railway station. There were also other buildings like the high court and the secretariat, which were wonderful examples of colonial architecture and were solid and impressive.

The Malayan government also started to build a new parliament house and a national mosque to represent their pride in an independent country. Also near the railway station was the traditional *padang* (field) which you find in every town colonized by the British. This field, also found in Singapore, was very useful. Usually at one or both ends there would be clubhouses, one for cricket, and the other for social or other purposes. The *padang* was thus the centre of outdoor social life for the British. The Selangor Club occupied one side of the *padang* in KL. Sundays would be spent watching a cricket match with a "tiffin" lunch at the club. Before the war, I don't think locals were allowed to join it. After the war, a few locals were allowed to join by election. After the British left, the locals had to be wooed to join or the club would not have been able to survive the loss of members and their subscriptions. The Selangor and Lake Clubs were the two main sources of entertainment for the expatriate community.

Margaret had never lived in a Malay state before so I drove her around most weekends to see the small towns and kampongs which were different from those in Singapore. I was relieved to see how quickly she adapted to local conditions as she prepared herself to give birth to our second child and first daughter. This time round, it was unlike the cold and impersonal conditions she encountered in London. In KL, she went to a leading hospital and came under the personal care of Derek Llewellyn-Jones, a distinguished obstetrician.

In 1959, there were dozens of high commissions and embassies in KL. Several of the countries represented offered help to develop the campus. I cannot recall the details, but I remember that New Zealand sent experts to the Faculty of Agriculture, and Australia helped with the establishment of the Faculty of Engineering. Both the British Council and the US Information Service (USIS) had good libraries and they were invaluable while the university was still building its own collection. Our Department of History received an annual Fulbright professorship to support teaching in American studies. Our first was Saul Padover, who was well known for his biography of Thomas Jefferson. He set out to introduce the liberal ideals that Americans believe have made their country so exceptional, but his presence also provided a kick-start to something new to us, access to American resources that were more generous than what we could expect from the British.

Indeed, I was an early beneficiary of that largesse. I had earlier met John Sutter of the Asia Foundation. He had just completed his PhD on Indonesia at Cornell University and was eager to connect our new university with their Southeast Asia programme. Also, he had served in Shanghai when I was in Nanjing. We shared some thoughts about the last days of the Kuomintang regime. He noted that I was a historian of China who had never been to the US, and came up with the idea that I write a report on the major Asia centres there for the Foundation. Having read while in "orientalist" Britain some of the research done on modern and contemporary China by social science scholars in America, I told him that I would be willing to try because I really needed to learn about American work on Asia.

To my surprise, a few weeks later, he offered me a four-month trip and consulted me about the centres that I would like to visit. I went to my head of department, John Bastin, for his advice. As I had only arrived in May 1959 and had been flying back to Singapore regularly to teach second year students there and would only start teaching our own second year students the next year, he asked the vice-chancellor to give me special leave for the first four months of 1960. I was very grateful for his support.

Before I describe the trip, let me quote Margaret for her reaction to my plan to be four months away, having just brought her up to this new place; now she had two babies and only a brother in KL to turn to for help.

I had to look after our two children by myself for four months from January to May 1960. Gungwu had a grant from the Asia Foundation to go to the United States for four months. There was not enough money for me to go with him. In any case, even if we had the money, there were the two babies. I knew it was important for his career to go as he was going to visit many universities and give lectures here and there. We had just moved from Singapore and I knew few people in KL. One of my brothers was living there, but he had his own job and concerns and I didn't think I could count on him for much. I was in the position again of having no family support, as both sets of our parents were in the south; there was nothing I could do but cope!

At that time, the Cold War was well and truly in place. The Americans had to rethink their foreign policy because China had a communist government. Vietnam was divided and the Americans were already in the South, helping the French to stem what they thought was a communist tide. The Americans were also active elsewhere in Southeast Asia, trying to influence the young and stop any more dominoes from falling. Thus there were scholarships and grants for promising young people to visit the US. Gungwu was one of them.

It was indeed a trip that broadened my mind about modern scholarship and helped me greatly in my career. I was a young academic from Southeast Asia who knew little about what American scholars were doing but who, as John Sutter saw it, might have some useful observations to make to the scholars there about the nationalist and ideological struggles in the region. I was lucky to have a wife who agreed I should go. She was someone who was unbelievably competent and determined and, most of all, believed in me. For four months, I sent her light-hearted reports of what I did and she kept assuring me that she was managing fine. That enabled me to make the most of the opportunities that I was given to learn and make myself known.

PART SEVEN

Globalizing?

Enter the Cold War

I WAS UNSURE how much I should say here about my US trip. For me, it was primarily a study tour to familiarize myself with the work of American universities. Today such a trip would be routine. American institutions of higher learning are highly respected and most students would know about the potential advantages of studying there. But, after going through notes of what I knew of universities in the US before the trip and what I learnt there, I decided to include a fuller account here. I had witnessed a power shift across the Pacific, traceable through some of the developments in knowledge making that I observed. Another reason for sharing more detail here was that I later realized I was observing the final stages of the American takeover of the global maritime project that the British had embarked on from the end of the 18th century. At the time, this was an opportunity to find out who were America's more lively scholars of Asia, including those who originated from UK, Europe and Asia. To what extent did they represent the coming together of a post-war Anglo-American or Anglophone world?

I never knew why John Sutter at the Asia Foundation asked me to write my impressions of the state of Asian studies in the US, or how he was sure that I was the right person to whom to award the grant that gave me access to some of the best universities in America. I doubt there was anything in my report that the foundation did not already know; perhaps what was of interest was how I reacted to what I saw and what it revealed of my politics. He could easily have found out that several of my closest friends in university were political detainees who had recently been released by the new PAP government in Singapore. I could only imagine that he judged that, despite that background, I was worth the risk and therefore acted quickly to enable me to go.

Reviewing what I knew about America before I set off made me aware that the British and the American had been placed in separate boxes in my early life. In Anderson School, America was almost never mentioned apart from being the place where brave British colonists settled among hostile Indians. There were few mentions of the rebels who took the 13 colonies out of the empire. However, in my Chinese home, I heard more about Americans. For example, the Chinese primary school textbooks introduced me to Washington, the father of the republic who could not tell a lie, and Lincoln who freed the slaves. During the Pacific War, Americans were the good guys on the side of the Chinese and my mother spoke warmly of the Flying Tigers and the American aid brought in by the Burma Road that enabled China to survive. When the war ended, it was President Roosevelt who made sure that China was given one of the five top seats in the UN Security Council.

In Nanjing, these positive images were politicized. American interventions had become unwelcome to many of my fellow students. They thought that the American military was siding with the corrupt Chiang Kai-shek government against more popular opposition parties. When I studied at the University of Malaya, I found that America barely featured in any of our courses. I read the American scholar Rupert Emerson's *Malaysia: A Study in Direct and Indirect Rule* (1937) but his "Malaysia" described the larger Malay world under both Dutch and British control. I also recall how many of our British teachers were patronizing about the naivety of American foreign policy; supporters of their Labour Party were openly critical of the capitalist ideology that American leaders boasted about. Those who liked America's anti-colonial stances also began to waver when the US backed the French colonial forces in the Vietnam War. Certainly, more voices for neutralism were being raised to oppose American efforts to pressure new nation-states to take their side in the Cold War.

Personally, my encounters with things American were always outside of the British education orbit. I remember popular films, such as those starring Shirley Temple, *The Adventures of Tom Sawyer* and *Gone with the Wind,* as well as war films depicting victorious Americans in Europe and the Pacific, not to mention the Westerns where guns talked louder than anything else. Two of the films I saw had displayed the power of

American theatre, based on Arthur Miller's *Death of a Salesman* and Tennessee Williams' *A Streetcar Named Desire*. As for American literature, we read it outside the classroom: from Walt Whitman to Edgar Allan Poe and Robert Frost, and those who made their names in Europe, T.S. Eliot, Ezra Pound, Henry James and Ernest Hemingway. And I met my first American writer, Wallace Stegner the novelist, in Manila at the writers' workshop I attended in 1950.

How many Americans had I actually met in Singapore and London before talking to John Sutter? There were a few adventurous students, but no academics at MU or SOAS. In Delhi, I met Stephen Schwebel, representing UN Students Association; in London, I shared my Japanese class with Philip Kuhn. But the only established scholar of Asia I had met was Benjamin Schwarz from Harvard whom I got to know at the Paris conference. It was not until I returned to Singapore in 1957 that I noticed that many more American scholars had been coming along. Two of them left important studies of Malaya: Gene Hanrahan's *The Communist Struggle in Malaya* (1954) and Lucian Pye's *Guerilla Communism in Malaya: Its Social and Political Meaning* (1956). And that interest grew stronger when Malaya became independent.

After I moved to KL, I met dozens of the American scholars and officials visiting our campus. By then, I was reading more about neighbouring countries in the region and realized that the Americans had long moved beyond the Philippines and were especially active in Vietnam, Thailand and the increasingly hostile Indonesia under Sukarno. They had also become involved in Burmese affairs after that country became independent and did not join the British Commonwealth. In comparison, the Americans saw that the British were well able to control Malaya and Singapore and their presence here was not so obvious. It was only after the Union Jack had been taken down in Malaya that the Americans seemed to have come in large numbers. At least, that was how it appeared to me. It was my first intimation of an Anglo-American agenda to manage the post-war maritime world order together.

New World Report

IN THE FIRST four months of 1960, I visited 14 different US universities. That enabled me to compare how each of them was responding to the changes in post-war Asia. What I saw also gave me a better sense of US concerns about its relations with East and Southeast Asia. The most important thing I learnt was that, while a few individual scholars were deeply interested, most American universities were not ready to give much attention to the study of Asia. All of them had been modelled on the great European universities and prided themselves as extensions of European learning that could hope to become better than their masters. For them, although the Pacific side of Asia was much further westwards, it was still seen from the European perspective as places that were really "Far East". It was the war against Japan, followed by "the loss of China" that led them to see the Cold War as a multi-directional threat to US interests in the post-imperial world. Even then, as the Asia Foundation was aware, there was really no understanding of the region where the small new nations created by European empires were left to save themselves from being dominated again.

John Sutter consulted me about the universities I would like to visit and the people I would like to meet and advised me about the time I needed to get a feel of each of the places I visited. He knew about the Association for Asian Studies conference in New York in early April and carefully took that into account when advising me how long I should stay in the west and midwest before getting there. And he thoughtfully allowed for some free weekends in various cities so that I could also learn something about the American political system and some aspects of culture and society. It was only after he had worked out the timetable for me that I realized how thorough and efficient he had been in arranging my itinerary.

I was away from mid-January to the middle of May of 1960. I flew Pan American Airlines (now defunct) and my first stop was Hawaii. The journey took nearly two days, stopping briefly in Manila, Wake Island and then Midway. Totally forgotten by today's travellers, the latter two stops reminded me how close we still were to the Pacific War. I had watched a documentary film called *The Battle for Midway* when still a schoolboy in Ipoh in 1945 that was about how the Americans pushed the Japanese navy back after their humiliation at Pearl Harbour. I was struck then how wide the ocean was, and thus how far the Americans had come to make their country the big player in the region it now was: how they made the Pacific an "American Lake" several times the size of the North Atlantic. To me, that flight was a measure of the extended American power that replaced the image of British "possessions" marked red on the map that my colonial school had implanted in my mind. It was a powerful start to my re-education.

My time in the US was full. I shall not describe everything I learnt but will focus on two areas. The first deals with the state of Asian studies, and what that might have meant for the field. The other concerns some of the exceptional individuals I met, among whom were those who made a difference to my understanding of past and present.

It was a short stopover in Hawaii. The university there was keen to be a bridge between east and west and was about to host a centrally-funded institution to bring scholars and students from Asia and the Pacific to learn about America. However, it was not until I got to Washington DC two months later that I learnt that congress was about to fund the East-West Center to bring eastern peoples closer to the US. The university had some Japanese studies, and the leading scholar I met there was a historian of the Russo-Japanese War. I did not meet anyone who taught anything about Southeast Asia.

The University of Washington in Seattle was much stronger on Asian studies, with its Far Eastern and Russian Institute focused primarily on China. I knew a fair bit about its strengths when still in Singapore from talking to Stanley Spector, one of its early PhDs in Chinese history. I remember asking him about Franz Michael, who had supervised him there and whose study of the origins of Manchu rule in China was one of the key texts used in teaching my course on the Ming-Qing transition.

He had also told me of Michael's grand project on the Taiping rebellion to which Stanley had contributed by studying one of the men who had helped to destroy it.

The institute's director was George Taylor, an Englishman who made me feel welcome by hosting me to dinner at his home. He knew I had studied in London so his wife served Yorkshire pudding as a special treat. Taylor had studied history both in the US and China and was especially interested in the Taiping Rebellion. It was his interest that led him to propose the Taiping Rebellion Project that Michael brought a team of scholars to study, and several fine volumes had already been published before I arrived. I was touched by Taylor's hospitality and impressed by the quality of the publications produced by his China programme, not least by its very impressive group of graduate students. Despite having recently lost such top scholars as Chang Chung-li 张仲礼 (author of the classic study *The Chinese Gentry*) who had returned to China and Karl Wittfogel (co-author of the authoritative study of the Khitan Liao dynasty as well as author of *Oriental Despotism*) who had gone to Columbia, the team was still very powerful. By the end of my US trip, I realized that Washington and Harvard were clearly the two best-funded centres of modern China studies in the Western world.

The institute's studies of the 19th century included Hsiao Kung-ch'uan's 萧公权 masterly *Rural China: Imperial Control in the 19th century*. Hsiao also wrote on Kang Youwei's Confucianism and I was intrigued by his interpretations of Kang's contributions to modern thought. At the same time, Kang's grandson Lo Jung-pang 羅榮邦, later known as the pioneer historian of early Chinese navies, was there preparing a new biography of his grandfather. When Lo Jung-pang heard that I had met Wu Xianzi, one of Kang's loyal followers in Hong Kong, he spent long hours telling me how he saw his grandfather's place in history.

This was my first encounter in the west with a university that attracted so many established scholars of China. What I thought extraordinary was that, apart from Hsiao, Lo, Chang, Vincent Shih Yu-chung 施友忠 who wrote on Taiping ideology, and the linguist Li Fang-kuei 李方桂, the others were Europeans like Taylor from the UK, and Michael and Hellmut Wilhelm (whose eight lectures on *The Book of Change* were a classic) from Germany, with the majority working on modern history.

None of the institutions in Europe combined the social sciences with sinology in their study of China. My first thought was that this institute had given the innovative "area studies" approach a flying start.

I went on to the Bay area in California and spent nearly three weeks there, the first week based in San Francisco and the remaining two on the University of California's Berkeley campus. After calling at The Asia Foundation's office, I visited Stanford University and was bowled over by the remarkable collections of contemporary documents in Chinese at the Hoover Library, including those of the CCP in China and the MCP in Malaya on how to fight guerrilla wars. It made me realize that, had I gone to study in California instead of London, I could have done research on the warlord period in 20th-century China and not gone back to ancient history. The deep bias in British Malaya, my leaving Nanjing in 1948, plus my own ignorance, had turned my eyes away from America. I recall, when looking through the catalogue of papers that the Hoover Library possessed, feeling some regret. It crossed my mind that, even in China, it would have been difficult to find such a specialized collection in any single library. At that time, I had just begun to study the overseas Chinese and was also struck by the collection of papers that covered the Chinese communities in Southeast Asia. It was the first time that I had come across a collection of this kind.

It was therefore not surprising that scholars of contemporary China were attracted to Stanford. When I was in London, I had followed some of the McCarthy attacks on American academics and had read Robert C. North's book about Russian and Chinese communists. I found his work enlightening and was delighted to meet him. I asked him whether communism in Southeast Asia was closer to that of the Russians or the Chinese. He explained how the Hoover Library was weak on this topic and that he was trying to collect more documents for study, but expected to find that China's influence was greater.

I was introduced to Claude Buss in the History Department. Up to this point, I had yet to meet anyone with any interest in Southeast Asia. Buss had served in the Philippines and had played a part in American planning for the region. He asked me to give a lecture to his students about Southeast Asia. I spoke of Malaya as a new nation and what it meant to be multi-communal and also made comparisons with what I knew of

Indonesia. Afterwards, Buss asked if I would consider a teaching position at Stanford. I explained that I was committed to developing historical studies in Malaya. But I was impressed by his interest in the region amidst the Cold War.

I spent more time at Berkeley after moving into its International House. At breakfast the first morning, I met, of all people, my former professor C.N. Parkinson who explained that he was on an extended lecture tour in the US as the man who discovered Parkinson's Law. Later in the day, another former MU professor, Paul Wheatley who had recently joined the Berkeley Geography Department, saw me and invited me to dinner at his home. We had known each other through our common interest in the ancient maritime trade with China; his study of the trading goods listed in Song dynasty records and my *Nanhai Trade* had both been published in the *Journal of the Royal Asiatic Society Malayan Branch*. It was encouraging to know that MU and Berkeley were not that far apart.

I had also found in the Berkeley Library a large collection of local Chinese newspapers dating from the turn of the century. Apart from local business news, they also had many reports of the activities of Kang Youwei's Protect the Emperor Society 保皇会 and Sun Yat-sen's anti-Manchu Tongmeng Hui 同盟会 that echoed what I had read in Singapore and Hong Kong. Other stories in the collection reminded me of the consequences of the Chinese Exclusion Act in California and not least of the San Francisco earthquake that destroyed much of the Chinatown area. They made me appreciate all the more the Chinatowns and the Chinese experience in North America and encouraged me to pursue my Nanyang Chinese studies in a broader framework.

UC Berkeley was more balanced than either Washington and Stanford. It had well-established scholars in ancient and modern China and a growing interest in Southeast Asia. There was even a student writing his Master's degree on Chinese communist policy towards overseas Chinese in Southeast Asia. The first sinologist I met there was Edward Schafer who knew just about everything worth knowing about Tang dynasty material culture and trading goods. When I was writing my master's thesis, I had missed reading his book *The Empire of Min* (1954) that described how the people of Fujian started its historical trading relationship in the East and South China Seas. I also did not know that, for his PhD in 1947, he had done a detailed study of Liu Chang 刘銀 (958–971), the last emperor of the Nan Han kingdom centred in Guangzhou, another major player in the Nanhai trade. When he told me that he had read *The Nanhai Trade* and showed me his card index that listed everything to do with foreign relations during the Tang and Five Dynasties (7th to 10th centuries), I felt truly humbled. He told me about the book he was about to finish on Tang exotics and the book that he would write after that on how Tang China imagined the south, including the world across the South China Sea. In addition, I was impressed to learn that he had led his colleagues to refuse to sign the loyalty oath demanded of academics by Senator McCarthy's committee and that he was widely respected for having done that. I wanted to meet Wolfram Eberhard, whose work on the northern Turkic emperors of the Five Dynasties had helped my research, but he was out of town. However, I did meet two younger scholars whose work I found awesome. The first was Eberhard's colleague Franz Schurmann, who made his name in Mongol Yuan history and whose linguistic skills had enabled him to study the Mongol descendants of Genghis Khan's armies in modern Afghanistan. I was astonished to find him now writing about contemporary China politics and examining Mao Zedong's ideological writings. The other was Joseph Levenson, whose study of Liang Qichao had led him to his second book, on the modern fate of Confucianism, the first volume of which I had just bought and begun to read. When he learned that I had come from Malaya, he invited me to lunch with his wife, whose brother was a senior officer with the British forces fighting the Malayan Emergency—a reminder of the Anglo-American power-sharing in our half of the world. The versatility of some of the scholars I met was breathtaking.

Unlike Seattle, there was here some interest in the insurgencies in Southeast Asia, if only as battlegrounds in the struggle against China and the Soviet Union. I recall visiting Robert Scalapino and Guy Pauker, in the Department of Political Science, who were encouraging their graduate students to work on Indonesia. But there were no signs that Berkeley planned to build a major Southeast Asia Centre like that in Cornell.

It was not all work and no play. I had a couple of weekends in San Francisco where I was taken to see the sights in the beautiful Bay area, north to the redwoods and the vineyards of the Napa Valley and south along the Pacific coast from Santa Cruz to Monterey. In the evenings, I was also brought to places where popular jazz and literary groups performed to appreciative young audiences.

⸺◦⧉◦⸺

My next three stops were deliberately chosen, with the advice of John Sutter, to represent new efforts to start serious work on Asia. They were the University of Arizona in Tucson, the University of Colorado in Boulder and Washington University in St Louis. I had heard of the first two through reading some newly-published books. In the case of Arizona, this was because a leading Ming historian Charles Hucker had moved there from the University of Chicago to start its Asian studies programme. I had used his work in my teaching of Ming history and very much looked forward to meeting him. In Colorado, I was familiar with Earl Swisher's *China's Management of the American Barbarians,* one of the first collections of Chinese documents available for American students. I was keen to ask him about his experiences before the war, when he taught at Lingnan University in Guangzhou. As for St Louis, I had asked to stop there to see Stanley Spector again, whom I knew well in Singapore and who was now the head of a new Centre for Asian studies. He was also someone who understood some of the problems facing the overseas Chinese in Malaya. I was keen to see him again and wanted to know how a new centre like his was faring in a university that had no known links to Asia prior to his arrival.

None of the three institutions had significant Asia programmes. All three asked me to lecture to their students. In each, I chose to talk about Southeast Asian history and politics as John Sutter had encouraged me to do. My talks focused on the reshaping of the island world of Malay peoples, especially the efforts to build nations out of disparate populations. Coincidentally, I had arrived in Arizona just after a local judge had declared that the state's prohibition of interracial marriages was unconstitutional. I was shown the offending clause, "The marriage of a person of Caucasian blood with a Negro, Mongolian, Malay or Hindu is null and void." Thus Malays and Chinese, the two main communities of Malaya, were listed together as people with whom Caucasians were not allowed to marry.

My lectures were thought to be timely. The students questioned me about the difference between the Philippines and the two newer states of Indonesia and Malaya; and the kinds of Chinese who were active in each. In Colorado, the miscegenation law had been invalidated a few years back so I could talk without difficulty about our Eurasians and other intermarriages and that many of them had moved to Britain, Australia and the Netherlands. As for Washington University, St Louis, I had been warned that interracial marriages, as in all the southern states, might be a sensitive subject so I avoided the topic. That was another reminder of how complicated a country like the United States was.

Although I had to give half a dozen lectures in three weeks, the visits to my chosen three cities provided happy breaks before I turned to the major Asian Studies centres in Chicago and the northeast. In Arizona, Charles Hucker took me for a day's outing to Nogales where we were allowed to cross into the Mexican half of the town without a visa, thus enabling me to say that I have been in Mexico. He also brought me to Tombstone, reminding me of the films I had seen some years back based on the town's history, *My Darling Clementine* and *Gunfight at the OK Corral*. I visited the local cemetery because some Chinese were buried there, including the grave of the chef who was accidentally shot in one of the numerous gunfights in the town. It surprised me how ubiquitous the Chinese were after China was opened up during the 19th century.

Images of the wild west were further enhanced by what I saw during the long day's flight on Pioneer Airlines from Tucson to Boulder via Albuquerque. The land was dry and rugged and our low-flying plane wove around many mountain ranges all the way. At the mile-high city of Boulder, I was often breathless after a bit of exertion, but that did not stop me from telling Malayan jokes in the lectures I gave.

I was even more relaxed in St Louis staying with the Spectors. They lived in a Jewish neighbourhood and Stanley, although no longer practising, educated me about Orthodox food and customs, and I enjoyed his favourite gefilte fish. Each evening, as the night wore on, he would play hymn-like Jewish music on his violin. I found the music deeply moving. He had trained to be a concert violinist before he enlisted for the Pacific

War and later turned to the study of Chinese history. He could still play beautifully. He had friends in the St Louis Symphony Orchestra and took me to two concerts. My stay was not only restful but also added another dimension to my understanding of America's immigrant past.

Chicago was more demanding. I called on the "orientalists" led by H.G. Creel and Edward Kracke. Creel was adamant that China could not be understood without a sound knowledge of classical ideas and institutions. Kracke had heard of my work with Denis Twitchett and asked what I thought was vital to the Confucianism of the Late Tang-Five Dynasties period. Both encouraged me to stay with sinology in my teaching and research.

However, I was impressed by the new American scholarship on modern China that I had encountered in Seattle and the Bay Area and also found in Chicago. I met Tsou Tang 邹谠, the son of Tsou Lu 邹鲁 a dedicated supporter of Sun Yat-sen, and heard him explain the Great Leap Forward and what was still unfolding in the PRC. His insights were eye opening and he convinced me that sinology was not enough if one wished to understand what was happening in the PRC. The way the social sciences were raising new questions seemed to me essential for us to explain how two revolutions had transformed China and what more might have to be changed. I also noted that Chicago had several scholars working on South and Southeast Asia, and thought that the work of the sociologist Edward Shils and the historian Bernard Cohn on the Indian sub-continent threw fresh light on traditional societies in ways that orientalism did not.

I was glad I found time to call on two men whose work did not raise difficult methodological problems for me. One was Donald Lach, a historian of the 16th to 18th centuries (the period that I was teaching at the University of Malaya) who was keen to explore the effects of Asian thought and institutions on the development of modern Europe. After talking to him, I vowed to incorporate the questions he asked into my lectures when I got home and continued to follow his writings for the next two decades. The other person was Tsien Tsuen-hsuin 錢存訓 the librarian in charge of Chicago's East Asian collection who was also a very fine scholar of ancient China. He was the younger brother of my father's schoolmate Chien Tsun-tien 钱存典, the diplomat in London who gave Margaret away at our wedding. I had set out to make a duty call, but our meeting turned into a most enlightening seminar on the history of the Chinese book before paper and printing, a subject I knew nothing about. Just before we parted, he told me that his wife was from the Xu 许 family and related to our Wang family—her aunt married one of my grand-uncles.

East Coast Centres

AFTER TWO MONTHS, I finally arrived on America's east coast. Curiously, there was no major centre for the study of Chinese and Southeast Asian history in Washington DC, the country's capital. I was advised to visit Johns Hopkins University's School of Advanced International Studies (SAIS) where I met, among other specialists in world affairs, Majid Khadduri. I heard that he had supported research in the Malay world through the Malaysian Social Research Institute based in KL. He was gracious and explained that the school's interests were global and Southeast Asia should be an area of concern. I was also brought to Howard University where I was introduced to Bernard Fall. He was known for his expertise on Vietnam and shared his insights on the war being fought in Vietnam, but there were no plans in the university to develop any work on our region.

The Asia Foundation was concerned that I should learn something about key American institutions and arranged for me to visit the Supreme Court and, when I went to the Congress Building, I was privileged to listen to the British Prime Minister Harold Macmillan addressing the Senate on the question of civil rights. Then there was a trip to pay my respects at Mt Vernon, George Washington's home. I had to miss seeing the Smithsonian museums because I wanted to spend more time at the Library of Congress. There was one of the world's best collections of books on things Chinese. I concentrated on the history sections and nursed the hope to do research there. Also, as an admirer of Abraham Lincoln, I did not want to miss the opportunity to see some of the historic sites of the American Civil War. During the weekend, I hired a car to drive to Gettysburg and Harper's Ferry, and then the next day to Fredericksburg.

In between, I contacted friends in the Malayan embassy and called on the ambassador, Datuk Nik Kamil, and his deputy, Tungku Ngah Mohammad, to get an update on Malaya's relations with the US. They were upbeat and convinced that the US was about to commit more resources to protect the region from communism. They made it a point to brief me about the black population residing in the city and made me curious about how they lived. Thus, when walking down one of the streets in their district one evening, I had the unforgettable experience of going to a theatre where a Southern Whites travelling group was performing. To my surprise, it turned out to be a show where young white males impersonated black female singers like Pearl Bailey and Ella Fitzgerald. The audience was all black, and I found it interesting how the audience enjoyed the impersonations and seemed to have thought that they were all well done. This was something I had not heard of and never came across again. I imagine this kind of show was later considered incorrect and abandoned.

My next stop was New York. I had read about the fine universities of the northeast and knew that this would be the high point of my trip. During the weeks on the road, I also heard a great deal more about them from the scholars I met, many of whom were products of those universities. I knew what to expect in universities like Columbia and, with New York as my base, had to choose which others I should visit. With advice from my Asia Foundation hosts, I chose Princeton, Yale, Harvard and Cornell. In retrospect, it was a mistake not to have gone to the University of Pennsylvania as well. But, asked to choose between UPenn and Princeton, I picked the latter because of Hu Shi's 胡适 connection with the Gest Library and because I knew that Frederick (Fritz) Mote had studied in Nanjing when I was also there. Also, Fritz had begun to build something unique, a centre that specialized in the history of the Ming, including the first half of the 1500–1800 period that I was teaching in Malaya.

For the next four weeks, I was soaking up information, much of which was most enlightening. Everything I was told about the four institutions was true. They were hubs of scholarly activity riding the wave of US superpower involvement everywhere that led to the determination to build centres of excellence to cover post-imperial Asia. I had been told when in Seattle and Berkeley that the new Ford Foundation grant for the study of contemporary China was galvanizing a new generation of graduate students. I saw evidence of that in every institution, especially in Columbia and Harvard.

My trip was mainly to learn about the state of China and Southeast Asian studies and I tried hard not to be distracted by the other fascinating developments around, including those in other New York colleges and universities. When I arrived in New York, my Asia Foundation hosts arranged for me to meet key officials of the Ford and Rockefeller Foundations and encouraged me to tell them what I had learnt from the first half of my trip, including my impressions of the smaller schools and what they might be able to do. I told them about the areas of my ignorance that I had set out to dispel, and on how much I picked up from the people I met as I crossed the continent. I assumed they knew more about the details of each institution than I did and were simply curious as to how the American world of Asian experts appeared in the eyes of someone from a new university in a newly independent country. In any case, just before I left New York, I gave the Asia Foundation representative there a preliminary report of my trip.

In fact, the picture overall was not a mystery. Looking back, I note that each institution has since recorded its history and these have been augmented by dozens of reports and memoirs by those directly involved. I cannot add anything to those accounts. I shall therefore only describe what I found memorable in my personal encounters. While doing that, I shall try to keep my comments on China studies separate from the studies of Southeast Asia.

Where China was concerned, my visit coincided with a major transition in academia when a dominant sinology emphasis was giving way to an area studies approach that needed the social sciences to help cope with the modern and contemporary. Harvard was clearly in the lead in the study of all aspects of China. It had begun to move early under the leadership of John King Fairbank. But both Columbia and Yale were moving the same way and picking up pace. In comparison, I was surprised to see how quickly the University of Washington in Seattle had moved to a modern platform and turned to the social sciences. UC Berkeley, too, with policy consultants like Robert Scalapino, was responding actively to the new American commitments in the Western Pacific and was paying more attention to Southeast Asia. I also sensed that Chicago was ready to do more in the social sciences, as it had already done in its work on Indian history and society. This became clear when I learnt that it had appointed Clifford Geertz, who was famous as the leading cultural anthropologist studying Indonesia. Princeton was more cautious. I visited its campus twice, coming away each time thinking that Fritz Mote's appointment was a clear signal that the university would not be behind the others for long.

I also visited Yale twice. Its decision to bring Arthur and Mary Wright from Stanford was truly remarkable. Arthur was mindful of sinology traditions and would ensure that they would continue to be seen as essential, while Mary would provide leadership for modern history. Together, they could kick off what would be a holistic perspective on China. I had heard of their move when visiting Stanford, where everyone was still lamenting the loss of them both to Yale. What I also thought was special about Yale was that it was still hoping to be another major centre for Southeast Asian studies and had appointed Harry Benda to lead its development. I had met Harry in Singapore and KL several times and thought he was the best person to lift Yale up in this new field. It was most encouraging to see him settling down to that challenging task.

Like Yale, Cornell had an early start in offering educational opportunities to China; many of its Chinese alumni became leading figures in the Chinese government and academia. It was never burdened by European traditions of sinology and its social scientists were drawn to the study of modern China earlier than in other universities. I met its leading historian Knight Biggerstaff, whose work I knew. He had deep personal experience of contemporary China. I had read about his struggle to clear his name after being accused of being pro-communist by Senator McCarthy's committee. I did not know if that affair had any effect on China studies on the Cornell campus. By the time I went to study in SOAS in London in 1954, it was already thought to be the leading university in the US for the study of modern Southeast Asia but its reputation for China studies was no longer so strong. Meeting George Kahin and Lauriston Sharp when I got there, and hearing their plans for Southeast Asian studies, I was sure that their centre would be unmatched for our generation.

For myself, coming from Southeast Asia and studying Chinese history had led to my belief that there were advantages in studying East and Southeast Asia together. From my work on early trade in the South China Sea, I was conscious that the Chinese coasts lined one-third of that sea while Southeast Asia formed the remainder. It serves as a constant reminder that the way the Chinese state had neglected the political changes in the region had given the China much grief. Hence my admiration for what Cornell had achieved and what Yale and UC Berkeley were seeking to do. Later, it became clear that the University of Michigan had also moved in the same direction and I was sorry that I had not included its campus on my list.

I have to say that Southeast Asian studies in America was but a blip compared to the interest in the Far East (mainly China and Japan) that filled up the rest of the screen. This was clear when I attended the Association for Asian Studies (AAS) conference that took place in New York in the middle of April. Panels on Southeast Asia were few, but they gave me a chance to meet several active scholars like Harry Benda, Bill Skinner, John Cady, Norman Parmer and Robert van Niel, and some of their graduate students who were later to lead the field. When I heard that Bill Skinner was leaving Columbia to return to Cornell, it confirmed that, where Southeast Asia was concerned, Cornell was clearly the place to be. I thus looked forward very much to my visit to Ithaca a week later.

This was my first AAS conference and I found it a valuable gathering not only for finding out what new research was being done but also what was happening in the transitions from "orientalism" to the social sciences. Not least, it enabled me to get to know scholars from parts of this huge country that I was unlikely ever to visit. As it turned out, it also prepared the ground for my visit to Harvard. For example, I met two Harvard graduate students: Philip Kuhn, whom I already knew from studying Japanese under Ronald Dore at SOAS, and David Roy, who, like Fritz Mote, had been in Nanjing when I was there. I did not meet David and Fritz in Nanjing because they were at Jinling University while I was at National Central, but meeting all three of them helped me feel that I was not entirely an outsider in this new Asian studies business.

An additional bonus was meeting Bill Holland of the Institute of Pacific Relations (IPR), a New Zealander whom I had long admired for his efforts to advance transpacific knowledge. I was appalled to read about the attacks on the IPR as a pro-communist organization by Senator McCarran's committee and was happy to learn that Holland, the IPR and the journal *Pacific Affairs* were about to find a new home in the University of British Columbia where, it so happened, my PhD examiner at Cambridge Ted Pulleyblank had gone. That move again reminded me that, despite their apparent historical differences, there was a broader underlying Anglo-American perspective on post-imperial world affairs that would become stronger as the Cold War progressed.

My Harvard friends might say that leaving Harvard to the last was to make sure my US trip ended with a suitable climax. It was certainly unforgettable. I was sorry to have missed seeing John Fairbank, who was away, but did see Benjamin Schwartz. When I was still a graduate student at the Paris conference four years earlier, Schwartz was very encouraging about my work on the Five Dynasties, despite the fact that he was famous as the leading scholar on Chinese communism. He told me he was working on a book on Yan Fu 严复, the man who introduced key modern European ideas to traditional Confucians, and was fascinated by the different ways late Qing Confucians thought of Yan's work. When I gave my seminar on an early devout Confucian of the 10th century, Feng Dao 冯道, Schwartz asked me questions that helped me rethink some of the assumptions that I had made. Chow Tse-tsung 周策纵, whose book on the May Fourth Movement had just been published, not only came but also took me aside to tell me about the various ways the last generation of Confucians responded to the May Fourth challenge. Both men made me realize how much I had missed, having made the decision to work on ancient instead of modern history. This point was further pressed home when I talked to Lucien Pye, Ch'u T'ung-tsu 瞿同祖 and Liu Kuang-ching 刘广京, some of the finest scholars of modern China.

It was a very full fortnight. Other highlights were Yang Lien-sheng's 杨聯陞 classes, a lecture by Ch'ien Mu 钱穆, and the time I spent in the rare books collection of the Harvard-Yenching Library. And, most enjoyable, I met outstanding graduate students who were preparing to be leaders of the next generation: Philip Kuhn, David Roy (later at Chicago), Yu Ying-shih 余英时 (at Yale and Princeton), Lloyd Eastman (at Illinois), and Ernest Young (at Michigan). They cheerfully took me around the campus and to inexpensive but healthy Chinese meals around Boston. My last evening with Philip, David and Lloyd was the true climax to my discovery of what Harvard had to offer to China studies.

I should also repeat that it was not all about China. There were several scholars of Japan, and Edwin Reischauer's extraordinary contributions to our knowledge of early Sino-Japanese relations during the Tang dynasty, coupled with his knowledge of modern Japan, was remarkable. As for Southeast Asian studies, I was told there were no plans to develop that. However, I admired Rupert Emerson's contributions to our understanding of colonialism in our region and his books on British Malaya and the Dutch East Indies. I had heard about his latest book, *From Empire to Nation*, and appreciated the chance to ask him for his frank comments on the future of the Malayan nation. He was carefully optimistic. An extra bonus was my success in getting to see Stephen Schwebel, the American student leader who had inspired the UN Students Conference in Delhi. He was now teaching in the Harvard Law School. We spent a day together, during which he stressed the importance of international law for the protection of the smaller post-colonial nations and why the study of Southeast Asian politics could not afford to neglect that. I was moved by his intense belief that respect for the law was the best instrument to ensure peace in the new world order. It did not surprise me when years later I learnt that he had become one of the judges at the International Court of Justice, and eventually its president.

I have left it to the last to say that, while I dutifully enquired about the study of Asia at every stop, I became increasingly curious about the American political system. John F. Kennedy had just launched his presidential campaign. He was not only the young Catholic war hero but also a Harvard alumnus. When I was in San Francisco, he was being compared to the Californian Richard Nixon (who had talked to us in Singapore about preparing to fight the Vietnamese communists). I was not convinced that a hot war was inevitable and wondered what Kennedy would say. In my innocence, I thought at the time that the Democrats would have been less warlike.

When reflecting on my takeaways from my four months' trip, I realized that, by the time I arrived on the US east coast, I was sometimes distracted from the state of Asian studies in America and was trying to follow the highly public mysteries of a special brand of democratic politics. What I knew of democracy came from the British parliamentary system and bookish studies of its origins in ancient Greece. I had seen versions of that a few months earlier in both Singapore and Malaya. None of that prepared me for what I encountered in the US week after week in early 1960. By the time I left, I found this mixture of a war of words and a cross between lively theatre and a soccer final quite addictive. Back in KL, I continued to follow the American campaigns and when Theodore White published his first *Making of the President*, I read it from cover to cover. That might not have been Asia Foundation's purpose for giving me the grant, but the trip certainly enabled me over the next five decades to separate America's highest ideals from the political discourse that often led to something I associated with demagoguery.

Years later, in 1967, in between my visits to conferences in Chicago and Ann Arbor, it was reported that the Central Intelligence Agency (CIA) had funded a large number of cultural and educational organizations worldwide to counter communist propaganda. By that time, the nature of the Cold War had become clear and I had lost most of my political innocence. I had read about the role of the CIA in Europe, Cuba and several Latin American states. In our neighbourhood, Hong Kong and Taiwan were obvious targets and we also learnt about CIA activities in Tibet, Laos and Vietnam and its recent success in Indonesia. I was not greatly surprised to read that the CIA was behind the Asia Foundation. It had been founded in 1954 ostensibly as a privately-funded foundation. After my return from my 1960 trip, I had nothing more to do with it. In turn, it had no further interest in me; it had done its job and satisfied my interest in the study of China and Southeast Asia in American universities. What did surprise me, however, was that the Congress for Cultural Freedom (CCF) was also a CIA creation. A large number of writers and thinkers whose work I admired had endorsed it, including Karl Jaspers, Bertrand Russell, Bernadette Croce and Arthur Koestler. I had been a regular reader of CCF's *Encounter* magazine and was disturbed that I had never suspected it of being a CIA front. While this did not make me totally cynical, it certainly confirmed how politically vulnerable we were.

Margaret's America

A FEW YEARS later, Margaret was asked to do a report on some of the English-language teaching centres in America. She also wanted to learn more about how the language was taught. She was rising in her profession as a teacher of English as a second language. She was only away for three weeks so I did not have to take care of household affairs the way she had for four months in 1960. But her interests were much more practical. She saw another side of the country and was much closer to the ground than I was. Two years later, in 1967, when Carrington Goodrich in Columbia asked me if I would consider coming to New York at the time when C.H. Philips offered me a professorship at SOAS and Jack Crawford invited me to the chair of Far Eastern History at the Australian National University, I was surprised how strongly Margaret felt about not wanting to bring up the family in the US or the UK. But she was prepared to go with me to Canberra. She had hinted of her reservations about aspects of American society in 1965 when she got back from the US but, on the whole, enjoyed learning about English teaching there and found her professional network useful for her work. Some years ago, she wrote about her trip for our children.

In March 1965, I suddenly got an invitation to do a job for the University of Hawaii. Johnny Hendrikson who had been professor of Zoology at MU in KL and specialized on the migration patterns of the giant turtles of Kelantan and Trengganu had joined the University of Hawaii as a vice-chancellor. The university used this term not to denote the head of the university but rather a dean. So he was actually the equivalent of an academic dean under the British system.

Johnny was interested in the teaching of English as a foreign or second language as Hawaii was full of Asian-Americans and this subject was getting to be an important one. Many foreign students needed enhancement courses in English when they went to the US for further studies, and the US was the forerunner in the development of the subject. Many linguists began to write about the nature of the language and so on, and I myself had spent quite a lot of time studying and teaching the subject.

I was asked whether I would write a report for the University of Hawaii on the teaching of English after visiting various universities and the courses they devised, to see what the University of Hawaii could do to improve their teaching of the subject. It so happened that I had a three-week holiday coming up in March and so agreed to do this job for Hendrickson. I naturally was very pleased to be invited, and prepared myself for it by doing quite a bit of research on where to go and whom to contact. I ended up with a list of universities like University of California, Los Angeles (UCLA), UC Berkeley, Michigan, Harvard and Radcliffe, and Columbia. I couldn't do very much in two weeks as I needed to stay in each place for at least two days to talk to people and monitor the courses. The University of Hawaii gave me US$20 a day. In those days it was enough, as a stay in a motel cost about $8 and a cup of coffee was 25 cents. It never occurred to me to ask for a fee as I saw this trip as an education for me!

My first stop on the mainland was Los Angeles. I visited the English Language Department at UCLA and talked to a lot of people. I also attended some classes. I found that a lot of people wanted to learn English as the language was already beginning to become the world's lingua franca. It would be the language for commerce and technology and also of entertainment.

What I discovered was most interesting. On the way from the west to the east coast, I encountered the same people, all attending the various conferences that were going on about language teaching and its problems. Many were huge conferences. It was like an industry, with academics going from one conference to another, probably learning nothing very much from each one but networking (this word didn't exist in 1965!) and establishing contacts with each other. By the time I got to New York and still found some of the same people at various events, I had established a camaraderie with them and felt quite at home attending these conferences. I found that most of them were women, many on the fringes of academia, and struggling to get jobs, especially tenured jobs. Women were still restricted in the fields they could enter and at that time, there were very few who were in business and finance. Teaching was the traditional profession for thousands of women. It was true even in America and Europe, let alone in Asia.

I returned to KL and wrote up my report for the university. I understand it acted on some of my recommendations. Later, Johnny Hendrikson left to go to the University of Arizona as he didn't really enjoy administration, and returned to his first love, the migration of giant turtles.

Malaysia

MARGARET WAS RIGHT to believe that my trip to the US would be good for my academic career, but neither of us anticipated how quickly that added to the range of my activities, and how that took up more of my time. I arrived home to start the new academic year. We now had our own batch of second year students in KL, and I began to teach the course on East Asia, 1500–1800, while continuing to do the same in Singapore, visiting the other campus for a couple of days every other fortnight. A few weeks after my return from the US, I received an invitation from Arthur Wright at Yale to attend a conference in New York on Confucian Personalities later that year, as he had heard that I had given the talk on Feng Dao 冯 道 at Harvard, an unusually conventional Confucian who survived a most turbulent period of war and destruction while serving his military masters loyally. I had been struck by how much Feng was excoriated by Confucian philosophers and historians for centuries afterwards for his un-Confucian behaviour, and wanted to understand why he thought he was a devout Confucian, why his contemporaries acknowledged him as such and why, a century after his death, his critics began to pick him out as one of the worst examples of betrayal of true Confucian ideals.

I recall how the 14 of us at the conference spent five days together dissecting the lives of 11 Confucians from the 5th to the 20th centuries. The papers presented and the discussions that followed opened my eyes to the complexities underlying our understanding of Confucianism's role in Chinese history. It was memorable not only because my sinology colleagues accepted me as one of them but also because I was surprised how comfortable I was working with them.

About the same time, I received an invitation to spend a year at SOAS as a Rockefeller Research Fellow in 1961. This came from a grant to fund three historians from Southeast Asia to use the resources in London to do research on our region: the other two were O.D. Corpuz from the University of the Philippines and Nugroho Notosusanto of the University of Indonesia. I had met them both, O.D. in Manila and Nugroho in Singapore, and looked forward to seeing them again. However, we arrived at different times and I did not see much of them in London. I was the first to take up the fellowship and spent the year working on early Ming relations with Southeast Asia. Nugroho did not stay long and went back to Jakarta to concentrate on the history of the Indonesian military, while O.D., who had written an excellent study of the Philippine bureaucracy, arrived not long before I returned to KL.

All three of us were hosted by D.G.E. Hall, so I was identified as a historian of Southeast Asia. During that year, I met numerous friends visiting from Malaya and Singapore and felt that London was very much the hub for everything pertaining to the two places. However, when I visited universities in Europe, I found that the major centres were focused on China and Japan and had very little on Southeast Asia, and I was greeted there as a sinologist. I did not realize it at the time but this ambiguity followed me back to Malaya. I found myself being identified as a historian or a sinologist depending on the person I was talking to. Very often historians saw the sinologist while many sinologists would consider me merely a historian. And there were even times when some thought I was some kind of social scientist. This gave me a strange in-between feeling that remained with me for years.

I spent the year focusing on the large set of Ming dynasty *shilu* 实录 (Veritable Records), especially on the reigns of the founder Zhu Yuanzhang 朱元璋 (Hongwu reign) and his son Zhu Di 朱棣 (Yongle reign). I was fascinated by the seven expeditions of Zheng He to the Western (Indian) Ocean and paid special attention to the nature of the relationship that was established between the Chinese emperor and the rulers of the states that Zheng He visited. That led me to write several articles probing the practice and meaning of *chaogong* 朝贡 (tribute) during that period and, with my interest in Malaya, included the exceptional relationship that the Yongle emperor and his successors established with the rulers of Malacca. It was a fruitful year that deepened my understanding of how China's relations with Southeast Asia were evolving prior to the arrival of the Europeans.

It was also during that year away that I gained a clearer perspective of what Malayan nationalism meant. When I was invited to speak to the Royal Central Asian Society, I spoke on "Malayan nationalism" and this was published in the Society's journal. In there, I offered the following description:

> If we were to venture a definition at this stage it would be probably be fair to say that "Malayan nationalism" consists of two component parts: a nucleus of Malay nationalism enclosed by the idea of Malay-Chinese-Indian unity. This is perhaps not the way which many Malay and non-Malay politicians would like to see it. There are some Malay leaders who equate Malayan nationalism with Malay nationalism and prefer to use "Melayu" instead of "Malayan" in every possible context. And many Chinese and Indian leaders who describe themselves as "Malayan" refer to an altogether new political identity and would refuse to consider it as in any way similar to "Malay". But what cannot be denied is that the dynamism, the single-mindedness and the leadership in Malayan nationalism has been ably provided by the present Malay ruling groups. These Malays have been supported by both Chinese and Indians, but they have at no time surrendered their claim to, or rights of, leadership.

I know this definition, made some 50 years ago, was meant to describe the Malaya prior to the Tunku's announcement about "Greater Malaysia". I was not fully cognizant of the role that the bumiputras of Sarawak and Sabah (Iban, Melanau, Murut, Kadazhan, Suluk, Bajau, and others) would play, and certainly did not think that Singapore would leave the new federation. However, looking back, I think the key point about Malay national leadership remains true; if anything, Malay leadership is even stronger now and can control any two-party coalition that might eventually emerge.

Margaret remembers the trip to London most of all as she was pregnant again. When my mother heard that Margaret wanted to go with me to London, she offered to look after our daughter Mei for the year. We thought it was a good idea. She doted on Mei, so there was no question that Mei would be in a loving home. Our son came with us because he was old enough to go to some kind of pre-prep school. Here is how Margaret remembered our visit:

> We went to London in January 1961 because Gungwu was given a Rockefeller fellowship for one year. This fellowship was awarded to promising young scholars from Asia. I was about six months pregnant then but felt quite well, even though we travelled once again by sea to England. This time we travelled on a Danish ship, the *Selandia*, a semi-cargo ship which had only about 80 passengers on it. We thus got to know everyone very well as we played, talked and ate together for almost four weeks until we reached Southampton. We were put at a table with many compatible people so enjoyed ourselves during those weeks. My and Ming's fares were paid by us as only Gungwu had his fare paid. I can't remember exactly how we had the money to pay our fares, but possibly the University of Malaya helped with some grant.
>
> I was originally going to take a course in English as a second language at the Institute of Education, London University, and was going to go to London in September 1960 by myself first, leaving the two children with Gungwu and the servants, but cancelled it when I found I was pregnant again. As the child would be born some time in April, when I would be right in the middle of the course, I decided that it would not have been possible for me to complete it. Although unplanned, the birth of our daughter Lan has brought great joy into our lives. I have not regretted not taking the course as I learnt just as much about the subject later by practice when I had to deal with the subject at the Malayan Teachers' College (MTC) in Pantai Hill.
>
> My sister Dorothy, who was studying in London at the time, came to meet us at Southampton, where the *Selandia* docked. Initially we stayed in a hotel in Russell Square and then found a flat in Muswell Hill, in the northern part of London, through the University of London's housing section. The landlord was a Jew from Czechoslovakia who had escaped to China during Hitler's pogroms. After the war, he made his way to England. Because at the time only the Chinese took in the Jews, he was grateful to them. He didn't object to my having a baby soon and was happy to rent us his flat.
>
> Our flat consisted of one large sitting/dining room, two bedrooms (one at the back of the flat) with a kitchen and bathroom also at the back. Dorothy stayed with us during this year and occupied the back bedroom, which was

just large enough for a single person. She had been sharing a flat with friends and I think was quite happy to be staying with us.

Ming slept on a divan in the sitting room. During the day, this divan was our sofa! The flat was rather cramped, but we didn't have very much, just a few suitcases of clothes. The flat was supposed to be fully furnished. In England that meant no refrigerator—something we took for granted in Asia—but Dorothy provided a small fridge which, to my amazement, actually worked! Clothes washing was done at a laundrette nearby. The kitchen was not large but big enough for a small table at which we ate. In any case, the shops were just downstairs fronting the main street so I made do with what we were provided.

Gungwu worked at a whole series of articles on the Ming dynasty's relations with Southeast Asia. This was a new field for him but was the beginning of what he was to become very well known for—his work on the Chinese overseas. In the end he fell into this field of study almost accidentally. His original thesis after all had been on the Five Dynasties of the 9th and 10th centuries of Chinese history.

When I got back to the MU campus early in 1962, I was elected dean of the Faculty of Arts. I agreed because I was very lucky to have had two spells away in two years (in the US and then the UK) and knew it was time for me to do my share of administration. The History Department had large intakes of students, but my head John Bastin supported my election as long as I did my teaching as planned. It was all very demanding and I needed all my strength to keep up with what was going on. But it was exciting to be learning something new all the time, whether teaching my students or providing administrative services to my colleagues. I must admit that I enjoyed every moment. Looking back, I spent most time after my return on two projects. The first came from the university's decision to add a Department of Chinese Studies to those of Malay and Indian studies. The other was triggered by the series of events that had led to five distinct polities of the diminishing British Empire to agree to establish a new federation of Malaysia.

The university had hoped to attract Cheng Te-k'un 郑德坤 of the University of Cambridge to head the new Chinese Studies Department, but he would only agree to come for a year as a visiting professor. As the dean, I was asked to act as head until we could fill the chair. I had some sinology background, so I took responsibility for recruiting new staff in preparation for an intake of students in 1963. With Cheng Te-k'un's help, we prepared the new syllabus and recruited the department's first set of teaching staff. Before he left, we managed to get Ho Peng Yoke 何丙郁, the physicist who had become a historian of Chinese mathematics and science, to agree to come from Singapore to accept an appointment as professor and head of the department. I then succeeded in persuading the other visiting professor, Wolfgang Franke from Hamburg, who was truly both sinologist and historian, to take over from me as acting head. Peng Yoke arrived the next year. This gave the department a good start. For myself, I learnt a great deal more about the sinology that I had first encountered at SOAS in London.

As for the second project, it was more to do with our quest to firm up our ideas of a Malayan nation, to understand the nation as something more than simply being a polity freed of British control. Living in KL after independence reminded me that there were different expectations of nationhood that still needed to be sorted out. These were apart from some of the extreme positions taken by individual leaders. For example, on one side, Malay nationalism linked closely to Indonesia Raya and the idea of an Islamic state had been set aside; on the other, the idea of liberation by the Malayan Communist Party was about to be defeated in the jungles. In between those extremes, there was still much space for political leaders to negotiate what kind of citizenship would be best for those who chose to make Malaya their country. There was a longstanding divide between those who thought that a Malay-led partnership with the Chinese and Indian communities was the only way to share power in the country, and those who believed that everything should be done to minimize ethnic differences wherever possible. For the latter group, the sooner our leaders focused attention on livelihood interests and reduced the gap between rich and poor the better it would be for the future. But the majority of people recognized that ethnic differences would be difficult to avoid.

What was at stake was the heritage of a colonial state built on a unique mix of various bureaucracies and feudal privileges that had been thrown together in a federation that above all would require strong central control. And at its core, although poorly understood at the time, was the ideal of democratic rights to ensure that its peoples could ultimately determine their own fates.

My experience with democracy had been superficial. It was limited to that in Britain in 1955 where I had observed the Labour Party being split between the supporters of Ernest Bevan and those who sided with Hugh Gaitskell. Back in Singapore, I had seen the PAP in action before I left. I arrived at the KL campus in time to follow the Malayan elections that took place three months later. Although each of the campaigns was conducted effectively, I was never in doubt in each case which party would win, so I paid little attention to the details that would make the difference between winners and losers. It was not until I visited the US in 1960 and encountered the campaigns of Kennedy and Nixon in every city I visited that I saw how democracy could be accompanied by sustained excitement and genuine suspense. Looking back, it is clear that I had taken democracy for granted as something inevitable that came with independence. I simply had not foreseen what a difficult institution it was to manage and how it needed a strong sense of commitment to freedom to be truly representative of people's wishes.

My KL friends were keen to take me around to see some of the action leading to the elections, especially my old friend from Malaya Hall in London Tharmalingam (changed his name to Mohd Tarmizi Abdullah after he had converted to Islam). Going around with them, I soon realized that I had some kind of built-in resistance to ethnicity-based communal parties. These were exclusive in ways that I thought could not help to develop a sense of nationhood. As expected, the three communal Alliance parties won. However, I was encouraged to see that they only won with a small majority of the popular vote. Although the parties not based on distinct ethnic communities did poorly, their performance left me hopeful that their position could improve. The fact that the Pan-Malayan Islamic Party (PMIP) did better than in previous elections did make me pause, but I felt at the time that it would always be a local and regional party and would not appeal to those who were trying to build the new nation. My belief in democracy was undiminished. While I continued to keep an interest in political developments, I was mainly interested in teaching my new classes and in helping the new university to get off the ground. I was optimistic that it was a matter of time before people would learn to build a democratic and non-communal Malayan nation, and was happy to be among those providing the education that would help that development.

Producing *A Survey*

ON 27 MAY 1961, Tunku Abdul Rahman proposed the idea of "Greater Malaysia". Margaret and I were in London at the time and I was surprised by his change of heart about Singapore. I wondered what the PAP leaders would think about being Malayan when the city would now be lined up with Sarawak, Brunei and Sabah. What did it have in common with those three? I did not know enough to understand what was at stake. Also, I was struggling to finish my research on Ming-China's relations with Southeast Asia and could only have one eye on the developments. However, during the months that followed, I saw how some of the leaders in KL and Singapore were working out an outline of a possible larger federation. By the beginning of 1962, on the eve of our return to KL, I was surprised to learn that the three northern Borneo states had indicated their willingness to join. It seemed that "Greater Malaysia" was on its way to being established.

This was not a matter of scholarship but one of understanding what this "Malaysia" was. I found my colleagues as puzzled as I was how the new venture might unfold. Many would agree with what my colleague Tan Tai Yong of the National University of Singapore later described as "a contrived and complex exercise ... an artificial political creation". When I was elected dean, I thought that our faculty was the best place to provide an introduction to this new state and offered to organize a volume of essays to describe the basic conditions that made such a state possible. I found that Terry McGee in the Geography Department was particularly keen, and we approached others on our two campuses. In the end, 27 of us agreed to survey what was already known about the various states involved, and thus help us re-imagine a different Malaya. There were 17 from KL, 3 from our sister campus in Singapore, and 7 others who were either visiting our university or associated with us in another capacity. Of the last group, Robin Winks, the Commonwealth historian visiting us from Yale University, also helped us find an international publisher. We gave ourselves a year, an ambitious deadline to meet the official plan to launch the larger federation by 31 August (National Day) of 1963.

As editor of the volume, I was sensitive to the fact that I knew little about the three Borneo states apart from what I had read. I asked one of our contributors, Tom Harrisson of the Sarawak Museum, for advice to help me visit Borneo and get a better sense of what the eastern half of the new country was like. I read what was in the news, including some serious doubts among Malay and Chinese leaders, the statements made by the Malaysia Solidarity Consultative Committee, and the Cobbold Commission's report.

But just before I left on the trip, the Brunei Revolt took place in December 1962. A few weeks later President Sukarno announced his *Konfrontasi* campaign against Malaysia's formation. I set out on the trip in February 1963 as planned: three weeks in Sarawak, one in Brunei and two in Sabah. In Sarawak, Alastair Morrison of the Information Office helped me to visit local leaders of the state's First, Second and Third Divisions. He also arranged for my long drive to Brunei. In that security-conscious city, I was shown around the city by staff of the Brunei Museum and then taken to the oil town of Seria. All was calm and our conversations were confined to lifestyle and cultural topics. In Sabah, I had time only for visiting either Sandakan on the east coast or travelling into the interior. I chose the latter and followed the Padas River to Tenom and then to Keningau.

It was altogether an exhilarating experience. I did not plan the trip simply to pursue matters political, but really wanted to learn everything I could from meeting people. As it turned out, I came across open interest in the Malaysia debates only in Sarawak, where the local communist party was supported by their PKI counterparts in Indonesia to rebel against British colonial rule. Brunei was still recovering from the Revolt and no one wanted to talk about anything political. In Sabah, I failed to meet Donald Stephens, the leader of the Dusun (Kadazan) community (he was not in Jesselton) and only managed to meet state officials who were supportive but without enthusiasm. The overall impression I had was that most people were satisfied that the Cobbold Commission had understood their concerns and were willing to accept federation if certain guarantees about state rights were secured and the states would join Malaya as equals. I was content to learn that. There was so much that was new that I had more than enough to absorb during the trip. Outside of Kuching, I became specially interested in land use among the indigenous peoples, and how they saw their relationship with the distinctive mix of Malays and Chinese brought together under the Raja Brooke family, the Brunei royal house and the North Borneo Company.

In Kuching, Alastair Morrison was particularly helpful and introduced me to Malay and Dayak and other community leaders. The most willing to talk, however, were the leaders of the Sarawak United Peoples' Party (SUPP), who openly opposed the Tunku's plan. Ong Kee Hui and Stephen Yong were critical of some aspects of the plan that seemed to place Sarawak under Malayan control. They explained that they had registered their concerns with the commission and hoped that the final agreement would reflect their worries. When they learned that we were producing a book that would introduce the new Malaysia to a wider audience, they asked me to make this point clearly. I also met a friend, my medical senior from the University of Malaya in Singapore, Wong Soon Kai. He gave me a sober account of how people were divided, but thought that the whole project had been thrust rather suddenly on them before they were ready to contemplate independence. Hence they had to count on the British to give them a fair deal.

On reflection, I had tried to do too much. I have been to East Malaysia and Brunei several times since and, after each visit, I realized how little I understood after my first visit about what it meant for the people of the three states to join Malaysia. For one thing, my visit to Brunei did not help me to expect their Sultan to withdraw from the federation. The cost of that decision was high for most of my contributors. I had to ask them to take back their essays and revise all references to Brunei, including the task of redoing several tables and charts. Our publisher was very understanding but that did delay publication of the volume by nearly a year. I have painful memories of the 15 months I spent on the book and promised myself not to get so involved in contemporary affairs in future.

I had waited to write the introduction after the new federation was launched in September 1963 and was carried away by the celebratory atmosphere at the time. As a result, what I wrote sounded more optimistic than how I actually felt when I first got back from my Borneo visit. For example,

> It is hoped that, taken as a whole, the studies in this book will provide a sufficiently comprehensive picture of the new and hopeful nation in Southeast Asia.... In this growth of a multiracial nationalism, the new states in Malaysia have also important roles to play. Singapore has already shown itself sufficiently sophisticated to develop a multiracial loyalty in a predominantly Chinese city. It now has the task of demonstrating the significance of this loyalty elsewhere in the country. Sarawak and Sabah are yet to face their tests, but there are indications that they will both evolve their own versions of multiracial loyalty. Whether these versions will blend easily with the loyalty developed on the mainland must, in large measure, depend on the wisdom of the new national leadership.

President Sukarno's *Konfrontasi* campaign soon turned violent. Malaysia moved quickly to ask the United Nations for help to gain international recognition. The new state was in the news everywhere and that helped the book receive wide attention. Additional interest was generated by the political battles in the Singapore elections that followed the federation celebrations, and then by the Malaysia elections the next year in 1964. After that, there were deadly race riots in Singapore that eroded whatever trust there might have been between the national and the PAP leaders. Together with other actions that heightened fears about the tense inter-communal relations, official negotiations between KL and Singapore also failed to resolve a series of sensitive economic and administrative differences. Despite these reactions and some sceptical remarks by reviewers of the book, I recall defending my concluding remarks:

> The concept of Malaysia (is) a strictly political decision to find a more permanent place for democratic institutions in Southeast Asia. This concept has been opposed, as one would expect, by international communism. It has also been opposed by Indonesia where parliamentary democracy has

failed. Malaysia still has to solve the problems out of its multistate system and plural society and it cannot be denied that these problems are great indeed. But the democratic nations of the world wish Malaysia well and recognise that it has a historic role in Southeast Asia. Malaysia is now expected to uphold some of the finest ideals of modern history: the ideals of freedom, of democratic representation and of equality before the law. These are values which deserve to survive.

Looking back, I realized that I had been eager ever since 1949 to find my place as a citizen of Malaya and saw what I wrote in 1963 as an affirmation of my faith in the country's new manifestation. I was aware that negotiations were still going on about the details of the Singapore state's relationship with the national centre. But I did not hesitate to make such a wishful statement. At the time, it sprang from a growing hope that a Malaysia that included Singapore was the best possible result following the many years of debates and confrontations. I was therefore shocked only a year after our book was published by the announcement on 9 August 1965 that the Malaysian leaders had agreed to the separation of Singapore. I also realized, from what I had learnt from those I had met in Sarawak and Sabah, that it was no less shocking to them because they had counted on having Singapore alongside in the larger federation.

PART EIGHT

Roots

Three Generations

MANY YEARS AGO, in answer to a question about how healthy he was in his 70s, an English friend replied in a wry tone that one should choose one's parents carefully. If one could do that, I could not have chosen better. I have written in my earlier book of my childhood, about what I learnt of my father and his traditional closely-knit literati family, and included my mother's accounts of what he and his family were like. I have in an earlier chapter written about my problems with the word "love", how inadequate and misleading it was when equated with the Chinese word *ai* (爱). *Ai* was used normally to describe a mother's relationship with her children which was understood as being dutiful and caring. The father's relationships where sons were concerned was to be stern (*yan* 严). This implied a degree of distance, to underline the father's authority with an expectation that he should always be obeyed. In return, the sons in particular were taught to be filial (*xiao* 孝).

When I grew up, my mother's *ai* was unspoken but obvious, my father was reticent but never stern and the word *xiao* was used only to describe how my father felt about his parents. I never knew how that came about but *xiao* simply did not enter my relationship with my parents. Looking back, it would seem that the word *ai* had taken over, and both father and mother could be dutiful and caring, perhaps with mother's *ai* expressed more intimately and father's only with discretion. My parents clearly did their duty and there was never any doubt about how much they cared for me. Years later, I came to understand that *ai* was the correct word for the love that was dutiful and caring, and that was the way my parents felt about each other.

One element of my childhood described in *Home is not Here* remained true in later years. I was never told what I should do with my life. There were only two points about which my parents were explicit: that I should study and learn as much as I could and that I become a good person (*zuohaoren* 做好人) when I grew up. As far as my mother was concerned, my father was an example of the latter. The classical texts that he taught me were to enable me to connect with our past as Chinese. Armed with both, I should be able to find my own way in life. It was not practical guidance, but despite moments of doubt when they were worried that I might go off the rails, they had faith in me and let me decide what I should or should not do. In their subtle way, they had prepared me for a world that was increasingly different from anything that they had known. Wisely, they sensed that the world would continue to change and that I would have to learn for myself how to find my place in it. Among Chinese, our nuclear family of three was something new. Conscious of that reality, they adapted to the modernity that many of their generation living in cities and in foreign parts had begun to accept.

Once I left home to study in Singapore, I never lived with them again. I visited them during university vacations in Ipoh and then in KL, normally staying a fortnight or so. When they came to spend a year in England after my father took early retirement to do his research in the British Museum, I was at least in the same city for two months before Margaret and I moved to Cambridge. By the time we moved to London, they were heading back to Malaya. On our return to Singapore in 1957, we were happy that they had chosen to live and work there. We saw each other most weekends. Less than two years later, we moved to KL. My parents had plans to move to KL too, but my father's appointment as principal of Foon Yew High School in Johor Bahru (JB) that year meant that we were again separated. When we built our new house in Petaling Jaya, Margaret planned an extension for when they would move in with us after my father retired. But before that happened, I had accepted a job at the Australian National University and we moved to Canberra.

Here I shall summarize our failure to live together as a three-generation family and jump ahead of our story to our time in Australia after 1968. My parents saw the two moves that I made, to KL and to Canberra, as being good for my career and accepted them without hesitation. They were content that, after my father's retirement, we would live together. It was not to be. After we went to Canberra, the 13 May 1969 riots in KL and the emergency turnarounds in national policies made it less attractive for me to return to the University of Malaya. By 1971, Margaret and I had decided that I should stay on at ANU. My father had retired by then and my parents visited us in Canberra, in part to attend the Orientalists Congress being held there but in part also to find out what it would be like to live there. Unfortunately, my father caught a bad cold and spent the last few days in bed. My mother decided that Canberra life would not suit them and that they would now plan to remain in JB. The next year, when we were to go to England for three months, we arranged for our children to stay with them and attend my father's Foon Yew School. My parents were really happy with that but, sadly for all of us, it was while the children were there that my father died of a heart attack. He was buried in JB and my mother wanted to remain close for a while and did not come to live with us until four years later.

Margaret and I rarely planned far ahead, but one of the few plans we did make was to prepare for the day when my parents would live with us after my father retired. We would then all be under one roof. Years later, when Margaret wrote of our time in Singapore and KL, she wanted our children to understand my parents.

What was happening to Yeye and Nainai (Gungwu's father and mother)? They had returned to Singapore from London and were living in some rooms in a Chinese school teachers' hostel. Like the housing provided for staff in China, Chinese schools in Singapore also provided housing for their staff. The housing wasn't very good, but if you needed somewhere to stay, you could rent a room or two in such hostels. Yeye and Nainai were settled in one of these hostels. They had a maid who stayed at the same hostel and cooked for them at the communal kitchen. Yeye did not get his master's degree from London University as he never really registered for a course. He may have thought it not worth his time or trouble. Gungwu never asked his father why he didn't do what he went to London to do. Among traditional Chinese fathers and sons, communication was always awkward. The mother was the conduit through which dialogue took place and the kind of open discussion that sons today have with their fathers was not so common then. Actually, it still is a problem among men. Daughters find it easier to talk to their fathers.

Nainai and Yeye had some idea that they would run a bookshop after his retirement. As Yeye had very little money, having saved little throughout the years, this didn't seem very feasible to me. Also he was the last person to be able to run a business. He would very likely have not accepted payment from customers if they were his friends and thus make huge losses. Nainai knew nothing of the world of business so it seemed to be an impossible dream.

Towards the end of 1958, the board of Foon Yew Secondary School in Johor Bahru (JB) tried to recruit Yeye to be its headmaster. At that time, the school was known for its radical students, low staff morale and poor financial circumstances. It was certainly not an attractive job to take up. Nainai thought he should do it, although Yeye didn't feel he could manage the school with all those negative features. However, after much soul searching, he decided to go to JB. It was to be one of the best decisions he could have made.

Yeye transformed the school. Firstly, he set a very good example by cutting his own salary from $800 to $700. Then he refused to have anything to do with money, leaving the finances entirely to the relevant section of the administration. The Wang family was noted for not having business connections. This stood them in good stead where financial probity was concerned. He left the tenders for books and so on in the hands of the financial director. This meant that no one could say that any money went through his hands. A lot of money goes through a school. The kickbacks for school supplies alone could make you rich if you were corrupt. Just imagine hundreds of copies of every textbook to be ordered and the opportunities for kickbacks would have been very tempting. But Yeye brought a culture of honesty and integrity to the school, so by the time he left, ten years later, the school not only had a few more buildings built for an increased enrolment, it had a surplus of $250,000 in its coffers, a huge sum in those days.

Yeye also improved the curriculum and tried to get better teachers. Chinese schoolteachers were paid less than government teachers. They had no tenure and were usually on one-year contracts. This was very demoralizing as you can imagine. The reason for this was that the school never knew whether their student numbers would remain stable. As private institutions, they depended on the fees for their operating funds so unless the students stayed and paid up, there might not be enough to pay all the teachers the following year. Yeye not only stabilized the student numbers, he increased the enrolment to double the number he started out with so that the school started to flourish. Today, the school has moved to new premises as its student numbers are now in the thousands.

By the time Yeye finally retired in 1969 he could truly be proud of his achievements. Although he was highly respected when he had been the inspector of Chinese schools, Yeye had been looked upon simply as a civil servant. In other words, he was merely seen as one who carried out British policies. He didn't initiate them. But as the headmaster of an independent school, he could shape the school to his vision of what it should be and this he succeeded in doing.

At his wake in February 1972, I will never forget what one of his former students said to me. He said that Yeye had turned him from a "liumang" 流氓, something equivalent to a gang member, to a respected citizen with a good job. Yeye inspired all his students to be good people. The young man then said that Yeye had gained a tremendous amount of "glory" from his contribution as an educationist, which he could take with him to his after-life. I was very moved to hear that Yeye was so much appreciated by his former students and colleagues. So, towards the end of his life, he finally received the recognition he deserved.

We Build A House

IT IS HARD to imagine today how a young couple could afford to build their own house after less than eight years in employment. This was possible because it was the University of Malaya's policy to encourage its local academic staff to build their own homes and offered housing loans at low interest rates to enable them to do so. That freed university housing for newly-appointed expatriate staff. Also it was fortunate that land was plentiful and inexpensive, especially in a new town like Petaling Jaya. When the policy came into effect, we looked at the new sections of the town that were being opened up and found a plot of land that suited us, big enough to build an extended house for us and my parents when my father retired, and in a cul-de-sac that assured us of privacy. Once again, it was Margaret who had the ideas as to what should be done.

After we came back from England (in 1962), we moved twice: once to a temporary house behind the Methodist Primary School in Petaling Jaya and then to a university house in Lorong Ilmu, new quarters which had just been built. The area was adjacent to the new university hospital and the houses were built around a horseshoe piece of land. They were spacious—four bedrooms, with the servants' quarters at the back, and totally undeveloped gardens. As the first tenants, we had to put in plants to give ourselves a pleasant garden to live with. University houses at that time were provided with "basic" furniture. That is, they were equipped with wooden furniture for the living and dining rooms, and beds and bedside tables for the bedrooms. There were also desks and chairs for the study. We had to supply mattresses, curtains, a refrigerator and other furnishings that we wanted or needed. I would say that the university was quite generous to the staff as the houses were also fully maintained by the estates office and we never needed to find workmen ourselves for any defects in the houses. We also bought one air-conditioner for the study and later, when we felt richer, another one for the bedroom. It was considered a luxury to have any air-conditioner at all and we usually used ceiling fans to stir the hot and humid air. We were accustomed to the heat and lived quite comfortably.

In 1962, there was a move to build private housing for the staff. The university was considering a loan system which would encourage the staff to buy their own home. The locals were mostly for it as it would mean that they would be able to own their own homes. I knew that Yeye and Nainai expected to live with us after Yeye's retirement.

Yeye and Nainai still had old notions of what retirement and a scholar's life meant. Yeye had the idea that he would help Gungwu with his research and they would write books together. That sort of dream would have been possible in the old China, but scholars were no longer reclusive people, spending their days discussing philosophy or poetry. Gungwu was an active person and he was as much an academic leader and administrator as scholar. I don't think Yeye really understood this about his own son. In any case, Gungwu never used any research assistants. He always preferred to do his own research as he felt he couldn't trust anyone else to see what he could see, or interpret what is or is not important. He has never employed a research assistant to this day. Yeye could not have lived his retirement through Gungwu's activities.

Yeye was still working, and though he had a tough time as headmaster of Foon Yew Chinese School, he also enjoyed the challenge of running a large school. He was highly respected by the Chinese community as he was a good headmaster, who brought the school to high standards of academic achievement and enlarged the school population considerably. As a result, the school board continued to urge him to keep on working and he did so until he was about 65.

I devised a method by which we could live together after Yeye's retirement but not in the same house. I decided to design a house which had separate quarters for the grandparents, now commonly known as a "granny flat" adjoining the main house. Petaling Jaya was still being developed and the PJ Corporation was eager to sell land to people. We were offered a very choice piece of land that had a large level area but was below the road level. It was bordering an old rubber estate to the east, with a slope like a ravine in front and half an acre in size. We had a great deal of privacy as we had only one neighbour to the left, facing the slope. We could build an extremely nice house on that site. I commissioned our friend Chen Voon Fee and his architectural firm, Design 4, to come up with a plan for a large house with four bedrooms, a large study, sitting room, dining, terraces for outdoor living and an attached flat for the grandparents. I had no intention of building a small pokey place for Yeye and Nainai as I wanted them to be happy with their new home.

Design 4 came up with a very grand plan, with the main entrance at the first floor, going down stairs to the ground level where the living and dining would be. Immediately to the right of the hall was a wide staircase which led downstairs to the main living rooms. There was a separate set of stairs at the back of the carport leading down to the grandparents' flat. The flat was spacious, being more than 1,000 square feet, with a sitting/dining room, large study and a bedroom with bathroom and its own kitchen. They also had a room for their own maid.

We had a multiracial group of friends and English was the language of discourse with them. Nainai knew no English and would be very uncomfortable with these friends. We also entertained a lot, so where would the grandparents eat when we did that? They had no idea of the kind of parties we had so it was impractical for us to share the same sitting and dining rooms, let alone the kitchen! This way, they could have their own servant and cook their own meals and entertain their own friends. The flat shared a common wall with us on the ground floor, their sitting room shared our living room wall and their whole flat was on one floor with ready access to the garden. It was a lovely flat and would be considered spacious even today.

So we started on this enterprise. It was quite exciting. I had already helped Yeye and Nainai build their investment house in PJ, a small bungalow near the university, so I could read architects' plans. We had also lived in numerous houses by then, so we had a good idea of what we liked and needed. Generally, I felt that space was the most important thing, as with adequate space no extensions would be needed for the future. We had our three children and didn't intend to have any more. We drew up a plan for a large bedroom for the girls that could be divided when they grew up. Our study was next to our bedroom. Unlike most people, whose study would be away from the sleeping quarters, we had already developed a habit of working late, especially Gungwu, so having the study next to the bedroom was sensible so that he could easily go to bed when he was finished for the day. We have stuck to this all our married life.

We managed to get everything done and started to build in the middle of 1964. Fortunately, Gungwu left all the decisions to me and only asked that we have a large study. The architects were grateful for that because couples often contradicted each other and gave conflicting instructions. We ended up with a magnificent design with spectacular views to the front as there was a huge gap between us and the house opposite, and we had greenery to our right with the forest reserve. The front of the house had a huge terrace where we often entertained.

It happened that at the time our house was finished, my youngest brother Henry and his wife Helene had to move as their lease had run out. We both got the idea that it would be marvellous to have them stay in the flat while Gungwu's parents were still in JB. It would give us a kind of extended family and the children would benefit from having an aunt and uncle in the vicinity. They moved in with us and stayed for three years. We lived very amicably with each other until they decided to build their own house and we prepared to leave for Australia. The children benefited greatly too by having someone other than parents and servants to turn to. They loved visiting their aunt, who was a scientist. She could encourage Ming when he needed to know something we couldn't provide him with. Henry and Helene didn't have any children then and were very indulgent towards ours. The children would often be found in their aunt's living room watching their TV in the afternoons, as they were only allowed to watch TV at restricted times in our house.

This experiment with a kind of extended family was very good for all of us and made me feel that the traditional extended family, provided there was enough space so that everyone had enough privacy, was a good thing. You certainly did not have the kind of pressure on parents that the nuclear family faces today.

We moved in sometime in May 1965 but we were to live in that house for only a little more than three years. I knew, when we decided to go to Australia, that we would never live in a house like that in Australia. It wasn't until we went to Hong Kong that we would have a grander house! I was sentimental about that house as we had built it and I had had so much to do with it, so I made the mistake of not selling it, hoping that we would come back after three years and live there again. In hindsight, that was impractical and subsequent events were to prove that I had been wrong.

Our new house in Petaling Jaya, designed by Chen Voon Fee to Margaret's specifications.

Settling Down

OUR SON MING had a good start in his education the year we were in London. At age four, he went to the pre-prep school at Muswell Hill where the teachers made sure he could read and write. I still recall the moment in London when he surprised us by reading a face cream advertisement on television. On our return to KL, he still had to wait another year before being able to attend school. He was always asking for books to read so we did what we could to satisfy him. We could see that his life of learning had got off to a good start. Margaret records her concerns as we began to settle down.

There were few kindergartens in those days. Children started school at seven so there was a long wait before a child had formal schooling. There were some private kindergartens, and one such was run by a pair of sisters who were friends of Yeye and Nainai. We sent our daughters there until they could attend a primary school. Ming already knew how to read and had a fantastic memory. So when he started school and found that he had to learn ABC again, he refused to go. Fortunately, the headmistress knew us and agreed that it was absurd for him to be in a class where no one could read when he was already reading children's encyclopaedias. She put him in the next class and he settled down to school.

So we lived this busy life while our family grew strong and healthy. Gungwu was involved in helping to develop his History Department and taking part in the governance of the university. I was busy trying to improve the language skills of my students and, apart from minor health and other normal domestic problems, our lives went on very productively.

During the weekends we would take the children out for drives and to visit playgrounds and so on. When there were holidays we went to the East Coast, to Kelantan and Trengganu. Once, I had to run a holiday course for teachers in Malacca, and Gungwu drove the children to see me at the weekend. We stayed at the Malacca Rest House. The British built such rest houses in each town in the country. These were like inns where officials on duty could stay. They were run mostly by Hainanese who, for historical reasons, were often owners of coffee shops and certain types of restaurants. These rest houses were cheap places to stay and members of the public could also stay in them. They were rather charming buildings, built in the bungalow style with wide verandahs and a restaurant inside. The rooms were spacious and were usually suites of a large sitting room and a bedroom with a bathroom attached.

The children in Trengganu, 1967.

When I was dean, we were all surprised when our history professor John Bastin suddenly announced that he was resigning to go to London. The university was still following British practice in having a single professor as head of each department. Whoever replaced John would have to be responsible for the department as well. I had been content to continue with my interests in the history of China–Southeast Asian relations together with some new work on the overseas Chinese in our region, and remain the lecturer teaching East Asian history. I certainly did not think I was ready to apply for the chair and headship of the department. My friends and colleagues encouraged me at least to put my hat in.

In August 1963, I was offered the appointment as professor. I thus felt that I should return full-time to the department and concentrate on building it up. I asked that I be allowed to step down after being dean for only one year. With my faculty and the university's agreement that I could do so, I accepted the appointment and moved back immediately.

The history headship was a challenging job and I loved every moment of the five years I was responsible for the department's development. The university was expanding and large numbers of students chose to take history. Our staff numbers were still small. Alastair Lamb and I had joined the department in 1959. Alastair taught South and Central Asian history and had a keen interest in early Indian influences and archaeological work in the archipelago. John Bastin invited two of our Singapore colleagues, David Bassett and Mary Turnbull, to join us to teach different periods of Southeast Asian history. Brian Peacock came to us from the National Museum as the region's archaeologist to work closely with Alastair.

As I recall it, the department recruited Jan Pluvier to be our first Indonesian specialist. John Frodsham whom I had met in Cambridge was recruited to be the other historian of China. He was working on the journals of Guo Songtao 郭松焘, the first Chinese ambassador to the UK in 1875–78, so he was asked to teach modern Chinese history. He was followed by a specialist in Sino-Russian history, a European history expert, a historian of political thought, and someone who could teach aspects of Malay-Polynesian history.

After a few years, while the department continued to grow, some of them moved on. So we not only had to recruit new staff but also had to replace those who left. I managed to get William Roff and Anthony Reid to join us, Bill to teach Malay-Muslim history and Tony to focus on the modern history of the Malay Archipelago. The department was also fortunate to get external help from visitors who offered our students some different historical perspectives: scholars from SOAS London and Yale University came, as well as five Fulbright visitors: two to start courses on US history, and three others who specialized on Indonesia, Thailand and Burma respectively. By this time, historians and political scientists interested in the region became regular visitors and we invited them to talk to our students. I believe our students were especially excited to meet Arnold Toynbee and hear his views on where Southeast Asia fitted into his history of civilizations.

We had also begun to recruit from our MU Singapore alumni: two to teach aspects of Malaya-Singapore history, one to teach economic history, and two others who worked on the Netherlands East Indies and modern Indonesia. I then persuaded Khoo Kay Kim and Rollins Bonney to work on 19th-century Malay States for their master's degrees. They produced two very fine studies that were accepted for publication by Oxford University Press and soon joined the staff. In addition, we looked out for local scholars who had graduated from other universities and we were able to get Zainal Abidin Wahid and James P. Ongkili (both from the University of Queensland), Stephen Leong from UCLA, and Goh Cheng Teik from Harvard to join us. Planning ahead, we obtained scholarships for our own graduates, one to Berkeley to work on the rise of American interests in Asia, another to study diplomatic history in London, and one who, in response to Afro-Asian aspirations, went to Ibadan, Nigeria to study sub-Saharan Africa. All three returned to teach in the department just before I left. I had hoped to persuade other promising students to study the history of the Malay states but in the end several chose to join the civil service instead.

We had also begun to attract graduate students from abroad. Among them were those who came on Commonwealth scholarships: from Australia, India, Hong Kong, New Zealand and East Africa. Several went on to academic careers in other universities. I was particularly interested in the research subjects of Raj Vasil from India, James Allen from Kenya and Michael Stenson from New Zealand. All worked on Malayan/Malaysian history and published their scholarly monographs. Together with a large number of bright young undergraduates, the department soon became a lively centre of activity and there was never a dull moment during the decade I spent there.

By the time I left in 1968, I could say that our department was developing into one that was not only diverse, with the capacity to teach in a wide range of fields, but also one of the strongest in Malaysian and Southeast Asian history. Our main interest remained that of Southeast Asian history, while building our capacity in Malaysian history to serve as its core. But we also provided courses that helped our students gain a good understanding of regions that would always be relevant to the country, especially South and East Asia, the West (Europe and America) and the Afro-Asian new nations. The foreign service thought our graduates performed well and its then head, Ghazali Shafiee, encouraged me to establish a division within the department that enabled the students to combine modern history of the region and beyond with a basic knowledge of politics and international relations. I believed that history was an excellent discipline for producing graduates whose historical knowledge helped them better serve the country, and made my position clear in my inaugural lecture "The Use of History". I believe that I had done my best to give our students a balanced range of courses that made them knowledgeable and useful citizens. Years later, I was proud to see Khoo Kay Kim as head of the department place on record the first 25 years of the department's work.

I continued to teach a full load but cut down on my Chinese history course to give a new course on the Theory and Method of History to those who wished to learn about the history of historical writings. I must admit that this was a course that I really enjoyed, not only in giving the lectures but also tutoring some of our best students in small groups. It was such a pleasure to see my students enjoy discovering the different approaches to the past among different peoples and learn to question the value of some kinds of history writing. After 1965, as we had larger intakes from the Malay-medium secondary schools, we began to grade essays, hold tutorials and conduct examinations in the national language. It was gratifying to know how well some of these students did after graduation.

While I was immersed in such new ventures, Margaret was making good progress as one of the country's experts on the teaching of English as a second language. In her story for our children about how we were settling down to our careers in the country, this was how she remembered the five years before we decided, for the sake of my professional development, to go to Australia in order to resume work on the Chinese history that I had set aside for some time.

In the meantime, I was working at the Malayan Teachers' College (MTC) at Pantai Hill, just next door to the university. This college was established to train teachers for secondary schools. They would teach the humanities and English as a second language.

There was a lot of controversy about the education policy at that time. The government wanted to introduce Malay as the medium of instruction for all national, that is, government-funded, schools. This would mean the phasing out of all English-medium schools. The Chinese language schools would have to teach the national curriculum and include Malay as a compulsory course. However, they were allowed to continue as private schools. For the pupils' good, they had to teach Malay or these pupils would not be able to enter any of the universities, then the only ones existing in the country. So a large number of teachers would have to be trained for these new schools, while still maintaining English as a second language in the country.

I found to my pleasure, that one of my former classmates at university, Dulcie Navaratnam, later to become Dulcie Abraham, was the head of the English Department at the college. I enjoyed teaching there very much. My main concern was that our students were not well-qualified in English. I argued that they should all have at least obtained a credit in their English, and not just with a pass, at the end of their sixth form or Higher School Certificate. I suppose there were just not enough students with a credit. Many thought of their time at the college, which came with an allowance, as a pathway to university, and many did indeed leave after teaching after a few years to go to university.

After two years, Dulcie transferred to the MTC in Johor Bahru. She became head of the English Department there and asked me to take over as head in KL. I took over because I was the most senior local by that time and I felt I could do the job. I was to head the department until we left for Australia in August 1968.

Margaret then goes on to tell our children what she thought I had achieved at MU and why they should be proud of me.

I realized that Gungwu was making a name for himself. He was appointed professor of History before his 33rd birthday, in 1963. Unlike his student days, he worked very hard, writing his lectures, writing for publications, being active in civil affairs and on the campus.

He had a phenomenal memory for names and could remember his students' names after meeting them once. This impressed them no end! He was also very level headed and his opinions much sought after. Most people did not realize how young he was. His early study on the Nanhai Trade was published in 1958. His series of radio lectures came out in Singapore as a history of the Nanyang Chinese. MU then published his thesis, "The Structure of Power in North China during the Five Dynasties", and this was reprinted by the Stanford University Press. In the meantime, he also wrote articles about the categories of Malayan Chinese and their political inclinations. Many scholars found the categories helpful when they tried to analyze the Chinese overseas.

When we look back at the University of Malaya, it was a great period in our lives. We were building a new university both physically and academically. Recruitment was worldwide so we had an interesting assortment of academics, some already famous. Our pay was good for those days and there was a lot of respect for university staff. There was C.J. Eliezer, the famous professor of mathematics from Ceylon. There were also Rayson Huang, the professor of chemistry who was also dean of the Faculty of Science and then vice- chancellor of Nanyang University in Singapore and, after that, of the University of Hong Kong. There were several other young academics who would later become professors in other universities after they left. And Gungwu made his early reputation there.

When we left KL, we still thought that we could return after a few years away. But when Margaret wrote for our children decades later, it was some kind of closure on a chapter in our lives. Our children were then very young, and happy where they were. I imagine that they might have been a little puzzled why we were moving again, this time to a country far away. I also think that this was Margaret's way of saying why she agreed to my move to the ANU. She made it sound as if she had no regrets about leaving the new house that we all liked so much. I know better, but Margaret was not one to let any regrets stop her from starting again. She would build another very liveable house in Canberra, one that we lived in for 15 years.

PART NINE

The Unexpected

1965: Down Under

IN AN EARLIER chapter, I mentioned the shock that I felt when, on 9 August 1965, it was announced that Singapore had separated from Greater Malaysia. That night, watching the news on TV, I was surprised to see Lee Kuan Yew cry. I was in transit on the way home from Australia at the time, and all the way on my flight back, I wondered how the break with KL happened. Was he not partly responsible? When our plane landed in Singapore to change planes to KL, I heard firecrackers celebrating the state's liberation and its unexpected independence as a republic. I did not share in the joy. Instead, what came to mind was that the economic fulcrum of West and East Malaysia had been removed. The original ideal of Malaya was now diminished and replaced by what was Tanah Melayu with Sarawak and Sabah added on under the new name, a country that was uneasily extended across a sea of fresh uncertainty.

Looking back, I had for too long taken for granted that Singapore was part of Malaya. When Malaysia was proposed, I was in London and thought that the idea would be acceptable for most people in the five polities concerned. Even when I heard a few months later that the PAP in Singapore was split on this issue, I felt confident that most people there would agree to join the federation. Thus, on my return in 1962, in my capacity as dean of MU's Arts faculty, I led my colleagues in introducing this Malaysia to the world. After my visit to the northern Borneo states, I was a little less certain that all was well but still thought that the "Malaysian Malaysia" slogan devised by Singapore, Sarawak and Sabah leaders would help the new political entity. Although controversial, the referendum that Singapore conducted in 1962 seemed to confirm majority support. Looking on from afar in KL, I was not convinced that my Socialist Club friends who sided with the Barisan Socialis and were detained by Operation Coldstore in early 1963 were communists. And I still thought that Singapore was essential to Malaysia for it to be successful. The federation was altogether a very complex mix of states and the leaders concerned had negotiated carefully to manage its creation and could therefore be counted on to persevere.

That was why I set aside any doubts I might have had and continued to spend much of my time dealing with matters related to Malaysia. After the launch of our *Survey* book in 1964, I was involved in a committee to investigate the 1964 Singapore race riots (it had a preliminary meeting in January 1965), and another to regulate traditional medical practices (report completed in May). I was also asked to chair a curriculum review committee to help Nanyang University in Singapore get its degrees recognized in the country, a report that was accepted to my surprise by the government of Singapore in September, after it separated from Malaysia.

At the same time, I was invited to be the inaugural Asia Fellow (May–August 1965) at the Australian National University (ANU). This was totally unexpected. It was the result of an embarrassing incident involving the ANU and the Australian government. Prime Minister Robert Menzies had, without consultation, announced that the King of Thailand would be awarded an honorary doctorate by the ANU. The university's professorial board thought this was contrary to university practice and declined to proceed. Menzies was furious but the ANU would not budge. Instead, a few months later, to show that the refusal was not directed against Thailand, the university established the Asia Fellowship in honour of the King. The first two fellowships were awarded in 1965, one to Prince Suphadradis Diskul, the Thai art historian and archaeologist of Silpakorn University and the other to me. I was given to understand that I was to help the ANU's Research School of Pacific Studies develop historical research on Southeast Asia, especially that of Malaysia. So 1965 was a year when Malaysia was very much on my mind. Therefore, coming back from the ANU on the day of separation to face yet another re-imagining of Malaya/Malaysia was something like having an unpalatable meal served up at a celebratory banquet.

As it turned out, the ANU invitation was a fateful one for us. It introduced us to Australia in the best possible way, as guests to its unique research university, with the opportunity to also visit other universities in three of its great cities, Adelaide, Melbourne and Sydney. We did not know it at the time, but the visit not only influenced my later career but also changed the lives of our family.

I had some knowledge of Asian studies in Australia and was aware that Sydney University long had a Department of Japanese Studies and had begun to develop China Studies and Indonesian Studies. I was also told that the new Monash University in Melbourne was starting a major Centre for Southeast Asian Studies. As for the ANU, I had heard that its Faculty of Asian Studies taught Chinese, Japanese and Indonesian, and its Asian Civilisation Department also covered South and Southeast Asian languages and cultures. The Research School of Pacific Studies had two History departments, one for Pacific history and the other for Far Eastern history. A third History Department was not justified, so Pacific history had made a start in Southeast Asian history. I also knew that the first scholar it appointed was my predecessor John Bastin, but he left shortly afterwards to join us in KL and was then in London.

Several of my historian friends and colleagues had New Zealand backgrounds: Harry Benda and Bill Roff had studied at Wellington, Anthony Reid was a New Zealander and so were two of our graduate students. And there were several others in our departments of Geography, Mathematics, Engineering and Agriculture. So I decided to take the opportunity to visit New Zealand first and call on my former colleague Terry McGee in Wellington and the British historian Nicholas Tarling in Auckland. Both had made their names writing on Southeast Asia and were actively promoting the study of the region.

At the ANU, I was hosted in the Pacific History Department, where Jim Davidson had been keen to locate Southeast Asian history. He had scholars like Emily Sadka, Png Poh Seng and Chiang Hai Ding from MU Singapore do their PhDs there. I also discovered that there were other students from the region at the ANU, but only two were doing history, both graduates from Nanyang University in Singapore: Yen Ching-hwang in the Far Eastern History Department and Yong Ching Fatt in the History Department of the Faculty of Arts. In short, despite the strong start, the field of Southeast Asian history was still unsecured. I was keen to see it developed, and Jim Davidson encouraged me to visit the other universities in the neighbouring states to find out what was happening.

I waited for Margaret to join me before visiting the other universities. We visited the University of Adelaide where Hugh Stretton assured me of his support for the teaching of Southeast Asian history but his colleagues seemed more interested in the history of China and Japan and his department later appointed Yen Ching-hwang. In Melbourne, however, the commitment at Monash University under John Legge to Southeast Asian studies was clear. Also, it had a close link with Malaysia through old friends like Jamie Mackie and my former colleague Cyril Skinner.

As for the many students from Malaysia in the Universities of Sydney and New South Wales, their interests were not in history. I was thus able to return to Canberra and urge ANU to develop historical studies in the Pacific History Department. I was familiar with conditions in the UK and the US, and had concluded that, through the ANU, together with the new centre at Monash, Australia could become one of the strongest centres of Southeast Asian research in the world. Looking back, I was to see many of the finest Southeast Asian historians do their graduate degrees at these two universities. Among those from MU's History Department alone, I recall Lim Teck Ghee and Cheah Boon Kheng graduating from ANU, and Lee Kam Hing and Khasnor Johan from Monash. All of them were later to make major contributions to the study of Malaysian and Southeast Asian history.

After reporting my observations to Jim Davidson, I felt that I had done my duty as Asia Fellow. But the task made me aware that my position was somewhat ambivalent. From the time I did my honours in history at MU, I had been moving towards the study of Chinese history, including work on Ming China's relations with Southeast Asia and the history of the Chinese in the region. My appointment as head of history did lead me to do more in Malaysian and Southeast Asian history, but my reputation in Europe as well as in the US was mainly as a China historian. And, during my visit to ANU, it was the Far Eastern History colleagues who knew my work: C.P. Fitzgerald knew that I was in Nanjing when he was head of the British Council there, Wang Ling 王铃 and Lo Hui-min 骆惠敏 had known me in Cambridge, and Andrew Fraser worked on Japan at SOAS when I was writing about 10th-century China. As for Igor de Rachewiltz, we had attended the New York conference on Confucian personalities together. Similarly, Goran Malmqvist, the head of the Chinese Department, and his colleagues Liu Tsun-yan 柳存仁 and Rafe de Crespigny all made me feel very welcome as one of them.

It was also during my visit that I managed to complete my paper for John Fairbank's conference on the Chinese World Order. Because of my commitments at MU, I was unable to attend, but sent the paper off to Fairbank. He included it in the published volume as a contribution to Chinese history and to our understanding of the Ming tributary system.

At the same time, others in Australia saw me as the editor of the new *Survey* book on Malaysia that officials dealing with Southeast Asia were consulting. I was invited to several meetings to talk about Malaysia and Indonesia. The night before I left Canberra, I had dinner with some of those in foreign affairs, and the next day, 9 August, I was meeting those in charge of the Malaysia desk for lunch when they were called away to deal with the news of Singapore's separation from Malaysia. I was struck by how they were equally in the dark about that sudden event. Thus, on the eve of my return to KL, I began to see that I might have to make a choice about the future direction of my work. Should my priority be the study of China or should I concentrate more on learning about Malaysian and Southeast Asian history?

1965: Reorient

I SUGGESTED EARLIER that 1965 was a transformative year, but I did not feel its effects until its second half, especially after August. The earlier months had kept me very busy, but I was happy to be active for what I thought were good causes and when everything seemed positive and predictable. That began to change when I thought that Malaysia was diminished due to Singapore's separation. But I had little time to get used to that before an even more dramatic event really shifted the goalposts for everyone in the region.

I refer to the coup attempt in Indonesia, which came to be known as Gestapu. We were hosting a friendly dinner at home for friends and colleagues and our guests included my dear friend Asraf and our Indonesian specialist Jay Maryanov. We were settling down after our meal when we heard a radio report of what had been happening that day following the assassination of six Indonesian generals in the early hours of the morning. The report called it a communist plot, and I recall that both Asraf and Jay could not believe that the Parti Kommunis Indonesia (PKI) would be that stupid. No one expected that what we heard was only the beginning and that the terrible consequences of the failed coup would follow for the next few weeks and months. In the end, to wide disbelief, the shocking events resulted in the total destruction of the PKI. No one could have imagined that the party, with its estimated two million members, could have been wiped out so quickly and thoroughly.

Many at the time were inclined to see communism in our region as largely one end of the anti-colonial nationalist spectrum. The PKI was, after all, a legal party that stood for elections and had shown its ability to win votes and seemed to have been nationalist in orientation. It was therefore all the more surprising to witness the nationwide fury that descended on the party, one that ended with hundreds of thousands killed, including a large number of Indonesian Chinese, and also with thousands of other Chinese being shipped to China.

I confess to have been horrified to learn what happened during the rest of the year. For a while, it was difficult to know whom to believe. My expert friends were themselves divided, ranging from those who grudgingly accepted the official accounts by the Indonesian military that blamed it all on the PKI, to those who claimed that it was the work of military factions that wanted to see the end of Sukarno. Some would argue that some of the factions were also collaborating with Anglo-American Cold War strategists who set out to counter Sukarno's anti-Malaysia Konfrontasi campaigns.

The events and the debates that followed led me to re-examine my own understanding of what nationalism in our region might mean. I began to realize how over-simple I had been in my hopes for Malaysia when I was producing the *Survey*. The events during the year that followed the book's publication were a rude awakening that forced me to reassess the difficult road ahead, especially for a multicommunal society like Malaysia that was still battling to define its path towards a new kind of nation.

Other transformative events later in 1965 were also reaching a climax, notably the advances of the Viet Cong in South Vietnam that led President Johnson to commit more US forces in preparation for a decisive war. And, further north, in China, reports of political infighting marked the opening shots of the Great Proletarian Cultural Revolution. I shall write more about the latter in the next chapter.

Closer to home that year, I was personally drawn into political developments that were not unrelated to the ideological struggles the Cold War was bringing to the region. I was actively involved in the building of a new university in KL and had just completed the Malaysia *Survey* volume where I was conscious of the higher education needs of the new Malaysia. So I readily accepted early in 1965 the invitation to chair a committee to review the Nanyang University curriculum. The committee consisted of three Nanyang University representatives and three other Singapore representatives (one from the Ministry of Education) and also professor of Physics, Thong Saw Pak. We had started meeting in January and completed our report in May, in time for me to leave for the ANU.

Most of our meetings were held on campus where, after we had been through the relevant documents, we also met dozens of representatives of the university's staff and students.

There had been two earlier reports in 1959 on the university: the Prescott Committee Report commented on the university's weaknesses and was followed a few months later by the Gwee Ah Leng Committee Report, which had a close focus on local conditions. This second report made a number of proposals but did not recommend recognition of the university's degrees.

The committee that I chaired looked at curriculum changes that would help the university to gain equal status as the third officially recognized institute of higher learning. It was concerned that the university should produce graduates who could serve the country the way the other two universities did. Recognition would enable its graduates to compete for positions they had not been able to apply for since the university's inauguration. Every member of the committee shared my view that this was most desirable, especially when we all knew that the Nanyang University students were the brightest students from all the Chinese high schools, whose services would be of great benefit to the country's future development. We took it as given that they would continue to teach in Chinese. Given that they were very efficient in the language they would have an advantage over other graduates if they had stronger English language skills and, for those who were fluent in Malay as well, that advantage would be even greater. We saw how they could become great assets in our multicultural society and were confident that would justify strong funding and full recognition of Nanyang degrees by the government. I was probably more optimistic than some of my colleagues in believing that most students could become more or less trilingual, but everyone agreed that if they did, they would not only have the skills to be good scholars but also be far more useful than those who were monolingual, or even bilingual, in meeting the country's needs.

Nanyang University was located in Singapore but served the whole of Malaysia and our report was written with that in mind. It would have been ideal if the education it offered could eventually also have attracted more adventurous students from English and Malay-medium schools who were prepared to become trilingual. But first of all, it needed to gain recognition from both the Singapore state and the national government in KL and be treated as equal to the two universities that were already recognized. No one anticipated that, three months after we submitted our report, Singapore and Malaysia would part ways.

Although we were aware that there were political considerations in the background, none of us thought of our report in terms of the political battles prevailing at the time. We thought we should only consider the educational ambitions that would ensure the official recognition of Nanyang University degrees, which could contribute to the uplifting of the nation. I do not know what the other committee members thought when Singapore left the Malaysia federation. When I returned from Canberra, three months had passed since the report's submission in May. We heard nothing about the report, and I was soon deeply immersed in my departmental duties in KL. I recall thinking that the report was no longer relevant since an independent Singapore would have to re-examine its *national* priorities. Thus I was taken aback when the Singapore government announced in September that the report was accepted and would be acted upon as soon as possible.

Nothing the committee did had taken into account the political struggles in Singapore, not least over the issue of joining Malaysia in the first place. We were conscious that elections had been held soon after Malaysia had been established, and that many leaders of the opposition, including several of my friends of the MU Socialist Club, had been detained without trial. The committee was therefore careful to concentrate on what was educationally appropriate for the third university in the larger federation, and avoided partisan politics altogether. However, when the separation created a newly-independent country, the struggles about who should now lead Singapore became more passionate. And our report had become controversial, in large part because the opposition focused on the threat it implied to the future of Chinese language education. Now that Singapore was independent and was a country with a majority Chinese population, such a threat in their minds was totally unacceptable.

Given the circumstances, the rejection of the report would have been understandable, but the ferocity of the attacks against it was greater than anyone expected. Similarly, many were surprised by the very tough measures taken by the government against the students who were thought to have supported the political opposition. I was disappointed by the extreme reactions, not least by parts of the Chinese press that singled me out for attack as someone who had set out to destroy Chinese education, something totally alien to my thinking. All these attacks are on record and the subject has been written up by a variety of people, including a number of historians. So I shall not dwell on the matter here. Suffice it to say that I gave thought to how I should respond to the distortions and the personal attacks. Given that the campaign had become part of the struggle for power in Singapore and that I was now a foreigner, I thought that it was futile to do so and decided not to do anything to aggravate the situation. Whether I was right not to answer back, I can now only leave for others to decide. I can understand disagreement and even the rejection of our recommendations but the practice of character assassination was both demeaning and hurtful.

National History

THE SUCCESSION OF events that followed after 1965 made it difficult for me to digest what the departure of Singapore meant for my life. During my 15 years of self-discovery, I had taken for granted that my adopted country Malaya included the island-city. How much would change with the establishment of Malaysia? Although I was aware of the tensions underlying the quest for balance in the new relationships, I had persuaded myself of the potential of this new country. The breakdown that led to separation reminded me how far I still was from appreciating the fundamental contradictions in post-colonial nation building. I realized that I needed to rethink my position as a historian who was poised between an emerging sense of patriotism and the attractions of studying larger issues of human accommodation and conflict.

I had no wish to be a cosmopolitan, and really sought the security of belonging to a country, not only for myself but also for my family. I was convinced that working in a modern university inspired by ideals of scholarship and truth could provide a firm platform for both belonging and reaching out. Because of that, I was even more determined to make the necessary commitments to make that happen. That meant, above all, that I would have to keep on learning and writing to remain a credible scholar in my chosen field.

Several events in 1965 had made me extra sensitive to a world that was becoming more uncertain. Singapore's separation was only a small manifestation of the hotting up of the Cold War. The bloody coup attempt in Indonesia and the brewing confrontations in the Indochina states happened close by. Not far away were the succession struggle in India following the death of Nehru, and the breakdown in Sino-Soviet relations. The latter led to a deadly split within the CCP in China, the forerunner of the "Great Proletarian Cultural Revolution" that almost unhinged the country from all its moorings. The months after my return from Canberra were some of the most sombre I can remember in my life.

After working on the Malaysia volume, I was convinced that our textbooks focused too much on what the British had done during the 19th century and did not cover enough of the history of the Malay states. Certainly, more attention should be paid to the earlier history outlined in the *Sejarah Melayu* and other historical texts. My colleagues agreed that we should introduce correctives to our courses and encourage more research on national history. When I became head of the department, I organized a meeting of our history teachers and talked about the teaching of history in the Southeast Asian context. I then asked Zainal Abidin Wahid to edit the volume on *History Teaching*.

I also thought that one way to highlight Malaysian history for our undergraduates was to use fieldwork trips as part of our courses. Thus, before I went to Australia, I had arranged to take some students to imagine 19th-century Perak on the eve of the British intervention, and asked Zainal Abidin Wahid and Khoo Kay Kim to provide detailed materials before we set off. On my return, we finalized arrangements and proceeded upriver from Telok Anson (Teluk Intan). We had not expected the 9 August separation of Singapore, but the event reminded us that it was British power based in Singapore that intervened in Perak in 1873. That was when the port city began to control the affairs of the West Malayan states, something that the Malay rulers did not welcome. We set out for Pulau Tiga and the historic Pasir Salak, where the state of Perak experienced a turning point fateful for the country's history. This was the place where Maharaja Lela planned the killing of James Birch. I still remember how, as we went upriver, Kay Kim explained what made the river so vital to Perak history. I recall the way our students listened attentively, and asked him searching questions when we reached Kampong Gajah and he pointed to the historic Pasir Salak not far away. The field trip was so successful that we organized a second one the next year. This time, we went to Larut and Matang in north-west Perak where the first railway on the peninsula was built from Port Weld (now Kuala Sepetang) to the former state capital at Taiping. Here were the sites of the Larut Wars that led to British intervention. We had asked the local police to escort us around the Chinese swamp settlements of the Sepetang river and they confirmed that these had long been used by smugglers and their secret societies and were still being carefully watched for illegal activities. The students were fascinated and imagined how those secretive Chinese kampongs might have provided the protagonists who fought over the Larut tin transported to Penang a century earlier.

My colleagues, notably Zainal Abidin Wahid, Khoo Kay Kim and Jagjit Singh Sidhu were keen to organize a National History Teachers Association (HITAM) to pursue our efforts further. HITAM would hold meetings where the teaching and research of national history would be discussed. This would be our History Department's contribution to the teaching profession. There was already the journal of the Malaysian Historical Society, *Malaysia in History* and that of our history students, *Journal of the University of Malaya Historical Society* (renamed *Jernal Sejarah*). We decided that HITAM could also produce a journal for history teachers. This was *Peninjau Sejarah*; Zainal Abidin Wahid offered to be its editor and the first issue appeared in July 1966.

I had made one further commitment on behalf of the department. In 1964, I had attended a conference organized by the University of Hong Kong that brought two streams of historians together. The first had met in Manila and founded the International Association of Historians of Asia (IAHA), while the other met in Singapore the same year at the Conference on Southeast Asian History. IAHA then met in Taipei in 1962, while the Southeast Asian historians invited IAHA to meet together at their second meeting in Hong Kong in 1964. There it was agreed to merge the two conferences and I was invited to be president of IAHA, and to hold its fourth conference in KL in 1967. When I came back with the news, the department was delighted and we set about to host our first international meeting. By the end of 1964, we had divided our responsibilities and invited colleagues from the Malay, Indian and Chinese studies, Geography and Economics departments to join us to make it a larger Asian studies gathering.

On my return from Canberra, I discovered that the Congress of Orientalists had announced that it would be meeting in 1967 in the US, the first time it was meeting outside of Europe. Everyone expected it would attract a very large number of Asian scholars. If we held our IAHA meeting in 1967, many would find it difficult to attend both conferences. I thought it wise to postpone ours till 1968. My organizing committee agreed we should advertise the IAHA meeting at the Congress meeting at Ann Arbor. We were all young and ambitious and hoped not only to organize the first international conference on history in Malaysia, but also the largest Asian history conference ever. I approached Deputy Prime Minister Tun Razak and he willingly gave us his support and promised to host the official dinner for the conference.

I had thought I could contribute to future developments by weaving the Malaysian Chinese story into national history but was now less confident I could do that in a region in which ethnic-based ideological struggles were surfacing. Since my radio talks about the history of the Nanyang Chinese, I had been collecting materials for a history of the Chinese in Malaya. In 1963, at a UNESCO conference held in Singapore soon after Malaysia was established, I read a paper on traditional leadership of the Malayan Chinese and saw how I could make a contribution to national history. In addition, the contacts I made in Selangor state around KL and the neighbouring states of Perak and Negri Sembilan made me conscious of what was happening to the Chinese communities now active in local politics. But the more I learnt about the Malayan Chinese Association, the more I was uncomfortable with communalist political parties. I admired K.J. Ratnam's study of *Communalism and the Political Process in Malaya* (1965), and agreed that it was probably inevitable that the three major communities in the country would dominate its politics during the first stage of democratic nation building. But I was already fearful that dependence on ethnic solidarity would become permanent and the only way politicians could find popular support.

I had tried to link current Chinese political divisions with the history of the Chinese coming to Malaya from different places and at different times. Tracing the efforts to organize Chinese society for different political goals, I had begun to see a pattern in Malayan Chinese politics. In my published radio talks, I had argued that the idea that Nanyang Chinese were the same everywhere in Southeast Asia was wrong. The Chinese varied considerably from country to country. What I learnt about the Chinese in Malaya suggested that they were more politically sensitive than most people realized. Their history showed that they had their own way of organizing themselves that was politically significant. Among other things, that enabled most of them to adapt quickly to different political systems and institutions.

I was now convinced that the portrayal of Chinese people as either apolitical or uninterested in politics was misleading. That perception came from a definition that drew on ideas of democracy and party politics developed in Europe and America and was further narrowed by the politics of national sovereignty. It neglected the power of social and community values that sensitized the political antenna of the Chinese when they dealt with local rulers and elites, especially on matters affecting their business interests. This was apparent in the Malayan Chinese Association (MCA), whose leaders came from the mining and plantation industries, the merchants and the manufacturers of consumer goods. They drew their strength from the welfare services they provided for the "New Villages" to wean the residents from any sympathy for the MCP, but they also focused on educational matters that ensured the preservation of Chinese culture. While they also worked with those involved in the rights of workers, they were careful always to stress traditional ideas of identity. What I tried to pin down were the different ways they could be described as having acted politically. When I attended the Orientalists Congress in Ann Arbor in 1967, I presented my preliminary findings about educational policies and the nature of Chinese politics in Malaya. But, given the keen interest in the PRC's Cultural Revolution, no one at the Congress was much interested in what I had to say in my paper. Instead, the focus was on what Mao Zedong was doing to destroy Chinese cultural values.

In trying to outline Chinese contributions to the national history of Malaya, I had to learn more about the wellsprings of their organizations. I found three groups that could be politically distinguished from one another. On one side were small numbers who always looked to China for what they should do. On the other end were those, also small in numbers, who wanted to take part in the shaping of the new Malayan nation and ultimately identify fully with it. In between were the majority of those Chinese who had settled in the country and saw their interests best served by active cooperation with official authority and by defending the cultural values that made them Chinese.

It would have been slick and eye-catching, for example, to call the first pro-China, pro-communist or Chinese patriots, describe the third as idealists or naïve neo-nationalists, even detribalized collaborators, and the large numbers in between as traditionalists, opportunists or cultural chauvinists. The more I learnt, however, the more I realized that any attempt to provide such shorthand labels to distinguish the three groups would be misleading. I struggled for years to find boundary lines and reduce the grey areas between the groups. In the end, I gave up and, when my paper on "Chinese politics in Malaya" was finally published in 1970, I simply dropped the idea of using colourful labels. Calling the first Group A, the second Group B and the third Group C, I turned to broad descriptions of what each group thought they believed in and how each group was inclined to act when called upon to do so. By that time, I had given up thinking I could really help to write national history. All I wanted was to be a scholar and a teacher.

Revolutions

I HAVE NOT been able to get away from the shadow of revolutions since I was a boy in Ipoh. In most Chinese shops and even some homes, I would see a photo of Sun Yat-sen under two flags, that of the Republic of China and that of the Guomindang (KMT). And on every 10 October, I would see celebrations of *Xinhai geming* 辛亥革命, the 1911 revolution. I had thought it amusing to say that I was born one day earlier, in time to join in the celebrations. We had to stop talking about that revolution for three and a half years when the Japanese occupied Malaya. By the time I left for China in 1947, the revolutions people talked about most were the anti-colonial ones, some of them closely linked with communist parties like the MCP, who were inspired by the revolutionary movements in China. When in Nanjing, my father brought me to the Sun Yat-sen mausoleum to see how the republic showed its veneration for the founder. But at the university, my fellow students were not so impressed. That KMT revolution was now characterized as corrupt and incompetent, and some social revolutions in the countryside seemed cleaner and more determined to save the country from the rot.

My parents did not believe that Mao Zedong's revolutionaries would be good for China. If they thought that back in Malaya there would be no more revolutions, they were mistaken. At my new university, we talked about the Indonesian and Vietnamese revolutions, and argued for Aung San's place as a revolutionary. The Malayan Emergency identified the revolutionary claims of the MCP as terrorism, but we were aware that many of the politically active in the community were less condemnatory. I recall going back to read about earlier revolutions, including the English and French that killed their kings, and still remember being horrified by the French revolution that ended by "devouring its children". The

American revolution was more successful largely because the 13 colonies were far away and had more space to turn the revolution into more constructive paths.

Then came the Chinese and the Russian revolutions. When the nationalists lost out to militarists carving up the country, the younger members turned to the Russian model. Japanese imperialism tormented the nationalists and exposed their disunity. The fact that the *xinhai* revolution would end by depending on American military support was disillusioning to the young. To everyone's surprise, American ambitions could not save the regime and, with help from the Soviet Union, the CCP won out. China needed a second revolution to stand up again.

My reading did not make me a revolutionary but drew me to a greater interest in history. When my fellow students talked about anti-colonialism, they observed the ethnic eruptions in British India's partition and the fate of Palestine and Cyprus. The new Federation of Malaya looked very vulnerable to communal terror. Closer to home, what was happening in Vietnam and Indonesia was also instructive. We saw no future in the use of violence. I accepted the negotiated approach that was taken by the Federation's political leaders and rejected the idea of revolution.

But revolution was never far away. Ho Chi Minh remained committed to the Russian and Chinese hostility against the capitalist west. Sukarno saw neo-colonialism in Greater Malaysia and swore to confront that by all means possible, including allying with the communists. The flags of revolution were coloured differently, but the word never stopped ringing in our ears. By the end of 1965, while Indonesia had turned away from its dangers, American intervention in the Vietnam War was in full swing and the CCP in China was imploding. Within months, Mao Zedong's Great Proletarian Cultural Revolution (GPCR) had become the biggest global drama on show. It was a perplexing outburst of "people's power" in the name of a continuous revolution, something that older revolutionaries could only mock and reject.

Thus 1966 became a year of bafflement for those who tried to understand what this new kind of revolution would bring to our region. With all PRC publications being banned first in Malaya and then in Malaysia and Singapore, it was impossible to make any sense of what was happening. Even the anti-communist propaganda that was available was too fragmentary for any clear picture to emerge. I was kept busy with the responsibility to build up the History Department and to deal with the large numbers who opted for the subject, not least due to a growing interest in national history and preparations to teach in the national language. I thus had little time to follow this alarming recasting of revolutionary zeal and could only desultorily read whatever news was available.

Nevertheless, my curiosity as to why some revolutions succeed and others fail was aroused. I was still puzzled by how thoroughly the PKI that had chosen to take the path of democratic elections was wiped out. All other communist parties in Southeast Asia had chosen violent revolution as the CCP had done. Thus when Juan Gatbonton, editor of *Asia Magazine* in Hong Kong, approached me to do a report on the communist parties that were still fighting democratic elections in India and Japan, I was interested. This was an opportunity to find out what the Indian Communist parties, the Communist Party of India (CPI) and CPI (Marxist) and the Japanese Communist Party (JCP) thought of the PKI's failure with its strategy of open participation in electoral politics. I had done a report for Gatbonton some years earlier when I reported on the Nanyang Chinese and their response to radical nationalist policies in the region. I told him that I would be interested if I could also visit Saigon to get some feel for what the Chinese there thought about the kind of revolution that the Viet Cong were fighting. Gatbonton was agreeable and added that to my itinerary.

I began in Delhi and called on my friend Romila Thapar who introduced me to her brother Romesh. He was the founding editor of the magazine *Seminar* and a member of the CPI (Marxist), but was also close to the Congress leader Indira Gandhi. At the time of the Sino-Soviet split and the Sino-Indian War of 1962, the original CPI began to divide, and the CPI (Marxist) had chosen to side with Mao Zedong's CCP. I told Romesh the questions I wanted to ask and sought his advice about the people I should try to meet. He gave me a bird's view of communism in various parts of India and steered me away from West Bengal because he thought the divisions there were particularly bitter and inchoate. Instead, he recommended that I go to Kerala to see its CPI (Marxist) leader EMS Nambudiripad, and then to call on the CPI leader Mohan Kumaramangalam in Madras (Chennai) to get a different point of view.

I was happy to take his advice because I had never been to South India before. On the way to Calicut, I read about "rice riots" on the borders of Kerala and Madras, but understood that this was a regular affair between those two states. More serious were the riots against the decision the year before by the Central government to replace English with Hindi as the official language. I was therefore surprised to learn that Nambudiripad had been jailed for his participation in the rice riots and was therefore unable to see me. I had to be content to talk to some of his supporters who did not think that the fate of the PKI was in any way relevant to the CPI (Marxist)'s electoral successes in India. I then went further south, first to Ernakulam in Cochin and then to Quilon (Kollam), but found no one with any concern for the future of communism in a democratic country. The local leaders I met were confident that their concern for the welfare of the peasant and worker classes would always win them broad support.

Having come this far south, I could not resist pursuing my historical interest in the Malabar coast, its ancient spice trade with the Mediterranean peoples, and the Jews, Christians and Muslims who settled there. Of particular interest was why, after 1408, Zheng He chose to leave an imperial inscription to the ruler of Cochin, then known as Kezhi 柯支国, to support him against his rivals. I visited one of the few surviving synagogues there and was told that most of their men had moved to Bombay and other cities to seek their fortunes. At Quilon, I was reminded that its cashew nuts were in great demand long before the Ming naval expeditions arrived. I could see why the Ming Chinese thought highly of all the Kerala ports.

The train journey from Cochin to Madras was memorable for the banners and graffiti at all the main stops that called for the rejection of Hindi as the language of government. There were a few references to the bans on the "rice riots" that had put Nambudiripad in jail, but they were submerged under the dark shadows of anti-Hindi demonstrations. At Madras, I was fortunate to be invited to the home of Mohan Kumaramangalam. He was a product of Eton and Cambridge with a distinguished pedigree, and one of the Cambridge communists of the 1930s. I was reminded of Lim Hong Bee, one of Singapore's Queen's Scholars at Cambridge about the same time, who remained a British communist all his life.

Kumaramangalam was a gracious host in his most attractive house. He was eloquent in his support of Soviet Russia but very regretful of the split within the CPI. He thought that Mao Zedong simply did not understand Karl Marx and that Mao's idea of revolution was really derived from China's peasant rebel traditions. His cool analysis of history reminded me of British Marxists who saw the communist revolution as inevitable for all societies: parties like the CPI could play its role in the democratic process and there would be no lack of popular support. He assured me that the CPI was in no danger of meeting the fate of PKI in Indonesia. In the meantime, the struggle against Hindi was no less relevant for the people's political education. Ours was a gentle encounter and I was not surprised when I learnt a year later that he had resigned from the CPI to join the Congress Party.

I felt very comfortable wherever I went to South India. What people did and how places looked seemed familiar and, when I told people I came from Malaysia, I invariably received friendly greetings, including knowing questions about which part of the country I came from. I made a trip to Mahabalipuram, a place that I associated with Huangzhi 黄支国, a polity which was recorded as having traded with China during the Han dynasty. It was one of the holy sites of Hinduism with some of the most beautiful temples I have ever seen. Also memorable was my visit to the Madras Museum. This was established under the British and still displayed some of the original collections. I spent hours there and was especially fascinated by the rich representations of the stories found in the *Mahabharata* and *Ramayana*. In comparison, the Buddhist sections consisted of hundreds of different poses of the Buddha. The contrast was so striking that I imagined I now knew why India chose to stay with its Hindu glories and left the plain and serene Buddhism to others.

My next stop was Tokyo. I had been to Japan a few years earlier and visited famous sinologists whose work had helped me most in my early studies. I met them in Tokyo and Kyoto University as well as in the Morrison Library at the Toyo Bunko 东洋文库. That was also when I discovered the new research being done at Kyoto University's Southeast Asian Centre. This trip, however, was not about scholarship; with its focus on contemporary politics, I was walking into totally new territory. In the end, I was unable to meet the JCP leaders Miyamoto Kenji 宫本显

治 or Nosaka Sanzo 野坂参三 and only met with some of the editors of *Red Flag* 《赤旗报》 the party's newspaper. They gave me a set of recent issues and a short history of the JCP and *Red Flag*.

I had heard that the party had for years been trying to avoid taking sides in face of Sino-Soviet rivalry. The editors carefully explained how the party was pressured to follow Mao Zedong's call for more militancy and lost support. On the other hand, they did not approve of Khrushchev's rapprochement with the US, who represented in their eyes a new imperialist power. There had been fierce debates within the JCP that led some of its factions to leave to join other socialist parties. They were particularly critical of the lack of socialist unity, but pointed to the divisive tactics of the ruling Liberal Democratic Party, backed by the US, as the cause of their fragmented condition.

After meeting communists in India and Japan, I was reminded of what I had read of the effects on the British, French and Italian parties after Khrushchev's "secret speech" against Stalin and the Polish and Hungarian revolts. Both the CPI and JCP reacted in similar ways, but did not openly divide on those events. It was only in reaction to China's Great Leap Forward that serious cracks appeared, and finally the CPI split into two and the JCP lost many of its younger members. When asked about the fate of the PKI, the people I spoke to stressed that Indonesia under Sukarno was unstable. There was no constitutional democracy and playing politics with the military was a serious mistake; as a result, the PKI paid dearly for that.

The CPI and JCP positions underlined the different experiences in Southeast Asia. The Viet Minh won against the French on the battlefield, and war was continuing in the south against a state that was backed by US forces. Communists had led armed revolts in Burma, Malaysia and the Philippines; when they did not in Indonesia, they were annihilated. I now wanted to learn what people in Saigon felt about the deadly fighting around them. I saw how close the war was when our plane landed at Tan Son Nhut Airport. I saw a row of planes that had been destroyed a few days earlier by Viet Cong and, as I went through immigration, I could hear bombs going off in the distance. My hotel was in a quiet, well-guarded part of the city. However, the tension around was signified by the number of houses marked by British, French and other European flags; I was told this was to ensure that Viet Cong supporters would not mistake their residents for Americans. I could not imagine US authorities being pleased by such displays.

I visited the Chinese quarter of Cholon several times and found the shops there doing well from the war. The people I spoke to in Cantonese said that they carried ROC passports but felt the pressure to make contributions to organizations that sympathized with the communists. Some assured me that the Viet Cong were really nationalists who hated those who collaborated with the imperialists. What they wanted was a united Vietnam that was truly independent. I was reminded that some of my friends in Malaya had similar views about the MCP. The obvious difference was that the Viet Cong leaders were indigenous while the Chinese who led the MCP were not only considered by the Malay majority as *pendatang asing* (immigrants, foreigners) but also identified as followers of the CCP.

On my return, I reported my experiences in the *Asia Magazine*, but offered no conclusions where our region was concerned. My main takeaway was to recognize that revolutions had many dimensions and some were likely to be ongoing for a long while to come. In Malaysia and Singapore, revolutionary voices were still heard, but the fighting on the Thai and Sarawak borders was no longer threatening to the two governments that were elected two years earlier, Singapore in 1963 and Malaysia in 1964. When I looked back after my return from Saigon, it reminded me of a local calm before the larger storm come.

East Asia Focus

TAKING ME BY surprise, the next year was one when the focus of events shifted northwards. In addition to three invitations to attend meetings that were directly or indirectly related to Mao Zedong's explosive Cultural Revolution (GPCR), I also received invitations to move away from MU to work in centres that specialized on Chinese history and politics.

I was first invited to attend the "China in Crisis" conference at the University of Chicago in February 1966. The "crisis" referred to China being in the midst of yet another revolution after having had two violent ones within a half-century of each other. The meeting was the culmination of a year's seminars and talks at the university dedicated to explaining what was happening in the PRC. It was meant to be a thorough examination of China's heritage and why its second revolution seemed to be devouring its children. The second invitation was to the Orientalist Congress in Ann Arbor mentioned earlier. There I found that the same subject threatened to dominate the China sections of the meeting. The Congress was primarily concerned with the pre-modern Orient but, unexpectedly, the sinologists were unable to avoid debating contemporary developments in the PRC. For me, that was not all. At the end of the year, I was invited to South Korea where I was asked again and again what China's revolution was doing to the core values of Confucian civilization.

These three meetings in quick succession in 1967 made me feel that I was not keeping up with the best work being done in my chosen field. It was becoming clear that I needed to get back to doing research where I could make a contribution to scholarship. That was what really mattered if I wanted a university career.

In the context of China, the revolutions were really about unifying China and regaining respect and pride. The idea of *geming* for revolution had several layers of meaning, the latest of which had been translated from what came out of the French and Russian examples. For the Federation and then for Malaysia, Indonesia's experience was the immediate challenge. How did Sukarno and the PKI become so powerful? But also why was the former so easily removed and the latter so utterly destroyed? The Harvard-trained Indonesian sinologist, Lie Tek Tjeng, told me that he had monitored President Liu Shaoqi's visit to Jakarta in 1963 and D.N. Aidit's visit to Beijing in 1965 and thought that the abrupt fall of the PKI could have influenced Mao Zedong's thinking about the need for continuous revolution, and might even have been a factor in the launch of the Cultural Revolution in early 1966. Working in KL and not having access to materials about what the CCP was going through, I felt inadequate because I was unable to respond to Lie Tek Tjeng's insights.

I recall talking about this to two of my colleagues at MU who had gone from Europe to work in the PRC in the late 1950s and had remained there until the height of the Great Leap Forward in the early 1960s. One was the Indonesia-born Tjoa Soei Hock in the Malay Studies Department, who had gone from the Netherlands to China in the 1950s. The other was Thong Saw Pak in the Physics Department, who had been invited to do physics research in Beijing but left when he found untrained party cadres trying to tell him what should or should not be done. Both of them said that they had felt the tensions growing within the CCP that led to the break between Mao Zedong and Liu Shaoqi, and had concluded that it had to do with questions of insufficient revolutionary commitment among senior party leaders.

The Chicago invitation asked me to be one of the commentators for the historical heritage section of the conference. I had met both the conference organizers, Ho Ping-ti and Tsou Tang, during my earlier visits to Chicago. They had invited some of the best-known historians in the West to examine the links between the Confucian-Legalist state of the 19th to 20th centuries and the ongoing Maoist struggles. Ho Ping-ti opened the conference with a masterly essay on the relevant features in China's political traditions, followed by two historical analyses, by Liu Kwang Ching of the 19th century and Martin Wilbur on the 20th. I was fascinated by the way they both tried to identify what was salient to the evolving PRC power structure. They were followed by three political scientists/philosophers—Benjamin Schwarz, Tsou Tang and Chalmers Johnson—who drew from the past to explain the thinking, leadership and mass behaviour displayed since the beginning of 1966. What was new was that Chicago had invited 14 commentators to add thickness to the six historical perspectives. I commented on Wilbur's paper by comparing periods of division in the past and what was necessary before reunification could succeed. Altogether, I came away greatly encouraged by the thought that historians could usefully contribute to understanding the present, perhaps even had the duty to do so.

I stayed behind to attend the second part of the conference and listened to 20 other social scientists who not only described what they had to do to collect the masses of pamphlet and interview data through Hong Kong, Taiwan and Japan, but also what skills were required to elucidate them. Of course, I was observing a group of "China-watchers" at work and they raised more questions than they could answer, but the experience left me with the urge to know more. In particular, I was intrigued by how revolutionaries who claimed to reject everything pertaining to the feudal past had become so obsessed with using the past to fight their current internal battles. I later realized that watching historians and social scientists entwined in this way was an experience that remained a strong influence on my work thereafter.

Unusual for Orientalist congresses, the one held a few months later in nearby Michigan was attended by many social scientists. I had found this so in the Southeast Asia section, where several comments on my paper on "alien education in Malayan history" came from social scientists. However, what drew the largest numbers of congress attendees was an ad hoc panel where I was asked to join John Fairbank and scholars from Europe to explain what was "cultural" in the latest revolution in China. This aroused so much passion among the sinologists that we found ourselves talking about politics rather than culture. For example, a senior scholar from the KMT in Taiwan accused Southeast Asian *huaqiao* of abandoning their heritage. As I was on the panel, he pointed to me as an example of what he meant: someone who called himself a Malayan *huaren* 华人 and not a *Zhongguo ren* 中国人 (a traditional reference to all Chinese but used by current regimes to identify a citizen of either the PRC or the ROC in Taiwan). In my studies of the *huaqiao*, I had observed the political sensitivities about nomenclature. The passions aroused at the panel encouraged me to study more closely the transnational mobility that lay at the core of the new identity politics. It was clear that what happened in China both past and present hung over many lives.

In an earlier chapter, I mentioned that countries in Southeast Asia tended to focus on their own national problems. Indeed, most of them had difficulties dealing with the borders they inherited from their imperial masters and the mix of different ethnic communities residing within those borders. As a result, few paid attention to the nature and potential of the region as a whole. The only exception was when Sukarno swore to destroy (*ganyang*) the neo-colonialist Malaysia. That did not do him any good and might even have contributed to his downfall. As a result, it was the scholars and policy makers of North America, Western Europe and Australasia who gave the region more serious attention.

By the mid-1960s, however, Japan's post-war recovery had enabled it to make peace with the new national leaders. Asian tigers like Hong Kong, Taiwan and South Korea followed export-oriented strategies and these three were about to be joined by an independent Singapore. The new Japanese scholarship, as seen in their new journals, was impressive, especially the research done at the new Centre of Southeast Asian Studies at Kyoto University.

I began to meet Japanese scholars at international conferences not only in Japan and the West but also in Hong Kong, Singapore, KL and Bangkok. And, at the Orientalists Congress in Ann Arbor, we learnt that their collections of Cultural Revolution documents were as good as if not better than those gathered in Hong Kong. At the Chicago conference, the China-watchers also acknowledged their debt to Japanese sources. Together with those from Hong Kong and Taiwan, the materials collected were invaluable to those trying to understand what was happening in Mao Zedong's China. The new developments occurring in East Asia were enabling scholars to develop a different perspective on the changes.

Thus when I was invited to spend a month in Korea I was intrigued and eagerly accepted. This was the initiative of the Korean ambassador to Malaysia, Choi Kyu-hah 崔圭夏. He was a senior diplomat who studied English literature and had a keen interest in the history of Sino-Korean relations. When he found out that, together with his friend Chun Haejong 全海宗, I was one of the contributors to J.K. Fairbank's *The Chinese World Order*, he persuaded his Ministry of Education to invite me to compare Korean and Chinese traditions of Confucianism. My reading of Sino-Vietnamese history after the 10th century had made me curious about what made the Koreans different. Chun Haejong's essay on the complexities that the Koreans faced when dealing with the Manchu Qing had whetted my appetite, and the chance to examine the Korean royal archives at Seoul National University (SNU) was irresistible.

I should mention here that this visit turned out to be a fateful one because what I saw in Korea led me to confirm my wish to get back to dedicated research on China and go to where I could have access to all publications about China. But let me describe what I experienced that made me sure that this was what I should do.

When I arrived at SNU, Professor Chun showed me around the university's archival collections, which included the last set of the Korean kingdom's documents. As I read a sample of them, all adopting the kind of officialese used in Qing China, I was struck by the proud resistance to Japanese efforts to take over the country altogether. Chun Haejong also introduced me to two of his colleagues, Koh Byong-ik 高柄翊, who was a specialist on Korean Confucianism during the Yi dynasty, and Kim Wonyong 金元龍, the archaeologist who had excavated the capital of the Baekche 百济 kingdom. They both stressed the ancient roots of Korean culture and the special relationship between different parts of the peninsula and Chinese expansionist power. That set the background for me to meet two other leading historians, Yi Ki-baek 李基白 at Sogang University and Kim Jun-yop 金俊燁 of Korea University.

Yi was an outstanding historian of the Koryo kingdom (918–1392). His work on the kingdom's foundation in the 10th century dovetailed with my own. He had studied how Koryo successfully resisted the Khitan Liao invasions, while I had dealt with the failure of the Five Dynasties of North China to keep them out of North China. Even after the Song had reunified most of China in 978, it still could not defeat the Khitan and was forced to accept a humiliating peace that surrendered all the border counties to non-Han rule for the next three hundred years. While thus sharing a common dangerous enemy, Koryo and Song China developed a relationship of mutual respect. Yi Ki-baek introduced me to *Koryo-sa* 高丽史 (*History of Koryo*) and pointed to parallels in the territorial divisions following the fall of the Silla kingdom and in the factors that led to the complete reunification on the peninsula. I greatly valued his insights and regretted that I had not returned to the study of 10th-century China to complete the story of the Song unification between 960 and 978.

Kim Jun-yop was the founding director of the Centre of Asia Studies. He had a remarkable story to tell. Recruited by the Japanese to fight in China, he escaped to Chongqing where he joined the Korean nationalists who received support from Chiang Kai-shek's government. There he studied at the National Central University, the one that I had joined after it returned to Nanjing, and also taught Korean to Chinese students and officials. In 1948, he returned to Korea. We worked out that we had overlapped for a brief few months when I was a freshman. Coincidentally, his centre was developing Southeast Asian studies, and he introduced me to his first doctoral student, who was working on the law codes of Annan (Vietnam). Kim Jun-yop planned to introduce Indonesian-language teaching and was especially curious about Malaysia. We became good friends and remained in contact for the rest of the century.

All this provided a running start to my introduction to two thousand years of Sino-Korean history. At the same time, Kim Jun-yop was deeply engaged in advising on urgent issues concerning the country's struggle against North Korean communism. He told me how he sought the help of Taiwan scholars to help him understand what Mao Zedong was doing with his Cultural Revolution. I had to confess I was totally baffled by what was happening to the young people of the PRC.

Chun Haejong then asked his graduate student Kwon Sikbong 权锡棒 to accompany me around the country for the remaining weeks. We began with Andong 安东, the hometown of Korea's greatest Confucian philosopher Yi Hwang 李滉 (better known as Toegyi 退溪). I was taken to the historic Yi Hwang home to perform Confucian rites before I could enter his library. Classes were still being held every morning for local schoolboys to introduce them to key Confucian texts. Although I was not sure how much was symbolic rather than substantive, the contrast with what the young Red Guards were doing in China against anything Confucian was striking.

What followed was a further leap into the past to the Baekche capital on the west coast that had just been excavated. The royal palace tombs were remarkable in showing the strong influence of Tang China. We then crossed the peninsula to the southeast to visit Kyongju 庆州, capital of the Silla 新罗 kingdom. Kwon Sikbong made sure that I was shown the best-preserved sites in the Bulguksa 佛國寺 temple complex. I did not know enough to tell how much the Buddhism there had been filtered via China and how much came from the Silla monks who were inspired by learning directly from India, but the artefacts certainly looked different from the finds in China from before the 10th century.

The best was yet to come. After visiting Pusan, the port closest to Japan, and the south coast where Admiral Yi Sun-shin 李舜臣 defeated the Japanese navy in the 16th century, I was taken inland to the Kaya mountains where the Haeinsa 海印寺 is located. This has been the home for over 600 years of the thousands of wooden printing blocks used to print the Korean *Tripitaka*. They are the oldest surviving printing blocks of the Buddhist scriptures anywhere in the world, and are so well preserved that they were, at the time I visited, still being used to print new copies of the texts. I saw the printing being done of several sets of the *Tripitaka*, which were to be presented to the counties that provided the United Nations troops to defend the south from northern invasion during the Korean War.

I was greatly moved by the deep sense of the past that prevailed in that whole valley and was sorry that our stop was so brief. The night before we left to return to Seoul, a party of Korean women was having dinner in the next room. When they burst into song, both Kwon and I recognized that they were singing Japanese war songs. I was surprised when Kwon was so upset that he nearly jumped up to go to the next room to stop the singing. It was my first taste of the depth of Korean feelings about Japanese imperialism. He explained how ashamed he was to hear such songs still being sung and told me that young Koreans in particular could not tolerate anyone who harboured nostalgic thoughts about Japan.

We returned to Seoul via Taegu and drove through the rural centre of the peninsula. Every bit of agricultural land was cultivated and it was obvious how densely populated Korea was. As we approached the capital, the landscape dramatically changed; the industrial capitalism of an Asian tiger took over, with rows of smoking factory chimneys demonstrating the country's determination to catch up with Japan and join the modern world.

Each day during my visit, the news reported on the Cultural Revolution in the PRC. I was not interested in the anti-communist analyses in the reports, but was reminded of the contrast between the cultural destruction that was taking place all over China and the respect still being shown to past treasures in Korea. I felt a profound sadness. It had to do with matters deep in Chinese history, and reminded me how much I did not know. What was in China's past that could help me understand the extraordinary happenings in the PRC? After several sleepless nights asking myself a range of similar questions, I rang home to Margaret to share my feelings. I told her that I was now ready to accept the invitation to take up the research professorship at the Australian National University.

Take a Break

I REFERRED EARLIER to the three invitations that asked me to leave MU and resume research on things Chinese. They came within weeks of one another, at a time when I had doubts about leaving the field of Chinese history to concentrate on the national history that I felt our department should be trying to shape. Although the temptation to accept was great, I did not really want to leave the country for more than two or three years.

Margaret and I had been mulling over the invitations, which were offering me professorial positions in the US, the UK and Australia. The first came from Carrington Goodrich in Columbia University asking me to join the Department of East Asian Languages and Cultures. When I last talked to him at Ann Arbor, he was especially interested in expanding work on the Ming period (he was preparing to produce the authoritative *Dictionary of Ming Biography*) and also in developing more research on Tang-Song history. The second invitation followed shortly afterwards. This was from C.H. Phillips, Director of SOAS, asking me to head the School's Contemporary China Centre. And, by extraordinary coincidence, the third came a few days later from Jack Crawford, director of the Research School of Pacific Studies at ANU, offering me the Far Eastern History chair held by C.P. Fitzgerald, who was due to retire in 1968.

What was significant was that all three addressed my work as a historian of China, although they also noted my research interest in China's relations with Southeast Asia. They were stark reminders that I was only dutifully involved in Malaysian history and had not produced anything significant in that field. It was the China side of my work that was recognized. I also realized that each of the offered positions could provide me with opportunities to go further. In contrast, as long as I was obliged to advance national history at MU and accept the limits on my access to books on

China, it would have been difficult for me to improve the quality of my work on Chinese history.

The invitations arrived at a time when I felt that I was not keeping up with the latest scholarship in my field. I thus found them difficult to ignore. I was loath to leave MU and wondered if I could take no-pay leave, say for three years, to accept one of them. We had only recently moved into our new home. Our children had all started school and there was no question of going without them. Margaret and I wavered for months as we discussed what each offer entailed.

Margaret was hesitant about bringing up our children in New York and, given her unhappy experiences with a modern secondary school in England, was doubtful whether we could afford to live in London and send our children to "public" (private) schools. As for Canberra, it was closest by and it would be easier for our families to stay in touch. For me, I was not sure if I wanted to stay in the pre-modern or "medieval" periods that Goodrich had in mind. Nor did I want to turn to the study of contemporary China, which I would have to if I chose to go to SOAS. At ANU, Crawford assured me that he wanted to see a more open Far Eastern history where I could also combine modern history with my work on the Chinese in Southeast Asia. We knew that Columbia and SOAS were more central to world affairs and more prestigious, and we also admitted that both New York and London were more exciting as cities, but taken overall, ANU seemed to provide more of what we preferred.

Thus we had agreed that we would choose ANU and make our final decision after my return from Seoul. But, after what I saw over those weeks in Korea, I could not wait to tell Margaret that my visit to Korea had made me feel that it was Chinese history that I wanted to spend my life doing, so I rang home first. As we talked on the phone and I heard her agree to support my decision, I could sense that Margaret was once again saying that she was willing to follow me where I thought I needed to go.

I wrote to the University Council and asked for three years' no-pay leave. I explained my wish to accept the invitation to join the research school at ANU because I would be free from teaching and could concentrate on my research. I also asked if the Council would agree to the appointment of a new professorial head so that, when I returned, I could be the second professor in the department. The Council pointed out that, if it were to agree, that would mean that the department would have two professors and this was against university policy. They could only agree to appoint someone junior to act as head during my absence. I could see that would not be in the interest of the department under a system of professorial heads. The ANU Research Chair was a position tenured to age 65. If I resigned, MU would fill their chair and the department would be well served. For myself, I would take my chances in three years' time when I felt ready to return. On that basis, I explained my reasons to the Council and tendered my resignation.

But I felt a lingering discomfort about leaving and it led me to do something that I had not wanted ever to do. I have been reluctant to tell this story, one that was both a story of friendship as well as of openly showing my political sympathies in the face of the social realities that I understood Malaysia to be facing. I had expressed my personal distaste for the ethnic-based politics that undergirded the Alliance Coalition of the UMNO, MCA and MIC parties. I had acknowledged that communalism might have been unavoidable in order to make sure that the British would leave sooner rather than later. But I had always felt that communalist power sharing could not be in the interest of nation-building in the longer run.

The friendship part of the story, however, was to do with Tan Chee Khoon who, as a member of the University Council, had supported my decision to spend time at ANU and had encouraged me to take three years' leave. He was sorry I decided to resign when the Council could not allow a second chair for the department, but expected me to return after a few years.

The two parts of the story came together when Chee Khoon decided to establish the non-communal Parti Gerakan Rakyat Malaysia (Gerakan) and asked me to help him before I left for Australia. Our friendship had begun when I was a student activist on the MU campus in Singapore. He was senior to me, in the medical school. After graduation, he not only became a beloved doctor in KL but also a dedicated parliamentarian. I had lost touch with him, but we met again years later in KL and became close friends. As a loyal alumnus, he developed a keen interest in building the new university and we did a fair bit together to keep the university attractive for new staff and students. He was by then very active in national politics as one of the leaders of the Labour Party of Malaya. In 1964, he was elected to represent the constituency of Batu in the heart of KL and remained a respected opposition voice for the next 12 years.

But when the Labour Party was radicalized and turned further to the left, Chee Khoon was ousted and could only stay on in parliament as an independent. He wanted to set up a political party that did not depend on ethnic loyalties but really cared for the poor in the country, and he asked me if I could help. He knew I had decided to leave for the ANU and that I was not interested in being a politician, so he only asked that I advise him on drafting a manifesto and a constitution. In the context of my resigning from MU, I thought this would show my commitment to Malaysia and agreed. I attended several meetings as friend and adviser. Eventually, Chee Khoon persuaded Syed Hussein Alatas to be the party's president, and agreed to Dr Lim Chong Eu's willingness to merge his United Democratic Party in Penang with Gerakan. After all was agreed, he invited me to attend the foundation meeting in 1968 and introduced me as one of those who helped him draft the constitution. Next day, it was reported in the press that I was one of the party's founders.

I tell the story here because, however peripherally, it was the only time I found myself publicly involved in partisan Malaysian politics. The identification with Parti Gerakan Rakyat Malaysia had added a thin but extra layer of sharing and belonging onto the inclusive ideas of home that I had discerned as relevant to our lives: those of country and fellow citizens, town and state, campus colleagues and students, family and friends, house and garden, even the multiple identities in my private thoughts. Margaret was bemused when I suggested that I had now added one more layer to my public persona. She knew me only too well and laughingly brushed that aside as merely another sign of excess sensibility.

There was one more memorable link in my memory of our last year in KL. This was the conference of the International Association of Historians of Asia, that we had postponed in order not to be overshadowed by the Ann Arbor Orientalists meeting. My colleagues knew I was leaving MU a few weeks after the conference and treated it as a farewell meeting. I appreciated their gesture, but what was really memorable was yet another event to mark the consequences of the revolutions of our age. This time it was the Prague Spring. Malaysia had established diplomatic relations with the Soviet Union in 1967 and we had several scholars from the Soviet bloc who came for the conference. The liveliest were three scholars from Czechoslovakia, all supporters of their leader Alexander Dubcek, and led by one of their finest sinologists, Timoteus Pokora. Our conference provided the platform for some dramatic scenes when the Russian ambassador to Malaysia confronted Pokora on his defiant public comments. As a result, the conference was punctuated by political exchanges, and it came as no surprise when Soviet armies crushed the Prague uprising a few days after our conference ended. Just before Pokora left KL, he told me that the Russian ambassador had warned him that the Spring was over. Soon afterwards, I learnt that Pokora was sacked and was not allowed to resume his career. My colleagues assured me that everyone who attended thought the conference was a success but I cannot help remembering it as a moment when the fragility of academic freedom was exposed. It reminded me that I was setting out to learn about the fate of the scholars who were humiliated by the Red Guards in the PRC. It made me all the more grateful to have started my career with the University of Malaya.

Wrapping Up

WHEN I SET forth from Ipoh to study at the University of Malaya as a newly-minted citizen of a future country, I was grateful to take the first step on the journey to a new home. Although I did not know which direction my studies would take, that did not seem really to matter. During those early years, my idea of home was still linked to some country that would take the place of the China that, in my mind, had slipped down a steep slope beyond reach. There was no other home I could imagine. In Ipoh, my parents had moved from a dingy-rented place to a two-room flat and then moved to KL to a rented semi-detached house where I had a room that I only used for two weeks in the year, when I visited them during vacations. For five years until I left for London, I stayed in university hostels in Singapore, from an open dormitory for 15 to a closed one of 20 partitioned rooms, and then to a shared twin room in one of the 40 semi-detached houses on Dunearn Road. I never mistook home for the places where I stayed.

In fact, during those years, I don't think the word was much in my consciousness. I believe that this was in part because the idea of home seemed to have taken on a form that I had not thought of before, that of a campus for continuous learning. MU was such a place, with its staff and students housed in buildings close to libraries and laboratories, and most of them engaged in lively exchanges. Not only that, it was also on the site of the beautiful Botanic Gardens that we could treat as our own. In fact, it was easy to identify this beautiful campus as home since I was there on average at least 45 weeks of each of the five years I studied there.

Then I went to London. Margaret joined me, we married and moved to Cambridge and back. England and especially London were places of culture, for literature and music. As for Connaught Hall in London,

Homerton College and the flat on Orchard Street as well as the one in Shepherd's Bush, they were all temporary places for us to work and sleep in. Once it was clear that Parkinson wanted me to return to MU as a new member of staff, I could expect that home would once again be my old campus. Of course, Margaret also saw hers in Singapore where her family had been for over 15 years and, with my parents deciding to move there as well, the growing Wang family in 1957 could begin to be located in one place at last.

Yet it was not to be. I looked to my adopted country of Malaya and its capital, where MU was housing its new campus. We exchanged university housing in Singapore for that in KL, long enough to have some pleasant memories of each of the four houses we stayed in from 1957 to 1964. However, all that time, home in another form continued to take shape in my mind, one tied to a campus, but increasingly linked with the university as a site of free and open learning. I was not really conscious of how significant that was to the idea of home, simply comfortable and content to be surrounded by people with inquiring minds.

Looking back, it was the coming together of many levels of belonging that led me to believe that we were settling down. The new campus was expanding its reach, not only in its academic fields and the size of the library collections, but also as each new building was occupied and the university idea was given physical frames. Being faculty dean and then head of the History Department brought me closer to the heart of the nation-building project, including the Greater Malaysia plan that I spent years trying to describe in the *Survey* volume. Abroad, Sukarno's Konfrontasi and the Americanization of the war against the Sino-Soviet communist challenge were also raising a nationalist consciousness.

On the ground, the new environment was now familiar. I could see KL and its satellite town of Petaling Jaya becoming lively and interesting, and felt the web of intimate ties in our local shops and among our neighbours. Margaret was doing extremely well as a teaching-of-English specialist, our son was ready for a fine primary school in which Malay and Chinese languages were available in addition to English, and my father was now the much-respected head of one of the top independent Chinese schools in the country.

My work in the university was immensely satisfying. The MU traditions I grew up with since 1949 were carefully sustained. I had ample support to bring a dedicated team of colleagues together. With their help, the department could make the study of history an enlightening experience for graduates who would be able to serve the country in a larger and more complex world. My efforts to set a good example for the development of Malaysian national history had also drawn me into fascinating new work, including the history of the Malaysian Chinese communities. Outside the campus, I was asked to support the Dewan Bahasa and Pustaka's programme of selecting major works of history for translation. I chaired its Istilah (Special Terms) Committee for History to ensure technical consistency.

Three generations together, this photo taken in Singapore, 1968, not long before the family moved to Australia.

What concerned me most then was to connect our graduate studies programme more systematically to local research on Malaysian history. Both were making progress, and holding weekly seminars by MU staff and graduate students, including those from other departments who shared our interests, was particularly useful. The regular meetings provided a great deal of stimulation for all of us. For more than three years, these seminars helped to inspire our team to plan and organize our first history conference of international historians in 1968. I still recall with pleasure how my colleagues worked so hard for the meeting that brought so many of the world's historians of Asia to KL.

As I mentioned earlier, I had become conscious that my administrative duties plus a heavy teaching load were affecting the quality of my research in Chinese history. The meetings I attended in Chicago and Ann Arbor in 1967 had highlighted my inability to keep up with the latest work being done. Every historian of China I met at those meetings seemed able to understand key features of the developments in the PRC. It was obvious that my inability to access books and articles on contemporary China had become a serious handicap to my ability to comprehend. Yet everyone I met expected me to know what was happening and explain why the young people in the PRC were following the destructive exhortations of Mao Zedong. Hence my month in South Korea convinced me that I must get back to Chinese history before it was too late.

Margaret and I had thought hard before we made this decision. But she was convinced that my career as a historian of China was at stake and encouraged me to go to Canberra. My parents too did not hesitate when we told them what we planned. As always, they believed that I should go on learning, and any move that would improve my ability to do so would be the right one. Malaysia was our country, the university was my intellectual home, and we had our house to come back to. All the same, it was a tough decision to make. The fateful events of 1969, after we left, transformed the national landscape, and were totally unexpected.

Margaret was, as always, practical and down-to-earth. The ANU offered university housing for three years, but we would have to bring all our household things if we did not want to buy anything new. We would rent out our house in PJ, and it would be easier to do that if we left it unfurnished. After the IAHA conference, we packed and were ready. On the eve of leaving our home in mid-September, she looked around the house, contemplated what we were bringing with us and turned to me saying, "Home is where we are." I nodded, I can settle for that.

Home is Where We Are

DID WE FIND home in Australia where we lived for 18 years? Does home have to be a country or a city? Like Hong Kong, where we were for nearly ten years? Or a unique multicultural city-state like Singapore, after living here for over 24 years? Or is home this house or that? Indeed we have lived in some very comfortable ones, including our apartments in Singapore.

We have been fortunate and never found home difficult to envisage wherever we lived and worked. For myself, it might have had something to do with the universities that have offered me the freedom to ask questions that have intrigued me no end, for example, China as a resilient ancient culture, as several kinds of empire over two millennia, and as a multiethnic modern state; and, for someone like me living outside its borders, the "Chinese" wherever they went to live. In every campus, Margaret and I made friends, and shared with our colleagues and students what we found so interesting about the world we knew.

Looking back, we left KL for Canberra over 50 years ago. We have been asked where we thought our home was and, because we could never pin it down, often replied that it was where we were, and all the places in which we had felt at home.

In Canberra, we lived for three years in a house that the ANU provided us. I walked to work at the Coombs Building 200 yards away and the research library was just opposite that. Margaret decided to study for another degree in Asian studies and walked to a building another 50 yards beyond that.

When our son's Canberra High School moved to the nearby suburb of Aranda and our girls could attend the primary school there, we built our new house in that suburb. Margaret was now more experienced and designed a comfortable one that we lived in for the next 15 years.

In 1977, I became an Australian citizen. Margaret kept her Malaysian citizenship for a few years longer.

I shall leave it to our children and grandchildren to tell their story of where they thought home was. We had rented out our house in Petaling Jaya and only sold it a couple of years after building our second in Canberra. When our son Ming went to study in Sydney, he never lived with us again. After his marriage, he settled in Sydney. Our daughters studied at ANU and were with us until Mei married and moved out. Lan had her own home after graduation. My mother had come to live with us and, for a while, there were just the three of us in Aranda.

60th wedding anniversary.

After 18 years at the ANU, I left for the University of Hong Kong where we lived in the rather splendid vice-chancellor's lodge and my mother came with us. We rented out our Aranda house expecting to return after my stint with HKU. That did not happen. When I retired, I went to the Institute of Southeast Asian Studies in Singapore and also became executive chairman of the Institute of East Asian Political Economy and later director of the East Asian Institute, National University of Singapore.

None of our children remained in Canberra, so we decided to sell our Canberra house and invest in a flat in Singapore. We had made no plans as to when to return to Australia or, if we returned, whether to live in Sydney where Ming was, or in Melbourne where Mei had bought her own house and Lan had hers.

As it turned out, we stayed on, now in our 24th year. We were forced to move out of our first condominium when it was sold en-bloc, and bought another flat in the next suburb. We are very comfortable and are prepared to remain here as long as we are in Singapore. All those 50 years, we seemed always to have been home.

Appendix: Writings Related to My Malaya Home

(entries are arranged in chronological order in each category)

My Life: Ipoh and Beyond

"Looking Forward, Looking Back: An Interview with Wang Gungwu" (生命之树长青一专访王赓武教授), in《地平线月刊》by Liu Hong 刘宏. Trans. Gregor Benton. Hong Kong, no. 1, 2000, pp. 13–24.

"前言". In *Wang Fo-wen, 1903–1972: a memorial collection of poems, essays and calligraphy*《王宓文纪念集》. River Edge, NJ: Global Publishing, 2002, pp. ix–xi.

李业霖主编.《南洋大学走过的历史道路》. 马来亚南洋大学校友会, 2002.

Philip A. Kuhn, "Wang Gungwu: The Historian in His Times". In *Power and Identity in the Chinese World Order, Festschrift in Honour of Professor Wang Gungwu*, ed. Billy K.L. So, John Fitzgerald, Huang Jianli and James K. Chin. Hong Kong: Hong Kong University Press, 2003, pp. 11–31.

Lee Guan-kin, "Wang Gungwu: An Oral History". In *Power and Identity in the Chinese World Order*, pp. 375–413.

刘宏, "从新加坡看华人世界: 王赓武教授与海外华人研究". In 《战后新加坡华人社会的嬗变: 本土情怀、区域网络、全球视野》, 刘宏, 厦门 : 厦门大学出版社, 2003, pp. 245–63.

Gregor Benton and Hong Liu, eds. *Diasporic Chinese Ventures: The life and work of Wang Gungwu*. London: Routledge/Curzon, 2004.

陈松赞 (C.C. Chin), "校长王宓文先生传略". In《宽柔论集》, ed. 郑良树. Skudai: Nanyuan Publishing, 2006, pp. 83–112.

Alan Baumler, "Rethinking Chinese History in a global Age: an Interview with Wang Gungwu", *The Chinese Historical Review* 14, no. 1 (Spring 2007): 97–113.

Vineeta Sinha, "In Conversation with Wang Gungwu", *ISA (International Sociological Association) E-Bulletin*, no. 6 (March 2007): 54–80.

Wang Gungwu: Junzi: Scholar-gentleman in conversation with Asad-ul Iqbal Latif. Singapore: Institute of Southeast Asian Studies, 2010.

Huang Jianli, "Conceptualizing Chinese Migration and Chinese Overseas: The Contribution of Wang Gungwu", *Journal of Chinese Overseas* 6, no. 1 (2010): 1–21.

"My Green Innocence", "Life had changed forever", and "A Nomad in Ipoh". In *Ipoh, My Home Town: Reminiscences of Growing Up, in Ipoh, in Pictures and Words*, ed. Ian Anderson. Ipoh: Media Masters Publishing, 2011, pp. 104–7, 144–5, 262–5.

Zheng Yongnian and Phua Kok Khoo, eds. *Wang Gungwu: Educator and Scholar.* Singapore: World Scientific, 2013.

苏基朗，"古今生民命、天下华人心". In《天下华人》. 广州：广东人民出版社，2016，pp. 1–9.

"王赓武：关注华人的忧患与命运".《各在天一涯：二十位港台海外知识人谈话录》, 李怀宇采访。北京：中华书局，2016，pp. 75–101.

"Childhood memories to the age of 12". In *Recalling*, ed. Nicholas Tarling with the assistance of Ooi Keat Gin and Rupert Wheeler. New York: Hamilton Books, 2017, pp. 217–33.

杜晋轩，"海外华人的史学家王赓武回忆录面世"，多维新闻网，18 September 2018.

Home is not Here. Singapore: NUS Press, 2018.

Rachel Leow, "Home is everywhere", *Mekong Review* 4, no. 2 (February–April 2019): 6–7 [also in *Los Angeles Review of Books* China Channel, 7 October 2019].

Wu Xiao An, Review essay, "Home is not Here", *Journal of the Malaysian Branch of the Royal Asiatic Society* 92, part 2, no. 317 (December 2019): 163–76.

王菁, "漂泊的学人——王赓武: 何处为家?"《东方历史评论》, 2019.

Madeline Y. Hsu, "Where Is Home? The Current State of Chinese Migration Studies", *Cross-Currents: East Asian History and Culture Review* (e-journal) 32: 140–5. <https://cross-currents.berkeley.edu/e-journal/issue-32/hsu>

毛升，"评王赓武回忆录 | 侨居与定居之间",《上海书评》*Shanghai Review of Books*, 12 February 2020.

Philip Holden, Anthony Reid and Khoo Boo Teik, "SOJOURN Symposium on Home is not Here". *SOJOURN: Journal of Social Issues in Southeast Asia* 35, no. 1 (2020): 138–59.

University

"A New Tradition at the University" and "Campus at Pantai Valley", *The Straits Times Annual for 1960* and *for 1966*. Singapore, 1960 and 1966, pp. 53–5 and 54–7.

"The University in relation to traditional culture". In *Proceedings, Asian Workshop on Higher Education*, ed. Li Choh-Ming. Hong Kong: Chinese University of Hong Kong, 1969, pp. 21–32.

"二十年前的一段往事 – 王赓武校长谈 '南大事件'", 香港大学《学苑》, 1986. Trans. Gregor Benton as "Wang Gungwu on the Nantah Incident: an interview". In *Diasporic Chinese Ventures: The Life and Work of Wang Gungwu*, 2004, pp. 31–42.

"The University and the Community". In *Proceedings, Second Asian Workshop on Higher Education*, ed. Rayson L. Huang. Singapore: Nanyang University, 1972, pp. 17–29, 111–20.

"Universities in Transition in Asia", *Oxford Review of Education* 18, no. 1 (1992): pp. 17–27.

"The University as a Global Institution". In *The Universities of the Future: Roles in the Changing World Order*. Richard, A. Harvill Conference on Higher Education, University of Arizona, 1994, pp. 38–43.

The Modern University in Australia and Asia, The Menzies Oration on Higher Education, 1 October 1996, University of Melbourne, 1997.

李业霖主编,《南洋大学走过的历史道路》. 马来亚南洋大学校友会, 2002.

Shifting Paradigms and Asian Perspectives: Implications for Research and Teaching. In *Reflections on Alternative Discourses from Southeast Asia*, ed. Syed Farid Alatas. Singapore: Pagesetters Services, 2002, pp. 47–54.

"Inception, Origins, Contemplations: a Personal Perspective". In *Imagination, Openness & Courage: The National University of Singapore at 100*. NUS, 2006, pp. 1–31.

"New University, three Generations: China, Malaya, Singapore", *s/pores: New Directions in Singapore Studies* 1, issue 2.1. <http://spores.wordpress.com/2008/02>

"Post-imperial Knowledge and Pre-Social Science in Southeast Asia". In *Decentring and Diversifying Southeast Asian Studies: Perspectives from the Region*, ed. Goh Beng-Lan. Singapore: Institute of Southeast Asian Studies, 2011, pp. 60–80.

"马来亚大学中文系成立往事: 王赓武教授专访". In《薪火相传、桃李芬芳: 国大中文系六十周年系庆特刊》, 2013, pp. 20–3.

Literature

Pulse. Published by Beda Lim at the University of Malaya, Singapore, 1950.

"Trial and Error in Malayan Poetry", *The Malayan Undergrad* 9, no. 6 (July 1958): 6–8. Reprinted in *s/pores: New Directions in Singapore Studies*, 10 January 2008.

"Twelve Poems". In *Litmus One, Selected University Verse, 1949–1957*. The Raffles Society, University of Malaya, Singapore, 1958, pp. 27–36.

"The Violin". In *The Compact: A selection of University of Malaya short stories, 1953–1959*, ed. Herman Hochstadt. Raffles Society, University of Malaya, 1959, pp. 85–94.

Awang Kedua, "Five Poems", *Varsity 1962*, Kuala Lumpur, 1962, pp. 71–2.

"On hearing of a friend's death", "If I was born to rule", "In a Silk-draped Hothouse", "I am not a soldier"; and "A New Sensation", and "A short introduction to Chinese Writing in Malaya". In *Bunga Emas: an anthology of contemporary Malaysian literature*, ed. T. Wignesan. London: Anthony Blond and Kuala Lumpur: Rayirath (Raybooks) Publications, 1964.

"The Pier", "Moon thoughts", "Ahmad", and "A New Sensation". In *The Flowering Tree: Selected Writings from Singapore/Malaysia*, compiled by Edwin Thumboo. Singapore: Educational Publications Bureau, 1970, pp. 21, 22, 23, 123–38.

Koh Tai Ann, "Literature in English by Chinese in Malaya/Malaysia and Singapore: Its origins and development". In *Chinese Adaptation and Diversity: Essays on Society and Literature in Indonesia, Malaysia & Singapore*, ed. Leo Suryadinata. Singapore: Singapore University Press, 1993, pp. 120–68.

Philip Holden, "Interrogating Diaspora: Wang Gungwu's *Pulse*", *Ariel* 33, Issue 3–4 (2002):105–30.

"无以解脱的困境?" (Writing as *haiwai huaren*: Dilemma without Relief?),《读书》(Beijing), 10/2004, pp. 110–20.

"Within and Without: Chinese Writers Overseas", *Journal of Chinese Overseas* 1, no. 1 (2005): 1–15.

"A New Sensation". In *Twenty-two Malaysian Stories: An Anthology of Writing in English*, ed. Lloyd Fernando. Singapore: Heinemann Educational Books (Asia), 1968, pp. 113–25. ["前所未有的感觉". Trans. 胡寶珠. In《回到马来亚: 华马小说七十年》(Return to Malaya: Stories by Chinese Malaysian Writers, 1937–2007), 张锦忠、黄锦树、庄华兴 (编). Batu Caves: Mentor Publishing, 2008, pp. 51–61.

"Learning Me your Language", *s/pores: New Directions in Singapore Studies* 1, issue 2 (2008). <http://spores.wordpress.com/2008/01/12>

"An Interview with Wang Gungwu by Robert Yeo from the mid-1980s". *s/pores: New Directions in Singapore Studies* 1, issue 2.1 <http://spores.wordpress.com/2008/02>

"Plus One", "Three Faces of Night" and "A New Sensation". In *Writing Singapore: An Historical Anthology of Singapore Literature*, ed. Angelia Poon, Philip Holden and Shirley Geok-lin Lim. Singapore: NUS Press, 2009, pp. 106–17.

"Three Faces of Night (poem)". In *& Words: Poems Singapore and Beyond*, ed. Edwin Thumboo. Singapore: Ethos Books, 2010, pp. 32–3.

"Six Poems". In *Malchin Testament: Malaysian Poems*, ed. Malachi Edwin Vethaman. Petaling Jaya: Maya Press, 2017, pp. 333–9.

"Moon thoughts" and "Three Faces of Night". In *Unfree Verse: Singapore Poetry in Form, 1937–2015*, ed. Tse Hao Guang, Joshua Ip and Theophilus Kwek. Singapore: Ethos Books, 2017, pp. 9–11.

"Two Poems 'The Pier' and 'Pulse'". In *Who are you my country? Writing about identity past and present*, ed. Winston Toh Ghee Wei, Theophilus Kwek, Joshua Jesudason and Hygin Prasad Fernandez. Singapore: Landmark Books, 2018, pp. 39 and 92.

Nilanjana Sengupta, "Foreword". In *The Votive Pen: Life and poetry of Edwin Thumboo* (2020).

History

"Johor Lama: An introduction to archaeology", *The Malayan Historical Journal* 1, no. 1 (1954): 18–23.

"The *Chiu Wu-Tai Shih* and History-Writing during the Five Dynasties". *Asia Major,* London, 1957, pp. 1–22.

"The University of Malaya Archaeological Society's Survey of Central Kedah, May 1958", *Journal of Malayan Branch of the Royal Asiatic Society* 31, no. 1 (no. 181) (1958): 220–3.

"The Nanhai Trade: A Study of the Early History of Chinese Trade in the South China Sea", *JMBRAS* 31, pt. 2 (1958): 1–135. ["南海贸易 — 对南中国海中国早期贸易史的研究",《南海贸易与南洋华人》, 姚楠译. 香港: 中华书局, 1988, pp. 1–204.

"Mr. Harrison and the 'Western Bias' in the Nanhai Trade", *Asian Perspectives*, Hong Kong, 1961.

"Feng Tao, an essay on Confucian loyalty". In *Confucian Personalities*, ed. Arthur F. Wright and Denis Twitchett. Stanford: Stanford University Press, 1962, pp. 123–45, 346–51.

"The opening of relations between China and Malacca, 1402–1405". In *Malayan and Indonesian Studies: Festschrift for Richard Winstedt*, ed. J.S. Bastin and R. Roolvink. London: Oxford University Press, 1964, pp. 87–104.

The Use of History. Inaugural lecture, University of Malaya, 14 December 1966, Kuala Lumpur; also published in Papers in International Studies, Ohio University, 1968.

"Early Ming relations with Southeast Asia – a background essay". In *The Chinese World Order*, ed. J.K. Fairbank. Cambridge, MA: Harvard University Press, 1968, pp. 34–62, 293–9.

"China and Southeast Asia, 1402–1424". In *Studies in the social history of China and Southeast Asia: essays in memory of Victor Purcell*, ed. J. Chen and N. Tarling. Cambridge: Cambridge University Press, 1970, pp. 375–401.

Community and Nation: Essays on Southeast Asia and the Chinese. Kuala Lumpur and Sydney: Heinemann Asia and Allen & Unwin, 1981.

"Southeast Asian Hua-ch'iao in Chinese History-Writing", *Journal of Southeast Asian Studies* 12, no. 1 (1981): 1–14.

"Lu Xun, Lim Boon Keng and Confucianism", *Papers on Far Eastern History*, no. 39 (1989): 75–91.

"Merchants Without Empire: the Hokkien sojourning communities". In *The Rise of Merchant Empires: Long-Distance Trade in the Early Modern World, 1350–1750*, ed. James D. Tracy. Cambridge: Cambridge University Press, 1990, pp. 400–21.

China and the Chinese Overseas. Singapore: Times Academic Press, 1991.

"The Status of Overseas Chinese Studies". In *Chinese America: History and Perspectives 1994*, Chinese Historical Society of America, San Francisco, 1993, pp. 1–18.

"Migration and Its Enemies". In *Conceptualizing Global History*, ed. Bruce Mazlish and Ralph Buultjens. Boulder, CO: Westview Press, 1993, pp. 131–51.

"Among Non-Chinese". In *The Living Tree: The Changing Meaning of Being Chinese Today*, ed. Tu Wei-ming. Stanford: Stanford University Press, 1994, pp. 127–46.

"Ming Foreign Relations: Southeast Asia". In *The Cambridge History of China, vol. 8: The Ming Dynasty, 1368–1644, Part 2*, ed. Denis Twitchett and Frederick W. Mote. Cambridge and New York: Cambridge University Press, 1998, pp. 301–32, 992–5.

The Chinese Overseas: From Earthbound China to the Quest for Autonomy. Cambridge, MA: Harvard University Press, 2000.

《海外华人研究的大视野与新方向：王赓武教授论文集》, ed. 刘宏，黄建立. River Edge, NJ: Global Publishing, 2002.

《离乡别土: 境外看中华》(China and Its Cultures: From the Periphery). Fu Ssu-nien Memorial Lectures. Taipei: Institute of History and Philology, Academia Sinica, 2007.

The Structure of Power in North China during the Five Dynasties. Kuala Lumpur: University of Malaya Press, 1963 and Stanford: Stanford University Press, 1967. 《五代时期北方中国的权力结构》. Trans. 胡耀飞、尹承译. 上海：中西书局，2014.

Huang Jianli, "Approaches to History and Domain Crossings: Wang Gungwu and his Scholarship". In *Chineseness and Modernity in a Changing China*, ed. Zheng Yongnian and Zhao Litao. Singapore: World Scientific, 2020, pp. 9–28.

Malaysia

"Memperkembang Bahasa Kebangsaan: Peranan Perseorangan dan Badan Kesusasteraan" [Developing the National Language: The role of individuals and literary bodies], *Bahasa, Keluaran Perseketuan Bahasa Melayu* 2, no. 2 (1960): 86–95. University of Malaya, Kuala Lumpur.

"Malacca in 1403", *Malaya in History* 7, no. 2 (1962): 1–5. Kuala Lumpur.

Latar Belakang Kebudayaan Pendudok di-Tanah Melayu: Bahagian Kebudayaan China [The Cultural Background of the Peoples of Malaysia: Chinese Culture]. Kuala Lumpur: Dewan Bahasa dan Pustaka, 1962.

"Malayan Nationalism", *Royal Central Asian Journal* 49, pts. iii and iv (1962): 317–25. London.

"The Melayu in *Hai-kuo Wen-chien Lu*", *Journal of the Historical Society* 2 (1963): 1–9. University of Malaya, Kuala Lumpur.

Malaysia: A Survey (editor). New York and London: Praeger and Pall Mall Press, 1964.

"The Concept of Malaysia", "Early Chinese Influence in Southeast Asia", "Political Malaya, 1895–1941", "The Japanese Occupation and Post-war Malaya, 1941–1948", and "Malaya: The Road to Independence and Malaysia". In *History of the Malaysian States*. Singapore: Lembaga Gerakan Pelajaran Dewasa, 1965, pp. 1–4, 12–16, 80–91.

"Political Symposium, The Great Split", *Varsity 1965* (University of Malaya Students' Union) 1, no. 5 (1965): 8–12.

"The Way Ahead", *The Straits Times Annual for 1966*, Singapore, 1965, pp. 26–31.

"1874 in our history" and "Malaysia's Social History", *Peninjau Sejarah* 1, no.1 and no. 2 (1966): 12–16 and 1–5. Kuala Lumpur.

"The Growth of a Nation". In *Ten Years of Merdeka, Straits Times*, Kuala Lumpur, August 1967, pp. 3–6.

"Political Change in Malaysia", *Pacific Community* 1, no. 4 (1970): 687–96.

Malaysia: Contending Elites. Sydney: University of Sydney, Department of Adult Education, 1970.

"Chinese politics in Malaya", *The China Quarterly* 43 (1970): 1–30.

"Reflections on Malaysian Elites", *Review of Indonesian and Malay Studies* 20, no. 1 (1986): 100–28. Sydney.

"Malaysia-Singapore: Two Kinds of Ethnic Transformations", *Southeast Asian Journal of Social Science* 25, no. 2 (1997): 183–7.

"Continuities in Island Southeast Asia". In *Reinventing Malaysia: Reflections on its Past and Future*, ed. Jomo K.S. Bangi, Malaysia: Penerbit Universiti Kebangsaan Malaysia, 2001, pp. 15–34.

"Chinese Political Culture and Scholarship about the Malay World". In *Chinese Scholarship on the Malay World: a revaluation of a scholarly tradition*, ed. Ding Choo Ming. Singapore: Eastern Universities Press, 2003, pp. 1–30.

Nation-building: Five Southeast Asian Histories (editor). Singapore: Institute of Southeast Asian Studies, 2005.

黄坚立，"南洋大学与新加坡的语文分化：1965年王赓武报告书的争议". In《南大图像：历史河流中的省视》, 李元瑾编. 新加坡 ： 南大中华语言文化中心 ：八方文化创作室, 2007), pp. 165–220. (The revised English version: Huang Jianli, "A Window into Nanyang University: Controversy over the 1965 Wang Gungwu Report". In *A General History of the Chinese in Singapore*, ed. Kwa Chong Guan and Kua Bak Lim. Singapore: Singapore Federation of Chinese Clan Association and World Scientific, 2019, pp. 445–75.)

"The Fifty Years Before", in *The Chronicle of Singapore, 1959-2009: Fifty Years of Headline News*, ed. Peter H.L. Lim. Singapore: Editions Didier Millet and National Heritage Board, 2009, pp. 15–27.

"Student movements: Malaya as Outlier in Southeast Asia", Review Article, *Journal of Southeast Asian Studies* 44, no. 3 (2013): 511–18.

"The Call for Malaysia" and "Malaya: Platform for Nation Building". In *Nanyang: Essays on Heritage*. Singapore: Institute of Southeast Asian Studies, 2018, pp. 11–35, 36–58.

Asia: Southeast Asia

"The Emergence of Southeast Asia", *Bakti,* Journal of the Political Study Centre, Singapore, no. 3 (1961): 9–11.

"Nation Formation and Regionalism in Southeast Asia". In *South Asia Pacific Crisis: National Development and the World Community*, ed. Margaret Grant. New York: Dodd, Mead & Company, 1964, pp. 125–35, 258–72.

"The Teaching of History in a Southeast Asian Context". In *History Teaching: Its Problems in Malaya*, ed. Zainal Abidin b. A. Wahid. Department of History, University of Malaya, 1964, pp. 1–11.

"The Vietnam Issue" and "Communism in Asia", *Journal of the Historical Society*, University of Malaya, 1965 and 1967, pp. 1–5 and 1–12.

"South and Southeast Asian Historiography", *International Encyclopedia of the Social Sciences* 6 (1968): 420–8, ed. David L. Sills. New York: Macmillan.

Scholarship and the History and Politics of Southeast Asia. Flinders University Asian Studies no.1, Adelaide, 1970.

"Southeast Asia between the 13th and 18th Centuries: Some Reflections on Political Fragmentation and Cultural Change" (1971). In *Historia: Essays in Commemoration*, ed. A.B. Muhammad, A. Kaur and Abdullah Zakaria. Kuala Lumpur: Malaysian Historical Society, 1984, pp. 1–12.

"Nationalism in Asia". In *Nationalism: the nature & evolution of an idea*, ed. Eugene Kamenka. London: Edward Arnold, 1973, pp. 82–98.

"The Study of the Southeast Asian past". In *Perceptions of the Past in Southeast Asia*, ed. A.J.S. Reid and D. Marr. Singapore: Heinemann, 1979, pp. 1–8.

"China and Southeast Asia: Some Recent Developments". In *Collected Essays in Sinology, dedicated to Professor Kim Jun-yop.* Seoul: Korea University Press, 1983, pp. 657–71.

"Introduction". In *Southeast Asia in the Ninth to Fourteenth Centuries*, ed. D.G. Marr and A.C. Milner. Singapore and Canberra: Institute of Southeast Asian Studies and Research School of Pacific Studies, Australian National University, 1986, pp. xi–xviii.

"Nationalism and its Historians". Keynote Lecture at the History of Nationalism Conference, 14th International Association of Historians of Asia, Bangkok, May 1996. In *Bind Us in Time: Nation and Civilization in Asia*, 2003, pp. 1–22.

China's Place in the Region: The Search for Allies and Friends. The 1997 Panglaykim Memorial Lecture, Center for Strategic and International Studies, Jakarta, 1997.

"ASEAN and the Three Powers of the Asia-Pacific". In *Southeast Asia's Changing Landscape*, ed. Gerrit W. Gong. Washington, DC: The Center for Strategic and International Studies, 1999, pp. 19–26.

"The Search for Asian National Histories". In *IAHA 2000: Proceedings, 16th Conference of the International Association of Historians of Asia*, Vol. I, ed. Ahmat Adam and Lai Yew Meng. Kota Kinabalu: Universiti Malaysia Sabah, 2004, pp. 275–83.

"Contemporary and National History: A Double Challenge". In *Nation-Building: Five Southeast Asian Histories*, ed. Wang Gungwu. Singapore: Institute of Southeast Asian Studies, 2005, pp. 1–19.

"The Pull of Southeast Asia". In *Historians and Their Disciplines: the Call of Southeast Asian History*, ed. Nicholas Tarling. MBRAS Monograph no. 40 (2007): 161–74.

"Southeast Asia: imperial themes", *New Zealand Journal of Asian Studies* 11, no. 1 (2009): 36–48.

"Party and Nation in Southeast Asia", *Millennial Asia: An International Journal of Asian Studies* 1, no. 1 (January–June 2010): 41–57.

"The Peranakan Phenomenon: Pre-national, Marginal, and Transnational". In *Peranakan Chinese in a Globalizing Southeast Asia*, ed. Leo Suryadinata. Singapore: Chinese Heritage Centre and NUS Museum Baba House, 2010, pp. 14–26.

"Before Southeast Asia: Passages and Terrains". In *ISEAS at 50: Understanding Southeast Asia Past and Present*. Singapore: Institute of Southeast Asian Studies, 2018, pp. 65–84.

Chinese Overseas

"Chinese Reformists and Revolutionaries in the Straits Settlements, 1900–1911", Appendix B: Wu Hsien-tzu 伍宪子, "A short account of K'ang Nan Hai in Nanyang" (1952). Trans. Wang Gungwu. University of Malaya, 1953.

A Short History of the Nanyang Chinese 《南洋华人简史》, 张弈善译。Singapore: Donald Moore, 1959. 台北：水牛出版社, 1969.

"Sun Yat-sen and Singapore" 《南洋学报》15, pt. 2 (1959): 55–68. Singapore.

"An Early Chinese Visitor to Kelantan" and "A Letter to Kuala Pilah, 1908", *Malaya in History* 6, no. 1 and no. 2 (1960 and 1961): 31–5 and 22–6.

"Traditional leadership in a New Nation: The Chinese in Malaya and Singapore". In *Leadership and Authority: a symposium*, ed. G. Wijeyewardene. Singapore: University of Malaya Press, 1968, pp. 208–22.

"Secret Societies and Overseas Chinese" (review article), *The China Quarterly* 47 (1971): 553–60. London.

"Political Chinese: an aspect of their Contribution to Modern Southeast Asian History". In *Southeast Asia in Modern World*, ed. Bernard Grossman. Wiesbaden: Otto Harrassowitz, 1972, pp. 115–28.

"The Limits of Nanyang Chinese Nationalism, 1912–1937". In *Southeast Asian History and Historiography: Essays Presented to D.G.E. Hall*, ed. C.D. Cowan and O.W. Wolters. Ithaca, NY: Cornell University Press, 1976, pp. 405–21.

"'Are Indonesian Chinese Unique?': Some Observations". In *The Chinese in Indonesia*, ed. J.A.C. Mackie. Melbourne: Thomas Nelson, 1976, pp. 199–210.

"The Question of the 'Overseas Chinese'", *Southeast Asian Affairs 1976*, Singapore, 1976, pp. 101–10.

"A note on the Origins of *Hua-ch'iao*". In *Masalah-Masalah International Masakini*, ed. Lie Tek Tjeng, vol. 7. Jakarta: Lembaga Research Kebudayaan Nasional L.I.P.I., 1977, pp. 71–8.

The Chinese Minority in Southeast Asia. Southeast Asia Research Paper Series 1, Nanyang University, Singapore. Singapore: Chopmen Enterprises, 1978.

"South China Perspectives on Overseas Chinese", *Australian Journal of Chinese Affairs*, no. 13 (1985): 69–84. Canberra.

《东南亚与华人: 王赓武教授论文选集》 [Southeast Asia and the Chinese], ed. 姚楠. 北京: 中國友誼出版公司; 新華書店北京發行所發行, 1987.

"The Study of Chinese Identities in Southeast Asia". In *Changing Identities of the Southeast Asian Chinese since World War II*, ed. Jennifer Cushman and Wang Gungwu. Hong Kong: Hong Kong University Press, 1988, pp. 1–21.

"The Chinese as Immigrants and Settlers". In *Management of Success: the Moulding of Modern Singapore*, ed. K.S. Sandhu and Paul Wheatley. Singapore: Institute of Southeast Asian Studies, 1989, pp. 552–62.

"Patterns of Chinese migration in historical perspective". In *Observing Change in Asia – Essays in Honour of J.A.C. Mackie*, ed. R.J. May and W.J. O'Malley. Bathurst: Crawford House Press, 1989, pp. 33–48.

"同化、归化与华侨史". In 《两次世界大战期间在亚洲之海外华人》, ed. 吴伦霓霞、郑赤琰. Hong Kong: Chinese University of Hong Kong, 1989, pp. 11–21.

"Greater China and the Chinese Overseas", *The China Quarterly*, no. 136 (1993): 926–48. London.

"Wealth and Culture: Strategies for a Chinese Entrepreneur", *A Special Brew: in honour of Kristof Glamann,* ed. Thomas Riis. Odense University Press, 1993, pp. 405–22.

"The Hakka in Migration History". In *Proceedings, International Conference on Hakkaology,* ed. Hsieh Chien and C.Y. Chang. Hong Kong: Chinese University of Hong Kong, Centre for Asia-Pacific Studies, 1995, pp. xxv–xl.

"Southeast Asian Chinese and the Development of China". In *Southeast Asian Chinese and China: The Politico-Economic Dimension,* ed. Leo Suryadinata. Singapore: Times Academic Press, 1995, pp. 12–30.

"Sojourning: The Chinese Experience in Southeast Asia". In *Sojourners and Settlers: Histories of Southeast Asia and the Chinese,* ed. Anthony Reid. St Leonard's, NSW: Allen & Unwin, 1996, pp. 1–14.

"Upgrading the Migrant: Neither Huaqiao nor Huaren". In *The Last Half Century of Chinese Overseas,* ed. Elizabeth Sinn. Hong Kong: Hong Kong University Press, 1998, pp. 15–33.

The Chinese Diaspora: Selected Essays (edited with Wang Ling-chi). Two volumes. Singapore: Times Academic Press, 1998.

"Chineseness: The Dilemmas of Place and Practice". In *Cosmopolitan Capitalists: Hong Kong and the Chinese Diaspora at the end of the 20th Century,* ed. Gary Hamilton. Seattle: University of Washington Press, 1999, pp. 118–34.

"A Single Chinese Diaspora? Some Historical Reflections". In *Imagining the Chinese Diaspora: Two Australian Perspectives.* Canberra: Centre for the Study of the Chinese Southern Diaspora, 1999, pp. 1–17.

"Ethnic Chinese: The Past in their Future". In *Intercultural Relations, Cultural Transformation, and Identity – The Ethnic Chinese,* ed. Teresita Ang See. Manila: Kaisa Para Sa Kaunlaran, Manila, 2000, pp. 1–20.

"Diaspora, a much abused word" (interview by Editor Laurent Malvezin). *Asian Affairs,* Hong Kong, no. 14 (Winter 2001): 17–29.

"再论海外华人的身分认同" [Chinese identity revisited]. In《汉学纵横》, ed. 李焯然. Hong Kong: Commercial Press, 2002, pp. 45–63.

Index